JOHN ON J

For Diana
with love & blessings,
Meg.
July. 1994.

Dedication:

To Friargate Bible Study group who went on this journey with me and to the memory of our dearly loved friend Kathleen Healey (1896-1992) who died before the project was completed

JOHN ON JESUS

A personal reflection

by

Meg Chignell

Sessions Book Trust
York, England

Acknowledgements: I am very grateful to the Joseph Rowntree Charitable Trust who funded my first year of work on the book, to the Sessions Book Trust for core funding, to Jo Farrow for her Foreword, to my sister Marion Willink for her encouragement and support. and as always to Barbara Windle, for reading and commenting on the manuscript with meticulous care.

Meg Chignell, 1994

All biblical quotations are from *The Revised English Bible*, 1989 (REB), unless otherwise stated, by permission of the Oxford University Press and Cambridge University Press.

ISBN 1 85072 141 6
(c) Meg Chignell, 1994

Printed from Author's disk
on recycled paper into 10/11 point Plantin typeface
by William Sessions Limited
The Ebor Press, York, England

Foreword

Jo Farrow

Formerly General Secretary of Quaker Home Service Committee of the Religious Society of Friends

A FEW MONTHS before I retired from working in Friends House I went to see the 'Monet in the '90s' Exhibition at the Royal Academy. Although I spent some time looking at Monet's serial paintings of 'Poplars at Giverny' and 'Morning on the Seine', it was his series of Grainstack paintings which so overwhelmed me that I found it hard, even after an hour or more, to tear myself away from them. It never occurred to me to ask 'Did the light really transfigure a few ordinary haystacks in a field behind his house at Giverny in just that way?' Nor did it occur to me to ask myself whether he had exaggerated natural effects or offered a faithful representation of the way the light fell across those stacks at early morning or at sunset. They would have been quite meaningless questions. What happened to me in looking at them was that I caught something of the sense of glory which Monet felt as he looked and painted with the eye of love. What he attempted in the series was to express what he *felt* when he looked at the fields behind his house and saw a landscape transfigured by the light. It was his experience of the sheer glory of it which he was trying to convey.

In *John on Jesus* Meg Chignell helps us to understand that this is what the author of the Fourth Gospel is doing in painting his series of pictures of Jesus. His concern is to return again and again to the same theme, but to show it in a different light; not to present us with a factual, historical account of what happened, but to draw out, in a variety of ways, the meaning of the Jesus event and, perhaps a bit like Monet, to tell us something important about the actual *experience* of seeing a landscape or a human being transfigured by the light . . . 'We beheld his glory' . . . writes John, giving us not a description of what Jesus looked like, but of how he affected those who responded to him.

For the first generation of Friends John's gospel was of primary importance because one of its main themes was the new age of the spirit which Jesus had inaugurated. Quaker worship was justified by the recorded words of Jesus to the woman at the well (John 4:23-24) and many of the key phrases in early Quaker parlance, eg. 'walk in the light,' 'children of the Light,' including the eventual choice of a name for the Religious Society of Friends were borrowed or adapted from either John's gospel or the Johanine letters. George Fox's reflections on the significance of the Jesus event are often extraordinarily close to those of the author of John's gospel. Both understand that in Jesus a new order has begun which is totally different from that which preceded it. They see in it the unmistakable 'signs' of the new age in which formal rites of worship or sacrificial systems are now obsolete. Many religious groups have grasped some of the implications of this. In our unprogrammed worship we have taken the risk of testing out those implications; creating, as an American Friend, Douglas Steere, suggests, 'a laboratory of the Holy Spirit'. John's gospel is the foundation text for that bold experiment in depth which is Quaker worship at its best.

It is valuable, therefore, to have a fresh interpretation of John's gospel from a Quaker author who has spent most of her life as an educationalist, teaching and writing about the Bible (in particular the New Testament) and its relevance to contemporary problems. Friends who were able to participate in her Bible Study groups at the Friends World Conference which met in 1991 at Elspeet, will have experienced at first hand her gift of making the New Testament come alive.

It is also refreshing to have a new exposition of John's gospel from a Friend who is not afraid of the difficult questions which this version of the Jesus story has posed for many of us. It is in this gospel that many of the most exclusive claims have been made which have so often reinforced religious dogmatism and buttressed the church's antipathy to, and persecution of, Jews in past centuries. It is in this gospel that Jesus appears to make claims for himself which have fuelled the bigotry of some fundamentalists and caused the scandal of particularity. Meg Chignell does not dodge these issues but deals with each of them with painstaking honesty and unobtrusive scholarship, offering alternative interpretations which allow us to see things in a new way or to understand the first century context and its particular cultural bias, and to see that we do not need to take it on board today.

No doubt others who read this book will be impressed, as I was, by her unquenchable enthusiasm and love for the Jesus who inspired the gospel, and also for the unfussed way in which she parts company with first century views of the story which are untenable. I often make heavy weather with my own brand of redaction criticism, arguing with the text in a way guaranteed to raise my blood pressure several notches or getting myself tangled in theological granny knots; Meg Chignell simply adds a quiet and unobtrusive footnote – 'I do not share this New Testament view' and compels me to see how idiotic my own feverish wrestling has been. Why on earth should any of us, in the late twentieth century, expect that our views will necessarily coincide with those of a first-century Jew!

As a belated, but now quite passionate feminist and universalist, I have problems with Jesus as the churches have so often portrayed him, and I have immense sympathy with those suffering from a surfeit of 'Jesusolatry', and the male emphasis of the Trinity. Meg Chignell's earlier book, *The Universal Jesus*, helped me to salvage some of my earlier fascination with the beatnik from Nazareth, and the implications of his message to our planet. *John on Jesus* takes me a little further in that process of recovery. It inspired me to go back to John's gospel and re-read it with a clearer understanding of its distinctive ethos; to unravel some of the tangled strands of my antipathy towards it in recent years, and to recover some of my original fascination with it. It was William Temple's *Readings in St John's Gospel* that first fired my enthusiasm for it. Meg Chignell's reflections on it have helped me to recover some of that initial relish.

Even more important, however, than my renewed sense of the significance of John's understanding of Jesus, is the experience of catching a glimpse of the gospel according to Meg Chignell. If I am honest, that is what blazed out of these pages for me and made me realise afresh the importance of our Quaker conviction that the teaching of the Spirit is always contemporary.

The book is an invitation to share in a journey of discovery and open ourselves to the spirit of truth which inspired the first gospel writers to express the impact of Jesus upon their lives. As she writes in the introduction:

> The same invitation is open to all readers of the gospel to whatever period or culture they may belong. In the last decade of the twentieth century, we will bring very different perspectives from those first century christians for whom probably the book was originally written ... for me this gospel forms a bridge between the Jesus of history, known only to a few, and the indwelling Christ of faith who has been the inspiration of millions of believers.

Leonard Hodgson, in his introduction to his Gifford Lectures, asks: 'What must the truth have been and be, if that is how it looked to men who thought and wrote like that?' He goes on to argue that we must struggle to understand what has been written, not because the gospel writers themselves hold the vital key to the truth we are seeking, or have the last word on the matter, but so that we in turn can make our own contribution from our different viewing points, leaving it open for revision by those who come after us. It seems to me that Meg Chignell's book of essays offers us an illustration of how to involve ourselves in that ongoing process of discovery and re-vision.

February 1994

Contents

                                                                                      Page

INTRODUCTION   xi

CHAPTER 1:   PERSONAL ENCOUNTERS   1

    John Baptist; the first disciples; Nicodemus; the Samaritan woman; the disciples blown off course on the Lake; the woman taken in adultery

CHAPTER 2:   SIX OF THE SEVEN SIGNS   26

    The marriage at Cana; the healing of the officer's son; the healing of the cripple; the feeding of the five thousand; the man born blind; the raising of Lazarus; the anointing at Bethany

CHAPTER 3:   CONTROVERSY AND CONFRONTATION IN
                    JERUSALEM   50

    The Cleansing of the Temple; opposition to Jesus after healing the cripple; Jesus at The Feast of Tabernacles; controversy following the healing of the man born blind on a Sabbath; repercussions to the Lazarus miracle; the Triumphal Entry; last public discourse in the temple area; Jesus' hour of inner trial; a note at the end of Jesus' public ministry

CHAPTER 4:   THE FINAL DISCOURSES AND JESUS' PRAYER   80

    The Last Supper - Jesus washes the disciples' feet; Judas departs; the new commandment; present reassurance and future promise; the Spirit of truth; the gift of peace; Jesus as the vine; loyalty to Jesus means attaining heavenly joy; hatred of the world; judgement by the Spirit; Jesus' final words to the disciples; Jesus' prayer

                                                                Page

Chapter 5:   The Seven I AM Statements   110

   The bread of life; the light of the world; the door; the good shepherd; the resurrection and the life; the way, the truth and the life; the vine

Chapter 6:   The Seventh Sign   130

   The arrest of Jesus; a preliminary trial before Annas and Peter's denials; trial before Pilate; the crucifixion; the burial; summary; the empty tomb; Mary Magdalene's encounter with the risen Jesus; the evening of the first day; the appearance to Thomas; conclusion; the appendix (John 21)

Chapter 7:   The Prologue   156

   Origins; background; comment on the text; difficulties and summary

Introduction

In the first chapter of John's gospel two of John Baptist's disciples are encouraged by the Baptist to go after Jesus. When Jesus turns to ask them what they are looking for, they reply that they want to see where he is staying. 'Come and see', says Jesus (1:35-39), which they do and remain with him for some hours. On the following day, Philip from Bethsaida having encountered Jesus and been invited to follow him, goes to find his friend Nathanael to tell him his news. Nathanael is frankly sceptical about anyone who originates from Nazareth, but Philip simply says 'Come and see', which he does, with dramatic results.

The same invitation is open to all readers of the gospel to whatever period or culture they may belong. In the last decade of the twentieth century, we will bring a very different perspective from those first century Christians for whom probably the book was originally written, but we share a common humanity and a common burden of fear and anxiety about the tumultuous times in which we live.

For me this gospel forms a bridge between the Jesus of history, known only to a few, and the indwelling Christ of faith who has been the inspiration of millions of believers. To explore the nature of this bridge is, I believe, a necessary and an essentially personal task.

In my previous book, *The Universal Jesus*, I used Mark's gospel as a primary source for establishing the complete humanity of Jesus. The Synoptics in general were also used to show how the innovative nature of Jesus' teaching still applies to our present situation. My own conviction is that we need Jesus' witness if we are to resolve our most fundamental and terrible problems. The New Testament picture is, of course, incomplete without a study of John and Paul with their very definitive statements about their own faith. Their influence has been enormous in the formulation of Christian doctrine. But all generations and indeed all individuals need to work out for themselves the basics of their own belief, for they bring to their reading and study their particular gifts and insights. I am myself a member of the Religious Society of Friends, or Quakers, founded by George Fox in the seventeenth century. It was this challenge to individual experience that moved Fox's listeners when he first preached at Ulverston: " Then what had any to do with the scriptures, but as they came to the Spirit that gave them forth. You will say, Christ saith this, and the apostles say this; but what canst thou say? Art thou a child of Light and hast walked in the Light, and what thou speakest is it inwardly from God?"

I have not attempted to write yet another commentary on John's gospel but have written instead seven chapters each of which could, if necessary, stand on its own. At the start of each chapter I have included a detailed list of the biblical passages covered. Although we do not know who was the author of the Fourth Gospel, I shall often call him 'John' for brevity's sake, or 'the Evangelist'. This latter term could apply to any of the four gospel writers but I use it solely for the author of John. I take the view that ancient tradition is right unless proved otherwise. Similarly, I think it may well be that Peter is the inspiration behind Mark's gospel. As many commentators assume that the writer of the Fourth Gospel knew either the written record of Mark or the strong oral tradition which lay behind the Synoptics, I shall look at John throughout the book in conjunction with the other gospels. I believe this will better enable us to appreciate his special contribution.

It is clear that the author of the Fourth Gospel wrote long after the events he describes and that the gospel may have had editorial additions especially in Chapters 16, 17 and the Prologue. Being Jews, those first disciples of Jesus searched their own scriptures for evidence to prove that their Master was the Christ. The Fourth Gospel does not contain as many 'proof-texts' as Matthew's gospel but more than enough to make this point. The modern reader may find this a disconcerting trait in the narrative but, given the cultural background of the time, it is understandable. I have commented on each of these Old Testament passages and given references for anyone who wants to look them up.

At first sight, we may find that this gospel is unacceptably anti-Jewish in tone; we need to remember that John uses the phrase 'the Jews' to represent the religious authorities who by their rejection of Jesus became, in his opinion, the opposition. I have also discussed in various places, the New Testament attitude towards "the world" (ie. non-Jewish and later non-Christian humanity) which is seen as being under the dominance of the powers of evil. Whilst recognising evil in all its terrible manifestations, I do not share this New Testament view.

The style of John's gospel is majestic and dramatic. The author is both ironic and profound. At times he is repetitive. He brings his readers back to the same point viewed from a slightly different angle. Because I am following the gospel story and the discourse, even if under different chapter headings, I also write about the same themes and return, of necessity and inclination, to the central topic of eternal life again and again.

The reader will find a movement towards increasingly personal comment in the course of the book. As the gospel emphasis moves from narrative to discourse, I have moved accordingly to place greater emphasis on my response to the author's ideas and his interpretation of Jesus rather than accepting his first century viewpoint without question.

By whom, where, why and when John's gospel was written

These are controversial questions on which scholars disagree because the kind of evidence which could be called conclusive by modern standards does not exist. Ancient tradition which goes back to the second and third centuries states that the Fourth Gospel was written (or caused to be written) at Ephesus by John the Apostle, the son of Zebedee and brother of James. This is the John who is known to us through the Synoptics as being not only among the first disciples called by Jesus, but also one of his three intimate friends (Matthew 4:21; 10:2; Mark 1:19; 3:17; 5:37; 9:2; 10:35; 14:33; Luke 22:8). Also from Acts (3:1, 11; 4:13; 8:14;) and Paul (Galatians 2:9) we learn that John was 'one of the pillars' of the young Christian community in Jerusalem.

In the gospel itself and its appendix (Chapter 21) there are five references to an anonymous beloved disciple:- at the last supper, 13:23,24; at the crucifixion, 19:16; at the resurrection, 20:2 and twice in Chapter 21: 7, 10. The claim to be an eyewitness of the events described in the gospel is made three times (1.14, 19:35; 21:24) and also in 1 John 1:14 - a letter which many scholars attest to being by the same hand as the gospel.

This tradition is based on the testimony of Irenaeus (bishop of Lyons c. AD170-200) and he clearly identifies John the Apostle with the beloved disciple. He says he got his information from Polycarp, whose pupil he had been. In turn Polycarp (bishop of Smyrna, martyred at the age of 86 in AD 155) himself had been a young disciple of John in Ephesus and had known others who had seen Jesus. Irenaeus also stated that John lived in Ephesus until the time of Trajan (AD 98), which would make him a very old man.

Modern scholarship on the whole rejects this second century tradition and several other candidates have been suggested for the beloved disciple. The one exception to this view, was John A.T. Robinson, who believed not only that John's gospel could have been the first written record of Jesus (The Priority of John, SCM Press, 1985), but also (Redating the New

Testament, SCM, 1976) that all the gospels were written before the Fall of Jerusalem in AD 70.

The Jewish Revolt began in AD66 and was finally crushed by the seizure of Masada in AD 73. At this distance of time it is difficult for us to appreciate how the devastation caused by this war completely ended an era. The way of life described in the gospels was gone for ever. Following the total destruction of Jerusalem in AD.70, the Temple with its sacrificial system and services, the Sanhedrin (the highest religious and official council of the Jews) and the role of the chief priests were all finished. A reorganisation of the Jewish faith was to emerge before the end of the century. In its new form, the local synagogue worship became central and with it the role of the rabbis who were the direct successors of the Scribal and Pharisaic traditions.

The only firm fact that can be stated about the date of the gospel is that it must have been written before the early part of the second century as fragments of gospel papyri have been found in Egypt dating from about AD125. Therefore AD90-100 is the date usually suggested for the gospel. Language experts agree that the Greek of the Fourth Gospel is adequate, if limited in syntax and vocabulary (unlike Luke's preface). It contains Aramaic (Semitic) idioms. It could well have been the spoken Greek of an eloquent Jew, as Greek was the *lingua franca* of the Empire.

We do not know who were the first readers of the Fourth Gospel. From the way in which the author explains Jewish customs, they could well have been Gentiles or even Greek-speaking Jews who were not familiar with Palestine. John, however, is quite specific about his reason for writing; he wants his readers to believe that "Jesus is the Christ, the Son of God and that through this faith you may have life by his name" (20:31).

As scholarly opinion about all these matters has differed so much during the decades in which I have been studying the New Testament, I have come to the conclusion that we need to concentrate less on problematic dates and more on the actual content of the gospels and letters, given that they are a record of people's actual experience expressed in terms which were appropriate to their own cultural background and history. This leaves me free to disagree with the way in which experiential truth is expressed and also stimulates me to try and formulate my own understanding of what is being said. I hope this book may encourage any reader to do the same.

CHAPTER ONE – PERSONAL ENCOUNTERS

		Chapter	Page
1.	John Baptist	1:19-34	3
2.	The First Disciples	1:35-51	6
3.	The Final Witness of John Baptist	3:22-30	9
4.	Comment by the Evangelist	3:31-36	11
5.	Nicodemus	3:13-21	13
6.	Comment by the Evangelist	3:13-21	15
7.	A special note on	3:16,17	16
8.	The Samaritan Woman	4:1-42	19
9.	The Disciples Blown off course on the Lake	6:16-21	22
10.	The Woman taken in Adultery	7:53-8:11	23

CHAPTER 1:

Personal Encounters

1.   John Baptist 1:19-34:

There is a rich Synoptic tradition about the Baptist. Mark's Gospel records that he came upon the scene dressed and behaving like Elijah: he was the Messiah's forerunner prophesied by Malachi (4:5) and Isaiah (40:3). He baptised Jesus in the Jordan (Mark 1:2-9) and later was indirectly described by Jesus as the returned Elijah (9:12f). There is a graphic account of the way in which Herodias (Herod's second wife) contrived to bring about John's execution. Matthew follows Mark but includes fuller details of the Baptist's preaching on repentance and comments on John's reluctance to baptise Jesus (Matthew 3:1-15). Luke gives us details of the unusual circumstances surrounding John's conception and the angel Gabriel's prophecy to John's father, Zechariah, the priest. When John is born, Zechariah, released from his dumbness, declares his son will be a prophet of the Most High, the Lord's forerunner sent to prepare people for his coming (Luke 1:5-25, 57-80). Luke goes on to give a more detailed account of John's preaching (3:1-20), the Baptist's later doubts as to whether Jesus is really the Messiah and Jesus' comments both about John's greatness and his limitations (7:18-35).

The Fourth Gospel tells us little of all this, perhaps because the Evangelist assumes that his readers already know it but also more probably because he wishes to put the emphasis elsewhere. In John we learn that the popular enthusiasm aroused by the Baptist caused an official enquiry into his credentials. A deputation of priests, Levites (minor Temple officials) and Pharisees from Jerusalem, question John Baptist about his identity but in reply he affirms nothing. He simply denies that he is either the Messiah, Elijah or the prophet promised by Moses (Deuteronomy 18:15) who was anticipated as part of the dawn of the Messianic age. When pressed further John describes himself in the words of Isaiah (40:3), as a voice crying aloud in the wilderness in preparation for the coming of the Lord. His baptism is one of water, a purely preparatory rite. His deep humility makes him feel unworthy even to act as a slave to the One who is coming after him, who is even then unrecognised in their midst.

On the next day, when John Baptist sees Jesus, he declares "There is the Lamb of God who takes away the sin of the world" (1:29). He says twice that he did not know the Chosen One until his eyes had been opened by a special revelation. He saw the descent of the Spirit as a dove upon Jesus. This was the outward sign of an inward permanent possession. He upon whom the Spirit came and rested was God's Chosen One (or Son of God), who from his own spiritual source could empower others with the gift of the Spirit. The Baptist reiterates that he has seen the truth and to this he can bear witness. Thus his ministry is brought to its climax and its focal point.

By making a comparison between the Synoptics' record of John Baptist and the Fourth Evangelist's treatment of this theme, we can see how they differ from each other in their approach. Working from the hypothesis that the Fourth Evangelist knew not only the oral tradition behind the Synoptics, but perhaps even Mark's gospel itself, and that he assumed this record to be common knowledge amongst his readers, we can more fully appreciate his distinctive contribution. Similarly, Paul's letters assume that his readers know the basic facts of the gospel story. Each of the gospels is the written record of preaching and teaching material. Each arose out of a particular community and was written with certain people in mind. In John's case, his declared purpose is given in his gospel (20:31). Although the truth about Jesus is stated at the beginning, it is only as the gospel proceeds that we come to understand the meaning of what has been said.

In John's version, the Baptist's recognition that Jesus is the Chosen One recalls the terms Mark uses in speaking of Jesus's own experience at his baptism (Mark 1:9-11). But what is important in John's gospel is that the Baptist himself makes the link between the Spirit and Jesus. Many Old Testament prophetic passages characterise the dawn of the Messianic Age by an outpouring of the Spirit (Joel 2:28; Isaiah 32:15, Ezekiel 39:29; Zechariah 12:10). The early Christians were convinced that these prophecies had been fulfilled through the coming of Jesus (Acts 2:16-18; 10-45; Romans 5:5; Galatians 4:6).

We know from Acts of two incidents where devout 'converts' had experienced only the baptism of John and did not know of the gift of the Spirit. We read (Acts 18:24-28) of a Jew called Apollos who came to Ephesus. He was a powerful spiritual preacher accurately informed about Jesus, but knowing John's baptism alone. Paul's two friends, Priscilla and Aquila took him in hand and instructed him more fully in the Way, i.e. about Jesus' Messiahship, after which he left Ephesus for Corinth. When Paul arrived at Ephesus (Acts 19:1-7) he met a group of about twelve 'disciples' who knew John's baptism of repentance, but had heard nothing of the gift of the Holy Spirit. However when these men were baptised into the name of the Lord Jesus and Paul laid his hands on them, they received the Holy Spirit. These two incidents show that John Baptist's influence was felt for many years after his death. But for the Evangelist the cleansing baptismal rite of John was entirely subsidiary to the gift of the Holy Spirit which came through an encounter with the person of Jesus the Christ.

The Baptist's title for Jesus - 'the Lamb of God who takes away the sin of the world' appears only in this gospel. There is much debate about its meaning. For the Jew the lamb was a sacrificial victim, offered daily in the Temple's morning and evening services. But in none of these services was the lamb related to a sin offering; rather it was associated with an act of praise and thanksgiving to God for all his mercies. Indeed, Moses had commanded (Exodus 12) that in perpetuity a lamb without blemish, a male of the first year, should be killed and eaten to celebrate God's deliverance of his people from the bondage in Egypt, hence the yearly celebration of the Feast of the Passover. The lamb was also a symbol of innocent suffering and was so used in the servant songs of Isaiah. The guiltless servant of God, who dies for his people is described as being led like a lamb to be slaughtered (53:7). The Synoptic record makes it clear that Jesus identified himself with Isaiah's suffering servant who bore the sin of many (53:12). In Mark's gospel, for example, Jesus says he has come to cure the sickness of sin (2:35-37); that he did not come to be served but to serve and to give his life as a ransom for many (Mark 10:45, cf. also Luke 22:37 with Isa.53:12). It is clear from Acts (8:32) that his early disciples also made the connection between Isaiah's servant and Jesus.

Although it is possible to understand the title 'Lamb of God' for Jesus in terms of the suffering servant of Isaiah which can also be Messianic in meaning, (one function of the Jewish Messiah could be to make an end of sin), in no sense does the Fourth Gospel treat Jesus' death as expiatory. A God who needed to be appeased or who demanded the making of amends for wrongdoing could not be the central figure in Jesus' all-embracing relationship of love with the Father whom he calls 'Abba'. When the Baptist names Jesus 'Lamb of God' he sharply points away from his own baptism of repentance to the new life which comes through Jesus.

2. The First Disciples, 1:35-51:

In the Synoptic record the first disciples, Simon, Andrew, James and John are called by Jesus when he is walking by the Sea of Galilee (Mark 1:16-20). It is not until much later, when they have been with Jesus for some time, that Peter, on being asked about his convictions, declares that Jesus is the Christ (Mark 8:27-33). Even then he does not in the least understand the implications of what he has said, as Jesus' subsequent conversation with him makes plain. Indeed Jesus binds all the disciples to silence because of popular misconceptions about the Messianic role.

By contrast, in John's gospel the Messiahship of Jesus is openly acknowledged from the beginning although the disciples are still presented as not fully realising either who their master is or the complete purpose of his mission. When the Baptist witnesses a second time to the Lamb of God (1:35-42), two of his disciples respond and go after Jesus but only one of them, Andrew, is named. Presumably the other one was either James or John and he too found his brother and brought him to Jesus as Andrew did Simon. Mysteriously, the sons of Zebedee and their mother Salome are never named in this gospel until chapter 21, although the unnamed beloved disciple is usually linked with Peter.

When Jesus decides to go to Galilee (1:45-51) he personally calls Philip to be his disciple. Philip's home is Bethsaida so John makes it clear that Jesus' ministry opened in Galilee, in accordance with the Synoptic tradition. Like Andrew, Philip immediately spreads the good news about Jesus by seeking out his friend Nathanael. Known only by name in the Synoptics, Philip plays a more important role in the Fourth Gospel and Nathanael, mentioned twice by John, is not found elsewhere. Because of his link with Philip, however, it has been suggested that Nathanael may be the same person as the Bartholomew listed in the Synoptic account of the Twelve Apostles.

In this gospel, ordinary words such as following, looking/seeking, staying/abiding/dwelling, coming, seeing, have deeper implications than the physical acts involved. To follow Jesus is to become his disciple: to stay/dwell/abide is indicative of the disciple's relationship with Jesus and of Jesus' relationship with the Father; to come to Jesus is synonymous with believing in him and to see can mean to know or understand. Thus when Simon comes to Jesus he becomes a disciple and is given a new name - Cephas is the Aramaic word for rock: Peter, the Greek equivalent. We know from Mark's gospel of Peter's impetuous even volatile nature, but through his relationship with Jesus he will develop and become a changed man (cf Mark 3:16 and Matthew 16:18 where the renaming is even more explicit).

Philip describes Jesus, son of Joseph from Nazareth, as the man of whom Moses wrote in the law (Deuteronomy 18:15). Nathanael is incredulous that Nazareth could produce such a man but when he meets Jesus he is overcome by Jesus' extraordinary perception not only of him as a person but of what he had recently been doing. Perhaps he wondered if Jesus even knew of his original scepticism? (The Evangelist's fine sense of irony is clear throughout the gospel.)

Jesus calls Nathanael 'An Israelite worthy of the name', who has 'nothing false in him'. The title Israelite is used in contrast to the Jews, John's collective title for the religious and judicial opposition to Jesus. In this gospel 'the Jews' is not used as a racial designation or as an anti-Semitic comment (after all, Jesus and the author himself were Jews), although the Jews of Asia Minor were strong in their condemnation and persecution of the followers of Jesus. John holds that everyone (Jew or Gentile alike) who believes in Jesus will be saved and have eternal life (3:16). The patriarch Jacob who was anything but honest in his dealings with his father and brother, was renamed Israel after his encounter with God (Genesis 32:28), so John uses the name Israel as a designation for the new people of God who recognised and accepted Jesus as the Messiah. For John, Jesus' rejection by the spiritual rulers of his own people and their failure to recognise him as the Son of God is a great tragedy indicative of how far they had wandered from their original destiny. The 'Jews', therefore, in his eyes, were no longer the true inheritors of the Promise and had become part of the pagan world.

Nathanael acknowledges Jesus as Son of God and King of Israel, but Jesus comments that Nathanael may believe him to be the Messiah because Nathanael has been moved by Jesus' unexpected knowledge of him, but he will see greater things than that. As the gospel unfolds seven great signs are given which show forth the glory of God as revealed through his Son. Then Jesus adds, 'In very truth I tell you all...' This phrase 'In very truth', or 'truly', in Hebrew 'so be it' i.e. Amen, normally forms the conclusion to prayer whereas Jesus in all the four gospels uses it to preface sayings with a particular note of authority. This distinctive use of 'in truth', 'amen', or 'amen, amen', which occurs twenty-seven times in John must be part of Jesus' authentic teaching style. Perhaps it was one of the things which antagonised the Scribes and Pharisees from the very beginning (cf Mark 1:22)?

The truth which Jesus declares to Nathanael is that he will see the heavens open and angels descending and ascending upon the Son of Man. This refers back to a famous episode in the Jacob story (Genesis 28:10-22). While fleeing from his brother Esau's anger, the young Jacob spends a night in a deserted place. There he dreams of angels ascending and descending a ladder, above which stands the Lord who speaks to him. Filled with awe, he believes that he has slept in the house of God, the very gate of heaven. The implication of Jesus' words therefore is that he, as Son of Man, is the place of revelation; he is the way to heaven or the door (9;10) through which people may pass to a new state of creative being. How this may be is not yet clear.

The title Son of Man appears fourteen times in Mark and must go back directly to Jesus himself. In Mark, however, the title carries a certain ambiguity. It could mean simply 'a man' standing for humanity in general as in Psalm 8:5, or it could be a veiled name for the Messiah, based on Daniel (7:13), a work written during a period of intense national suffering when loyalty to their ancestral faith involved the Jewish people in persecution. It is not always clear from the text in which sense Jesus is using it; in the controversy about Sabbath observance, for example, did Jesus mean that humanity is greater than its institutions or that he himself, as Messiah, is sovereign over the Mosaic law (2:27)? I believe the former interpretation is preferable but a case could be made out for either.

In John's gospel Jesus uses the Son of Man title eleven times and once (12:34) the crowd quote his use of it. We shall look at each of these in its context. In verse 51, the meaning is clear. John sees Jesus as the mediator between God and humanity, the one through whom the glory of God is to be revealed. It is impossible for the modern reader to know how John interpreted this self-designation by Jesus; did it stand for the true Israel whose real priestly vocation was mediation (cf. Exodus 19:6) or did it mean the sum total of human potential realised in one actual human being? One thing is certain; John and the other disciples knew their master as a real human being who loved, suffered, was thirsty, tired, anguished in spirit and who died, just as any other mortal man must do. In Jesus, however, there was a supreme quality of compassion, of perceptive illumination, of selfless authority and power - all of which sprang from Jesus' own relationship with God.

Reading the witness of John Baptist and the first disciples, we are struck by the time sequence of four days. This could, of course, be a literary device by the Evangelist to heighten the drama of the situation, or it could be a vividly spoken personal memory which says 'This is the way it was'. There is no reason to doubt John when he tells us that two of Jesus' disciples had previously followed John Baptist. It actually clarifies the Synoptic record, making it more credible that the two sets of brothers should leave their work and follow Jesus when he called them (Mark 1:16-20).

In this first chapter, we have been introduced to a Jesus who is described by a variety of impressive names; he is the Lamb of God who takes away the sins of the world; God's Chosen One on whom the Spirit rests and who will baptize with the Holy Spirit; the Messiah or Christ; the man of whom Moses wrote in the Law; the man foretold in the prophets; son of Joseph from Nazareth; Son of God; king of Israel: and the self designated Son of Man.

3. The Final Witness of John Baptist: 3:22-30:

There are two points to be discussed here. First, the additional information given in John's gospel that Jesus' ministry overlapped with the Baptist's for a short period of time; second, the words John Baptist uses to describe Jesus.

With regard to the overlap of Jesus and John, the Synoptic record states that Jesus was baptised by John. The Fourth Gospel implies this baptism in John's words about his recognition of Jesus (1:32). It also implies a certain link between John Baptist and Jesus since the latter's first disciples had been encouraged to follow him by the Baptist. Initially, Jesus may even have been part of John's following.

The Fourth Evangelist says Jesus went into Judaea to a place whose name literally means Fountains near to Peace. Although chapter 3:22 states Jesus and his disciples were baptising, it is clear from chapter 4:2 that Jesus himself did not baptise, only his disciples did it.. Presumably they were also giving a baptism of repentance for at that time they could not fully understand the gift of the Spirit which was to come after the resurrection. Further, John's gospel itself is emphatic that Jesus taught that the Counsellor or Advocate would come (cf.16:7-15) when he had gone from them.

In Jesus' day, many devout Jews practised purification by water on a daily basis (cf.Mark 7:1-8 and John 2:6). John Baptist used this purification rite in his call to a baptism of repentance in view of the Coming Day of the Lord (Mark 1:4,5). According to our passage, Jesus' disciples continued this baptism and people flocked to Jesus, inspired by his charismatic personality. This led to controversy among the Baptist's disciples and some Jews about the relative efficacy of the two rites. When appealed to, John Baptist made his final statement about Jesus.

The Synoptic account is different but not necessarily contradictory, although Mark states that Jesus did not start his preaching until after the Baptist had been arrested (Mark 1:14) and gives no hint that baptism formed part of his ministry. However, at the beginning of Acts, after the gift of the Spirit at Pentecost, (2:37-39) we read that a baptism of repentance in the name of Jesus the Messiah, was used by the disciples as a form of entry into the newly created community. Perhaps this meant a continuity of practice with the initial baptismal rites mentioned by John.

According to Matthew's gospel (28:19), the risen Jesus instructed his disciples to go to all the nations of the world, baptising believers in the name of the Father, the Son and the Holy Spirit. Succeeding generations of Christians have disputed about infant and adult baptism. There has also been bitter and deadly controversy in the Christian body on such matters as when the Spirit is given; the significance and value of the sacraments; the necessity for and the means by which Apostolic succession and authority has been maintained. Each firmly held conviction about these things relies on scriptural backing, but each depends upon a particular interpretation of the New Testament evidence. Yet the first century picture reveals young and struggling communities in a fluid state about their practices and organisation. For Quakers, whose silent Meetings for Worship exemplify a different approach, it is the awakening sense of the indwelling Spirit which is all-important; and this awakening is a matter of personal response, not of ritual.

God's Spirit, of course, has been present from the beginning of time in all places, to all people, according to the capacity of humankind to recognise its presence. But what the Evangelist believes, and what he says the Baptist stresses, is that because Jesus is the Son of God, he is able to endow others in a particular way with the gift of the Spirit.

Moving on to the second point; John's words about Jesus reveal his own deep humility and selflessness. People only have the gifts with which they are endowed and in John's case he knows he is not called to be the Messiah, but his forerunner. He uses the symbolic language of a marriage, in which his role is that of best man. His joy is simply that of rejoicing in the presence of the bridegroom. As the greatness of the groom is revealed, so his own importance diminishes.

The Old Testament prophet Hosea was led by personal experience to see God's compassion for his people and his righteous anger at their infidelity in terms of the relationship between husband and wife. He couched the hope of a renewed covenant between God and Israel in words of tender love (Hosea 2:14-17). The image of Jesus the Christ as the bridegroom of the new Israel therefore arises from Old Testament usage. Today, women in religious orders may still take vows of chastity, poverty and holy obedience as the brides of Christ and it is important to value and respect their devotion even if we, personally, cannot accept either the image or the language. Although feminists understandably object strongly to the masculine-oriented language of the bible, it is important for us to see beyond this to what is actually being expressed. Love seeks for reciprocity in all relationships even where there is great dependence as between a child and its parents. As humanity is created, it cannot have an equal relationship with its creator, the source of its being, but it can and needs to be aware of both giving and receiving in the realm of the Spirit. Depicting God as male is a cultural reality that belonged to past centuries and is not really appropriate for today. God is Spirit, which both embraces gender and is beyond it. Biblical writers idealise the submissive, dependent and self-surrendering role of woman as wife in order to speak of the worshippers' attitude towards their God. Again, in its cultural setting, this was not downgrading women but saying that both sexes need these qualities in their religious observance. The need for a restatement of the truth behind these symbols is obvious.

In finishing this chapter with the Baptist's witness, the Evangelist is clearly continuing his theme of the relationship between the old order and the new which he began in Chapter One where John Baptist recognised Jesus as the Lamb of God who takes away the sins of the world. John's water baptism of repentance was to be superseded by a baptism of the spirit. Jesus in himself will replace the inadequate rites, rituals and sacrificial system of Judaism. He is the new wine of abundant life which is offered to everyone. But to accept it means a rebirth of spirit, even for such a man as Nicodemus. As Jesus himself declared (Luke 7:24-28). the Baptist stands for all that is best in the old order, but his preparatory job, being fulfilled by the coming of the Messiah, is now at an end. Even so perhaps, Judaism itself must be seen as the forerunner of the new Israel which Jesus as the Christ, is creating. We see the Baptist's greatness in his acceptance of his limited role.

4. Comment by the Evangelist, 3:31-36:

The Revised English Bible and other translations clearly note the change from narrative to commentary by using inverted commas at the end of 3:30.

The totally inspired person of Jesus is contrasted with all others; even John Baptist is limited, however fine. God has enabled Jesus to speak the truth of God which itself is life. People do not understand or accept what Jesus has to say. But those who do believe recognise God's boundless gift of the Spirit. Such is the Father's love for the Son that he has entrusted all things to him.

In Luke's gospel, after the seventy-two disciples return from their successful mission, Jesus opens his heart to them and speaks in visionary and poetic words of power. 'Everything is entrusted to me by my Father; no one knows who the Son is but the Father, or who the Father is but the Son, and those to whom the Son chooses to reveal him:' (10:20). This exclusive claim can be off-putting to twentieth century readers, aware of the great mystic teachers of other religious faiths. We shall discuss this further when we come to study the 'I AM' statements. Luke has shown how Jesus at an early age was aware of a special relationship with God (2:29), whom he called Abba, . At his baptism he received inner confirmation, through empowerment by the Spirit, that he was indeed God's beloved son. In the symbolic account of the mental anguish he went through in the desert (the 'temptations', Luke 4:1-11), Jesus decided that messiahship for him was the way of sacrificial love. He saw himself as the servant of the Lord. And he demonstrated, in a way that was uniquely his own, the universal truth that God is love. His articulate, though rarely expressed awareness of his own intense relationship with God was sufficient for his disciples to see him, in an exclusive sense, as God's own and only Son through whom alone salvation comes.

We know, of course, that others also experience and teach of union with God/the Absolute, knowing nothing or little of Jesus the Christ. The validity of their witness is not in question; rather it shows that Eternal Truth is one, despite humanity's inability to comprehend it.

The chapter ends with the stark contrast between faith and unbelief, life and death. Those who disobey the Son incur the wrath of God - the first and only place in the gospel where this controversial concept is mentioned. I believe we must interpret 'wrath' as the inevitable working out in the moral and spiritual sphere of a law of cause and effect. Humanity has not yet fully understood or faced up to the truth of experience that it is self-destructive and self-defeating to be governed by violent bitterness, hatred, and revenge. Jesus initiated a new way of inner resolution to outward strife, a personally sacrificial and inordinately hard way yet full of joy and fulfilment for those with the love and courage to pursue it.

Eternal life is a life lived with Love at the centre of our being. Spiritual death is the denial of that human potential, when supreme egocentricity shuts off the possibility of ever reaching out to another because it sees all others not as persons in their own right but as objects to be used, regardless of suffering. As for wrath and ultimate judgement however, I do not believe we can possibly know or understand the final reckoning, for that is in the hands of Love itself.

5. Nicodemus: 3:1-12:

Only John tells us of Nicodemus and he is mentioned on three occasions in the gospel: in this passage we learn of his background; second, he protests at the Council meeting that Jesus (and indeed any man) should be given a fair hearing (7:50-52); and third, he helps Joseph of Arimathea to bury Jesus (19:39-40). Although doubts have been expressed about the genuineness of this record, there seems no good reason for them. John has a habit of giving his readers information which is absent in the Synoptics. It is also interesting to note, although it does not prove anything, that in Josephus' *Antiquities,* the name Nicodemus is associated with several generations of wealthy, influential Jerusalem Jews.

Nicodemus was a Pharisee, a member of the Sanhedrin, a religious leader and teacher of his people (and possibly a member of the wealthy, aristocratic and distinguished family to which Josephus refers). He has been deeply impressed by what he has seen of Jesus and his healing miracles. Unlike some of his contemporaries he does not attribute Jesus' power to black magic or Satanic influences (Mark 3:22) but freely admits that Jesus must be a teacher sent by God. Despite the sincerity of his admiration for Jesus and his desire to seek truth, he dare not openly admit to his interest and comes to see Jesus under cover of the dark. Jesus is very uncompromising with him. Nicodemus cannot have it both ways. There is a conscious decision to be made, so Jesus tells Nicodemus that a person has to be 'born again' to see the Kingdom of God. The words 'born again' can mean 'from above', 'from the beginning' or 'a second time'. Nicodemus interprets the words in the latter sense of a second time and expostulates that it a physical impossibility to re-enter the womb.

Jesus is a little more explicit but not much! No one can enter the Kingdom, (which means that the previous use of 'see' has the deeper meaning of 'experience'), unless he is born from water and spirit. From the word 'water' Nicodemus would recognise the reference to John Baptist, about whom everyone was talking. John's baptism of water was a preparatory act of repentance for the coming of the Spirit; true repentance necessarily involves knowledge of inner motivation.

Normal human birth is described by Jesus in terms of 'flesh' but spiritual birth is a different experience. I believe it to be an awakening of the conscious self to the inward spiritual source of being. 'You must all be born again' says Jesus, so for me this rebirth is a universal need to realise human potential. Jesus then likens the movement of the Spirit to the desert wind which cannot be contained and controlled by human will. It is enough to experience the wind, without knowing its source and its destination.

Openness and acceptance are hallmarks of the spiritual life. In the English language we miss the nuances of this wordplay as the Greek (and Hebrew) for Spirit can also imply breath or wind.

The comparison of Spirit with wind seems to alarm Nicodemus further for he cries out 'How is this possible?' He has become rigid and institutionalised in his religion. His fixed points perhaps are the letter of the law and the oral tradition of the Elders. His literalism has made him forget the many instances in his people's history of the free movement of the Spirit, the burgeoning and flowering of new truths. He deserves Jesus' rebuke.

To illuminate this encounter further we need to know Jesus's radical attitude towards the Judaism of his day, as shown by Matthew's account of his teaching in the Sermon on the Mount. Jesus says clearly that he has not come to abolish the law and the prophets but to fulfil or complete them (Matthew 5:17). He then proceeds to give six brief examples of what he means (5:21-48). In each case he quotes the law of Mosaic regulation regarding murder, adultery, divorce, vows and oaths, revenge and love. He then adds, 'but what I tell you...' Each comment shows that Jesus is always concerned with a person's inner disposition. It is often anger or hatred which leads to murder, lust which leads to infidelity, dishonesty to perjury. Therefore, he says recognise and deal with the springs of action. Instead of revenge or even paying back injury with strict justice, ie. 'an eye for an eye', Jesus advises an astonishing change of attitude, a spirit of active love which is able to overcome evil even to the extent of treating the enemy with understanding and compassion. He sees that the human personality can be transformed when motivated by Love. His disciples therefore have to show themselves 'far better' than the Scribes and the Pharisees to enter the Kingdom (5:20).

In John's gospel this 'far better' state, a 'righteousness that exceeds' that of Scribes and Pharisees, is expressed in terms of rebirth. In this sense John has shown a more profound understanding of Jesus' intent than Matthew.

The Synoptics are full of examples in parables about seed, yeast, hidden treasure and so on, of how Jesus used everyday things to point to spiritual truths if the hearer was capable of making that connection. His use of poetic imagery could equally fire the imagination of his listeners and lead them to explore further. This could have been true for Nicodemus if only his faith had been sufficiently flexible and open. But at this stage in his development, Nicodemus' inability to understand Jesus' words is used by John to illustrate a type of Jew who could not even recognise the truth of Jesus' teaching in an 'earthly' or material context, never mind the 'heavenly' or spiritual significance of his words (3:12).

6. **Comment by the Evangelist, 3:13-21:**

These verses appear to denote a change of presentation. The setting is no longer a private conversation between Jesus and a righteous Jew, but is rather the Evangelist uttering his mature convictions based on his own and his community's experience. The verses witness the power of the Spirit as manifested in Jesus' life, death and resurrection and yet the Jews did not believe. For the author and his contemporaries, heaven was the dwelling place of God. To speak of going up into, down from and being now in heaven was a way of expressing the intensely personal and intimate relationship which his disciples knew that Jesus, their master, had with God, the Father. The gift of the Spirit which came to them later was proof positive that Jesus had now returned to the Father. The presence and power of this Spirit amongst them was a fulfilment of Jesus' promise to them and a prophetic foreshadowing of the Messianic age.

As discussed before, it is understandable that his Jewish disciples should make constant use of Old Testament passages to authenticate Jesus as Messiah even though this does not appeal to us. Thus John now uses a verse from a Mosaic story which for him symbolises the purpose and efficacy of Jesus' death and resurrection. The passage from Numbers is both unbelievable and legendary (21:4-9). During their wanderings in the desert, the Israelites constantly lost faith both in God and his appointed leader, Moses, who had a very difficult time of it. On this occasion, they were punished for their rebelliousness by a plague of serpents whose bites caused inflammation and even death. On their repentance and appeal to Moses for the Lord's forgiveness, Moses is instructed by the Lord to make a brazen serpent and erect it on a pole so that those who looked at it could recover from their bites - an early illustration perhaps of the power of sympathetic magic! The relic of a bronze serpent housed in the Temple, became an idolatrous object of worship by the people and was destroyed by King Hezekiah in his reforming zeal (2 Kings 18:4). In later Jewish thought, however, the serpent became a 'symbol of salvation' (Wisdom of Solomon 16:6). John certainly uses it in this sense - just as Moses lifted up the serpent, so the Son of Man must be lifted up. The Greek 'lift up' can also mean 'exalt'. It has supreme significance for faith in Jesus brings eternal life.

The phrase eternal life occurs at least seventeen times in John's gospel. It is not quite the same idea as everlasting life, which suggests length of time. Eternal can mean that which is outside time and begins here and now in relationship with God. It is the quality of a life that is lived in the power of the spirit of Love itself.

7.   A special note on verses 3:16,17:

The love that is of God is now defined in well-known and hallowed words, used for centuries of Christian worship. What do they mean for the modern reader who may have difficulty with the anthropomorphic and male-orientated picture of the divine Father and Son? If the Son was 'given' for the sake of the world's salvation, did he have any option in the matter?

First, the writer of the First Letter of John (who could have been the Evangelist himself) twice states that 'God is love' (1 John 4:7,16). This belief arose out of his experience of both the human Jesus and the indwelling Christ of faith. To say that God is love is a much more comprehensive statement than to talk about the love of God, which implies that loving is one of the divine attributes. If God is love, then where there is love there is also God. The Epistle writer also clarifies that this is not simply esoteric knowledge of the divine nature, but knowledge acquired through human relationships. To claim to love God, yet hate your neighbour is a travesty of truth, for your neighbour is someone whom you know and see, whilst God is an unseen reality.

Behind the words of the Epistle lies the Synoptic record of the one absolute commandment Jesus gave when he summarised the whole law in terms of love. We are bidden to love God with all our being and to love our neighbour as ourselves. Jesus re-enforced these words by the example of his own self-giving. In fact Jesus by his life and death demonstrated the self-giving quality of Love itself. But the story does not finish here, for Jesus' faith in Love was vindicated. The resurrection experience and the disciples' subsequent empowerment by the Spirit witnessed to the fact that the spirit of Jesus was alive and present in the midst of his followers. Death is not the end. Life in the spirit continues in eternity.

Second, we should not take the anthropomorphic terms too literally. They speak of a relationship which is always personal because we cannot feel that we are loved by an abstraction. Jesus in conversation with the Samaritan woman defines God as Spirit. But he also called God "Abba" or Father. Therefore, the two concepts are not incompatible in his experience.

Third, we have to understand the biblical use of sacrificial language. All ancient religions practised actual sacrifice in some form or another. In primitive times sacrificial systems were inaugurated to placate, appease, influence or to celebrate the beneficence of the divine powers who managed the universe. These deities controlled those areas of life which humanity could not at that time understand or control. In the Old Testament we see the Israelites, through inspired leadership, coming to understand more about the divine nature of the one true God. Abraham was prepared to offer his only son, Isaac, as a sacrifice to God, but his willingness to do so was accepted as sufficient proof of his faith without the act being performed (Genesis 22:1-19). This ancient story of Abraham's inner conflict, as to what he conceived to be God's wish, is understandable, living as he did amongst Canaanite peoples who practised child sacrifice. He discovered his God did not require this of him.

Despite the insights of certain prophets, eg Micah, who emphasised that what the Lord required of his worshippers (6:8) was more integrity, fidelity and humility, rather than elaborate sacrifices, the sacrificial system continued until the destruction of the Temple at the fall of Jerusalem in AD.70. In the Jewish calendar, the Day of Atonement (Yom Kippur) was the most solemn day of the Jewish year, when the High Priest entered into the Holy Place and offered sacrifice to make amends for his own and his people's sins, which had been committed in ignorance during the past year. Yom Kippur is kept by modern Jewry as a day of fasting and repentance.

These sacrificial terms are part of the language of myth and symbolise much in our religious heritage. From long usage they speak to a deeper level than our conscious minds, as poetry speaks to the imagination and intuition. But in the latter part of the first century AD, the good news about Jesus was a fresh and dynamic message which contained truth for all humanity. We have to recapture and attempt to express this truth in terms of our own culture today.

Jesus himself, was of the prophetic mould and cleared the Temple of animal merchandise, yet he used the language of his people's past to explain his own self-offering. At the Last Supper as recorded by the Synoptics (Mark 14:12-16) he described the bread and the wine as his body and blood. They were symbolic of his self-offering and he believed that through this total giving of himself, he would establish a new relationship between God and humanity. By asking his intimate disciples to share in this supper with him, he had begun the new community. Although this offering of himself has been seen by some in previous centuries as expiatory, the God who is Love does not call for appeasement or need to be placated. Nor is it credible that Jesus by dying could make amends for the sins of others. He was not the sacrificial victim in an act of atonement. The God who is Love seeks and yearns for the willing repentance and response of each individual.

Jesus' aim was to bring enlightenment so that we may learn more truly the basis of our own spiritual wellbeing. He taught by profound example. He was the living illustration of what Love in its essence could mean. In this sense he was, as the son, the willing gift of Love, the Father. He could have avoided arrest and death. His opponents wanted to silence him, for his teaching was too disruptive of their religious practice. He refused to run away and compromise even though he knew what the outcome of this resistance would be. At his trial and crucifixion, he was not corrupted by agonising pressures or deviated from his task by terror. The powerful impact of his fidelity, reinforced by its subsequent vindication, acted as a great liberating force for humanity. But there is even more to it than that: because he has shown that God, the source of our being, is Love, those who follow his way are also energised by the indwelling Spirit of love and truth.

To return to the text, (3:18-21) to reject the way of love leads the individual to a deep morass of unfulfilled potential and decay. Judgement, therefore, is self-imposed. It is the product of a profound working out of the moral and spiritual law of cause and effect, referred to earlier. The fact that some people choose 'darkness' rather than 'light' is the inevitable cost of free will but one that strikes at the very heart of Love itself. Love is willing to suffer this rejection as part of the cost of being true to one's nature. Love treats each individual as a being capable of responding freely. This is the dignity the creator accords human beings, even though we have not yet realised it and do not treat each other in this way. According to Jesus' teaching in such parables as the Lost Sheep and the Lost Coin, it is not God's will that any child of his should be lost. The parable of the Prodigal Son shows the father's love calling him home. Jesus conceived of his mission as retrieving these lost souls. But the choice had still to be the person's own, otherwise it was non-productive of real growth and development.

The First Letter of John (1:5), defines God as light. In him there is no darkness at all. To be in the light is to be with God. These images were potent for John's day, even if in the twentieth century we cannot accept their absolute validity now that Jung has shown us the shadow side of ourselves. We may not necessarily associate darkness with moral and spiritual evil but see it as an opportunity for growth. To understand the shadow is the path of true self-discovery. Even so we may also argue that the divinity by definition has no unconscious and therefore no shadow. This may help us to read the gospel with more sympathetic understanding of John's outlook.

The light of Jesus' being was rejected by some. They preferred the darkness in which they could hide their evil deeds. We use the phrase 'in the dark' to signify lack of comprehension; this is John's meaning too, but he uses it with deep spiritual significance to mean spiritually blind and obtuse and therefore unaware of God. The illumination of God's Spirit seen in Jesus was too much of a challenge for some of his contemporaries. They shunned and rejected him because they were afraid of their own self-exposure. In this sense they judged themselves, because when they were offered spiritual life they chose spiritual death.

8.   **The Samaritan Woman 4:1-42:**

Background: The Samaritans were of mixed descent. When the Assyrians conquered the Northern Kingdom in 721 BC, the Israelite population was taken captive and replaced by a number of foreign settlers (2 Kings 17:24ff) who brought with them their own gods. The religious tradition of the Northern kingdom, therefore, continued with difficulty. After the Southern Kingdom was conquered by the Babylonians in 587 BC, the Judaic leadership was taken to Babylon but allowed to remain as a separate captive enclave for about fifty years. When Babylon itself fell to the Persians, the Jews were given permission to return to their homeland, which they found in a parlous state. They eventually rebuilt the Temple, the city walls and their religious life, based on their sacred literature. Nehemiah and Ezra, two outstanding figures in the post-exilic period, were disinclined to include the Samaritans in their restoration.

Consequently, in the middle of the fourth century BC, the Samaritans built their own temple on Mount Gerizim. Although this temple was destroyed some two centuries later, the Jews and Samaritans disputed bitterly about the relative values of Mount Zion in Jerusalem and Mount Gerizim. The Samaritans, who held sacred only the Pentateuch, or first five books of the Old Testament, believed themselves to be the True Israelites. Nevertheless they were greatly despised by the Jews as being members of a hybrid race, neither Jew nor Gentile.

Comment: Jesus leaves Judaea because of increasing hostility from the Pharisees who resent his growing popularity. He is making for Galilee and goes by the shortest route through Samaria, although more often than not Jews would avoid this territory. At Jacob's well, which was probably a little way from the nearby town of Sychar (possibly Shechem, Genesis 33:18f and 48:22), Jesus sits down. As he is tired and thirsty, his disciples go to buy food. When a Samaritan woman approaches the well, she is astonished that Jesus asks her for a drink. This woman is a remarkable character, an individual in her own right, but in this gospel, she also stands as a representative of her own people, as Nicodemus did for his.

The woman is surprised at Jesus' approach for three reasons; Jews would not normally have any dealings with Samaritans; a rabbi would not speak to a woman (not even his own wife) in public and, furthermore, a Jew would consider a common vessel offered by a Samaritan woman as ritually 'unclean'. But Jesus, looking at her and understanding much, simply forgets his own needs and offers her what he has to give - the living water of the eternal Spirit.

The woman naturally takes Jesus' words literally, just as Nicodemus did, but in this case the conversation is progressive. She points out that the well is deep - and Jesus has no bucket; she could feel indignant that Jesus may imagine himself superior to their great ancestor, the patriarch Jacob. Jesus, however, explains that he is not talking about water which temporarily satisfies ordinary thirst, but about an inner spring of spiritual vitality which can become a permanent possession. She immediately responds to his offer even if she persists in taking his words at their face value. Jesus then replies that she must bring her husband to share in his gift. When she simply answers that she has no husband, Jesus reveals that he knows more about her than she could possibly have imagined. She has had five husbands and is now living with a man not her husband. However, there is no condemnation in Jesus' words, a fact which must have deeply shaken her. If he knew so much, why had he spoken to her in the first place?

With growing faith and awareness, the woman now recognises Jesus is a prophet; perhaps he is the one foretold by Moses (Deuteronomy 18:15, cf. John 1:45). She has confidence to ask him to clarify the Jewish/Samaritan controversy about holy places. Jesus takes her question perfectly seriously and continues the discussion, which reflects his regard for her even if some of his words seem at first arrogant. To understand, we need to appreciate the background to his thought. Jesus says that the time is coming when the place of worship will have no significance. He states that the Samaritans do not know what they worship, whereas the Jews do. 'It is from the Jews that salvation comes.' Yet the first three chapters have made perfectly clear the inadequacy of Judaism - its purificatory rites (see p.28, its sacrificial system, its Temple (see p.51), and its religious leadership (as exemplified by Nicodemus).

However, Jesus himself is a Jew and he inherits a rich and purposeful past, hence the word *from*; Jesus comes from Jewish tradition and he is himself salvation. Fundamental to Old Testament theology is the belief that out of all the nations of the world, the Creator God chose to make a covenant relationship with the seed of Abraham (Genesis 12:1-3; 15:5,6). God's purpose in calling these people to be his own was that they should become 'a kingdom of priests', a holy nation (Exodus 19:6), implying Israel's vocation of service to all humanity. But the priestly role of intercession and mediation had often been forgotten in the nation's struggle for survival, except by a faithful few. It was the prophetic vision which interpreted the law afresh and recalled people to their principal reason for existing and to the moral nature of the divine being who had called them; the Wisdom school, the poets and the apocalyptic writers had all contributed to the rich tapestry of their sacred literature.

In Jesus' day, Israel hoped the coming of the Messiah would free them from bondage and establish God's kingdom on earth. But John Baptist, the greatest of the old order, saw the Messianic role in universal terms by recognising Jesus as the Chosen One who would take away the sin of the world. We can see from 1 John and Paul's letters that the disciples of Jesus came to appreciate what it meant to say that he was the true fulfilment of all that had gone before in Israel's history. He was the supreme revelation to humanity of the nature of the one true God, the Father of all. It is amazing that Jesus should be speaking privately to a woman, when in one of the profoundest passages of the Fourth Gospel, he defines God as spirit. True worship is spiritual. Externals are not essential. The divisions between Jews and Samaritans will come to have no significance. What is all-important is the inner attitude of the heart and mind of the worshipper. Those who worship God must do so in spirit and in truth.

The Samaritans also had Messianic expectations, so the woman begins to understand the deeper levels of Jesus' meaning. She believes the coming Messiah will clarify spiritual matters for them. Jesus replies 'I am he'. It is to this Samaritan woman at a well, that he first reveals his identity. And it is first to another woman, Mary Magdalene, that the Risen Jesus does the same (John 20:16). So Jesus breaks all racial, sexual and social barriers to meet people simply as people.

At this moment the disciples, returning with some food, are amazed at the scene in front of them, but make no comment. The woman rushes off to the town to broadcast her discovery, leaving her empty waterpot behind. She is coming back! The disciples beg Jesus to eat, but he has gone way beyond physical hunger to the exhilaration of spiritual fulfilment.

Jesus comments on the saying 'One sows, another reaps'. When the crop is eternal life, both sower and reaper can rejoice together. He sees the

Samaritans coming across the fields to greet him, so now the disciples will reap what others have sown (cf Mark 4:26-29 and Luke 10:2).

It is another remarkable tribute to the woman herself, whatever her past life may or may not have been, that so many Samaritans believe her testimony and come to Jesus. On their request he stays with them for a couple of days and many more believe in him thanks to their own personal encounter. We see the woman (who surely had a name!) fulfilling the role of a true disciple because through her witness many of her people become followers of Jesus. In fact they declare their conviction that he is the Saviour of the world. This brings to completion the opening words of John Baptist (1:29) when he recognised Jesus as the Lamb of God.

9.   The disciples blown off course on the lake; 6:16-21:

In Mark (6:45-52, cf. Matthew 14:22-31) this incident is presented as a miraculous act by Jesus who walks on the sea to meet his disciples, blown off course by strong winds. As we have come to expect, John makes different points, although some commentators make this a 'sign' story.

Following the feeding of the five thousand the disciples went down to the sea, and boarded their boat to cross to Capernaum. After rowing three or four miles in complete darkness, they may well have been nearer to land than they supposed. Meanwhile Jesus probably walked from the eastern side of the lake in the direction of Capernaum and was actually by the shore or in the surf, when they saw him. The same Greek word 'on' can also mean 'by' (It is so used in Chapter 21:1). When the disciples made to take Jesus on board, they discovered that they had landed on the beach near Capernaum.

If John deliberately minimises any miraculous walking on water, why does he include this story? Perhaps partly because it was an actual happening but primarily because of its symbolism. The disciples have been blown off course by heavy wind and turbulent waters. They are in the dark, which John always uses as an image of ignorance. They are terrified when they see a mysterious figure seemingly walking towards them. But all is well for it is the Master who comes to meet them and greets them in self-revelatory words, ' It is I; do not be afraid.'

(For further discussion on the 'I AM' statements which follow this incident, see p.110).

10.   The woman taken in adultery, vs. 7:53-8:11:

Textual background: There is no doubt amongst scholarly opinion that this is an authentic Jesus story but it is felt to have a 'floating' even if venerable history and to be more in keeping with the Synoptic tradition than John. At what point it became attached to the Fourth Gospel is a matter of conjecture. Certainly Jerome regarded it as part of John, hence its inclusion in the Latin Vulgate. Ambrose and Augustine both treat it as Johannine and tradition goes back to Papias recollecting a similar story. However, modern scholars say that it is missing from the best Greek manuscripts.

It has been suggested that the incident takes place during Jesus' last days in the Temple when, according to Mark, he is subject to a number of 'tests' or trick questions by the authorities in the hope that he will betray himself (Mark 11:28-33; 12:13-17; 12:18-27; 12: 28-34). In this eventful week, Jesus goes back to Bethany each evening and then returns to teaching in the Temple (Mark 11:11,12;19,27).

Whilst appreciating the validity of all the textual and ancient codex evidence, it seems to me that the scribe who inserted this story in this particular place did so for sound theological reasons even if the incident seems to break the flow of controversy which continues again in 8:12.

Comment: Jesus returns to the Temple from the Mount of Olives very early in the morning and continues to teach a large crowd gathered to hear him. A contingent of scribes and Pharisees bring before him a woman who has been caught in the very act of adultery. According to the Mosaic regulations (Leviticus 20:10; Deuteronomy 22:22) both the guilty man and woman should be punished by death, but on this occasion no guilty man is produced. In other Old Testament passages, it is either the betrothed maiden (betrothal being tantamount to marriage) who is discovered not to be a virgin, who shall be stoned to death (Deuteronomy 22:21), or if a betrothed virgin willingly submits to intercourse with a man not her future husband, then both man and woman should be stoned. According to Deuteronomy (17:7), it is the duty of the witness to be the first to execute judgement. These barbaric customs are deeply embedded in the ancient cultural assumption that a woman was a man's property and as a mother of his children must be pure and 'undefiled' before marriage. However, such beliefs have nothing to do with the point of the gospel episode, except as background information.

The deputation appears to be asking Jesus' advice about the matter but as John indicates, they think they have got him on the horns of a dilemma. If Jesus supports the law and agrees that the woman should be stoned,

Roman officials could charge him with inciting murder; as a subject people, the Jews were apparently not allowed to execute the death sentence. (The fact that the Jews managed to stone Stephen, Acts 7:54-60, presupposes that the martyrdom occurred during an interregnum when Pilate had been recalled to Rome, AD 36). On the other hand, if Jesus advocated mercy, he could be criticised as a poor Rabbi for not supporting the rigours of the law.

Jesus does not answer them immediately but writes on the ground. He does this twice (8:6 and 8:8). Jesus's first words after further pressure from the deputation, are totally unexpected. The first stone should be cast by the man who is without sin. As all, under the law, are guilty of some infringement and therefore sinful (even if not necessarily guilty of some sexual misdemeanour), everyone, beginning with the eldest, is stricken and ashamed and leaves the scene, while Jesus again writes on the ground. The woman is left standing where her accusers have placed her. Jesus looks at her and addresses her directly as a person. He asks if no one has condemned her. When she replies, Jesus says he will not condemn her either, adding, 'Go; do not sin again' (cf. the healing of the lame man, 5:6,14 , see p.32).

If we attempt to see why a scribe might have placed the episode in this context, we have to admit that in some ways the story is a fitting example of what Jesus has been saying. In chapter 7:24, Jesus has spoken out against the Jews' superficial judgement on him as a law breaker and asked them to consider being just in their assessments. In 8:15,16, he accuses them of judging by worldly standards and says that he passes judgement on no one. If he does judge it is only on behalf of the one who sent him. Further, in 8:46, he asks the assembled company if any of them can accuse him of sin. They do not recognise the truth when they see it because they are liars themselves.

For the Jew, sin, transgression, meant breaking God's holy law. Jesus, in the synoptic tradition, clearly summarises the whole law in terms of love of God and love of neighbour as oneself (Matthew 22:34-40. Mark 12:28-34, Luke (10:25-28). Sin, therefore, for Jesus was the unloving thought, word and deed, of which we are all guilty and from which we can all endeavour to change.

The meaning behind the phrase 'the judgement of God' is a vexed question, but I believe it has a two-fold application. On one level it is the working out of the moral law of cause and effect, hence Jesus' advice to do as you would be done by (Matthew 7:12). On a much deeper level, the revelation of God's nature, which has come to us through Jesus, is that Love is the ultimate reality. We have not begun to assess what this may mean in terms of human destiny. Jesus was very aware of human fallibility; none is good but God, he said to the rich young ruler (Luke 18:19). He also told his disciples in graphic detail not to be judgemental in their attitude to others (Matthew 7:1-5). In John's gospel his way of dealing with people is to reach them at their deepest level and awaken in them a desire to become whole through union with the one who is Love itself. Fear of punishment, hell fire, the devil, all can act as a partial deterrent, just as the promise of heavenly and earthly rewards can be a partial incentive to right behaviour. But Love is the only motive which can both bring self-illumination and engender a transformation of the self.

CHAPTER TWO – SIX OF THE SEVEN SIGNS

		Chapter	Page
1.	The Marriage at Cana	2:1-11	27
2.	The Healing of the Officer's Son	4:43-54	30
3.	The Healing of the Cripple	5:1-15	32
4.	The Feeding of the Five Thousand	6:1-16	33
5.	The Man Born Blind	9:1-41	36
6.	The Raising of Lazarus	11:1-43	40
7.	The Anointing at Bethany	12:1-11	46

CHAPTER 2:

Six of the Seven Signs

1.   The Marriage at Cana, 2:1-11:

Jesus is now in Galilee with his newly found disciples, all local men. He goes with them to the wedding of a friend of the family. We can assume that it was a family friendship as his mother, who is present, is able to take some responsibility for the servants' actions. A minor crisis arises in that the wine runs out and Jesus' mother appeals to her son for help in an embarrassing situation. Luke indicated in the opening chapters of his gospel that Jesus' mother had some inkling of her son's special nature. This is now implied in the Fourth Gospel as Mary (like the beloved disciple, she remains unnamed in this gospel), seems to be aware of a power within her son which gives him the ability to resolve problems. At first Jesus refuses his mother's request. It seems he must assert his independence from her and not be subject to the emotional pressure of family; perhaps he feels that what has happened has nothing to do with either of them and he does not want to take any responsibility for the situation. In any case the real point is that he will act upon his own initiative, in his own way, at his own time and his mother must understand and accept this state of affairs. Perhaps the full impact of what he is, what he has to do and what he has to give has not yet been fully realised within him.

Jesus is somewhat abrupt with his mother, but apparently she implicitly trusts him and is not abashed. She instructs the servants to do whatever Jesus tells them, so she clearly anticipates that Jesus will take some action! We are then given precise details about the six stone water jars, used for Jewish ceremonial washing which the guests might require on arrival. Being non-porous, they were thought to be uncontaminated by 'uncleanness'. The REB states each would hold twenty or thirty gallons - a lot of water and subsequently a great deal of wine to unload on to the guests who have already drunk freely. The servants are told by Jesus to refill these jars and the water which is then drawn off from them becomes the best wine the wedding party has tasted. Only the disciples, the servants and Jesus' mother know what has really happened. But, says John, this is the first of the signs in which Jesus' glory is revealed and which leads his disciples to believe in him.

First, we have to look at the cultural background of this story. The Evangelist makes a time link with the preceding chapter. The wedding takes place on the third day but it is also the seventh day in the time sequence of the gospel. In Jewish numerical symbolism (especially in the Apocalyptic books of Daniel and Revelation) three, seven and twelve are the numbers of completion and perfection. The seventh day is 'hallowed' in the Genesis creation myth (2:2).. Six, being short of seven, was seen as a symbol of the incomplete, even of sin. So the six water jars could represent the Mosaic law in its limiting, restricting emphasis on observance and its reliance on religious rites rather than a change of heart. In contrast, the best wine, which came from the transformed water, stands for the new life of the Spirit which as the gift of Jesus is overflowing and abundant in quantity and quality. The Baptist has already stated that his water of baptism would be superseded by Jesus' baptism of the Spirit and this story could be seen as a foretaste of that promise.

Second, it is useful to refer to the Synoptic record. According to Mark, Jesus went away into the wilderness after his baptism to think through his particular interpretation of messiahship. Mark gives no details of Jesus' temptations - these are supplied by Matthew and Luke. Then Jesus returns to Galilee, and begins his preaching ministry by declaring that the time has come, the long period of waiting is over for the Kingdom of God has come upon his listeners. He urges repentance and belief in the good news he brings. By contrast, John does not mention Jesus' temptations at all and the theme of the Kingdom, the main topic of Jesus' teaching in the Synoptics, appears only twice in his gospel. John prefers the phrase 'eternal life' which contains much that is involved in the idea of the Kingdom of God, but has fewer associations with Jewish aspirations and is more comprehensible to a wider range of readers.

In Mark, it is after Jesus has begun to preach that he calls his first disciples, performs several healing miracles and then enters into direct conflict with the Scribes and the Pharisees. The third so-called 'conflict' story (Mark 2:18-22) would appear to have some slight relevance to John's account of the Marriage at Cana. It was a Pharisaic custom to fast twice a week and the Baptist's disciples also fasted regularly. When it was observed that Jesus' disciples did not fast, Jesus was asked about this omission. He replied that it was unnatural to fast at a glad time, such as a wedding, but if the bridegroom were to be taken away, then his friends would fast out of sadness and grief. Jesus then told his questioners two little parables in which he contrasted the old with the new. It is not sensible to patch an old garment with a new piece of cloth because the strong new cloth would tear away the old: nor is it wise to fill old unelastic bottles with new wine, because the effervescence of the new wine would cause the old wineskins to crack and the wine would be spilt. It is quite clear in Mark's gospel, that Jesus is comparing his radical approach with that of the Pharisees; the new life he brings is liberating in its strength and power, in contrast to the old limitations and restrictions of the Jewish legal system. In the Synoptics, this mistaken emphasis on outward conformity rather than inward renewal was the basis of Jesus' criticism of the Scribes and the Pharisees.

The Wedding at Cana is not represented as a story parable; in the Fourth Gospel, Jesus does not use this form of teaching. Neither is Jesus the bridegroom, nor the family wedding symbolic of the Messianic Feast. The Evangelist has quite deliberately changed the emphasis. He says specifically that this wedding was an incident in the life of Jesus. It was the first of the signs in which Jesus revealed his glory. A sign can be interpreted as an acted parable but in John it is an act of symbolic spiritual truth. Compared to the Synoptic record of 'miracles', John records only a limited number of 'signs'. For example, he never mentions exorcism or even the Transfiguration. In the Synoptics, miracles are a manifestation of the Kingdom of God. In John the seven signs are symbolic acts which show forth God's glory in Jesus.

The Evangelist also has a strong feeling for irony. From time to time he reports someone unwittingly making a remark which has a profound double meaning. Here it is the toastmaster, or steward, who comments to the bridegroom that he has kept the best wine until the last. In fact this is what the story is all about. John writes on two levels: there is the ordinary human event and its extraordinary and deep spiritual significance.

Problems: Is the story true or false? Did Jesus have this kind of magical power to turn water into wine and even if he did, would he so have used it? From the Synoptic record it is clear that Jesus was totally opposed to the use of this kind of pressure to persuade watchers. (Luke 4:9-13). He refused to dazzle people into belief in him by some spectacular show of power (Mark 8:11-13) and left people free to make their own choices. He met people where they were, provoked them by enigmatic and paradoxical statements which encouraged self-knowledge and therefore the possibility of spiritual growth. What he looked for was the response to love which must be freely given.

How then can we approach this story? At this distance of time we do not and cannot know what actually happened. Therefore the question 'Is it true or false?' is an unanswerable one. My personal view is that even if

Jesus had the power to turn water into wine, he would not so have used it. I find myself trying to reconstruct the experience of those present and how the story came to be symbolically interpreted afterwards. The gospel writer's outlook and approach were quite different from our own. For him, every year, through the providence of God, the rain brought to fruition the greatly valued grape harvest. Can we use our imaginations to see with his eyes? The gospel was written many years later with the lived experience of the guidance of the Spirit of love and truth. There cannot have been any deliberate attempt to dissemble. The fact for John was that Jesus by turning an embarrassing family occasion into something other, revealed his transforming power. Water into wine was the symbol of that power. Its links with the witness of the Baptist were deeply significant bcause John Baptist contrasted the outward rite with the inward transformation. Water and wine can be seen also as a theme for the whole gospel.

2. The healing of the officer's son, 4:43-54:

Jesus now leaves Samaria (where he has had a successful mission) and returns to Galilee. His wry comment on the inevitability of a prophet being rejected by his own country indicates his deep hurt at the reception he received in Jerusalem, despite apparent but obviously superficial success. Mark reports that Jesus made this remark after rejection by his home town at Nazareth (6:4). The fact that John places Jesus' observation here, reflects the pattern of his gospel. The Jewish leadership have not received Jesus even though Nicodemus, the best of his kind, has sought him out. The Samaritan woman, although she did not recognise Jesus at first, responded eagerly to him and brought along others. Now we read of a Gentile who both knew his need and believed in Jesus.

Many commentators assume that John is here retelling the incident found in Luke (7:1-10) where the Roman Centurion's servant was healed thanks to the faith of his master. Luke's story is an alive and detailed account of the sensitivity of a "God-fearing" Gentile who is aware of Jesus' great spiritual authority. It ends with Jesus' comment that he has not found comparable faith among God's chosen people. Other commentators believe that the differences between the two stories are such as to suggest that John is writing of a separate healing.

In John, Jesus meets the officer at Cana, the place where the first sign took place. The officer, in the royal service, visits Jesus to implore him to go to Capernaum to heal his son who is mortally ill. Like Jesus' mother, in the previous story, the officer seems to be repulsed by Jesus. It is possible that Jesus is expressing disillusionment with a faith that depends on miracles and he needs to know for sure the officer's calibre. It is more probable, however, that Jesus discerns in this man a faith that is ready to blossom, so he stretches it further, as he did in the healing of the Syro-Phoenician woman's daughter (Mark 7:24-30). The man does not disappoint him. He is not put off by Jesus. In some deep place in his heart he trusts Jesus and renews his request. This time, Jesus does not fail him.

The officer is told to go home; his son will live. Astonishingly, the man believes and accepts the miracle without the need for Jesus to see the child. On his return, he is met by servants who tell him his son is recovering and that the moment of recovery coincides with the time when Jesus spoke. The conclusion notes that the officer and all his household become believers.

Three points need further discussion. First a casual reading might suggest that the man believed because of the exact synchronisation of Jesus' words with the boy's recovery. But the story has shown that the officer's faith was already there and had deepened through his encounter with Jesus. The detail of timing was simply an added confirmation of the miracle.

Second, we notice the cultural view of the family as a corporate whole. Thus in the Marcan story, the girl is healed through her mother's faith. We read also in Acts (18:8) of entire households, including servants and domestic slaves, becoming believers when the head of the house takes that step.

Third, for the Evangelist, writing to people living years after the actual Jesus event, it was important to establish the power of the indwelling spirit of Christ who continued to be active in their midst. The 'healings at a distance' as recorded in the gospels were but an illustration of the many great things which were and would be done in Jesus' name.

However, for the Fourth Gospel, the emphasis is always on belief and life - from the one springs the other - and it is the Gentile who responds without complication to that which Jesus offers. The symbolism of the first sign when water was changed into wine, speaks of the new and abundant life which Jesus brings. Here, in the second sign, an example of the healing power of Jesus to restore physical vitality, serves to demonstrate the springs of eternal life which are available to the officer and his whole family through his belief. The first four chapters are thus a unit which deals with the relationship between the old, in the form of Judaic practices, and the new, in the person of Jesus and his gift of the Spirit and eternal life. (For comment on 2:12-25, see chapter 3).

3. The healing of the cripple, 5:1-15:

The scene now moves back to Jerusalem, where Jesus again goes to celebrate one of the Jewish festivals, possibly Tabernacles in October. Recent archaeological discovery has established the existence of an ancient healing sanctuary in what must have been a relatively new area of the city for Jesus' era. This site was probably fed by intermittent underground springs, rich in mineral resources and therefore of some benefit to sufferers. It would have been completely destroyed during Titus' siege of Jerusalem in AD70. A copper scroll from the Qumran community establishes the name Bethesda, which means, literally, 'house of mercy'.

The sick people who lay there in great numbers, hoping for healing, would have been excluded by their infirmities from the temple ritual. But Jesus is always shown as caring for these people. From the crowd of sufferers, he speaks to one man, a cripple for the last thirty-eight years. He asks him the simple question, 'Do you want to get well?' The man's answer shows confusion. He seems to be making excuses for his present plight, but Jesus replies by telling the cripple to arise, pick up his pallet and walk. The man responds and is cured. However all this took place on the Sabbath, so the man is accosted by the Jews as a Sabbath breaker - to carry his bed on the Sabbath was work (cf Jeremiah 17:21) and Exodus states (31: 14, 15; 35:2) that work could profane the Sabbath, death being the penalty. The cured man genuinely does not know who it is who has healed him so all he can say is that he obeyed the words of the healer.

Whenever it was possible, Jesus seems to have kept an eye on those whom he had healed (cf John 9:35). In this case he found the man in the Temple and impressed upon him the need to live a disciplined life and to give up his sinful ways, which would be hard after years of imposed idleness. If he did not now continue the healing process by his own endeavour he would find himself in a worse case than before. This is not to say that Jesus regarded sin as the cause of the man's illness. Despite the fact that this view was current in much of the Old Testament and indeed was popular in New Testament times, Jesus himself has a different attitude (see p.36) He does not associate illness with sin (John 9:3) but he discerns people's needs and this man's particular weakness could be the inertia caused by thirty-eight years of inactivity to which he had grown accustomed. The man then went and told the authorities that it was Jesus who had healed him. This was not necessarily a betrayal for Jesus made no secret of his ability to heal.

We are reminded in some ways, but not in others, of Mark's story of the healing of the paralysed man (Mark 2:1-7). Both cases show a hopeless cripple cured by the instruction to get up and walk. In Mark, however, the man's friends sought out Jesus and went to a great deal of trouble on the cripple's behalf to present him to Jesus. Moreover, Jesus, clearly seeing the man's psychological and spiritual state which had probably contributed to his paralysis, forgave him his sins. He then had the faith to obey Jesus and was cured. In John's story Jesus takes the initiative without any preamble about forgiveness of sins and the episode happens on a Sabbath. Later, Jesus warns the man that his initial response to Jesus has awakened the dormant spirit within him but is not enough; now he himself must foster its growth with all his new-found energy.

Looking back on the preceding chapters, the symbol of water runs throughout the text. First it was used by John Baptist in a baptism of repentance, but he foretold that Jesus would baptise with the Spirit. Second, the water of Jewish purificatory rites was transformed into the wine of the new and abundant life which comes through faith in Jesus. Third, the water which quenches thirst was compared with Jesus' gift of the inner springs of eternal life. And lastly, here, the Bethesda water which had been used for healing was superseded by Jesus' word.

Some commentators see the cripple as a representative of his people and the duration of his sickness as symbolic of the thirty-eight years the Israelites spent in the wilderness (Deuteronomy 2:14). To my mind an alternative suggestion is preferable, that the crippled man represents humanity. Unable to help himself, he had become inured to his condition of semi-existence. Only on the initiative of Jesus, was there any hope for him. Even so, he must work on the development of his spiritual self. There must have been something within him which still struggled for wholeness. It was this that Jesus saw and was able to reach, for he obeyed Jesus without question and was physically healed. He could have scoffed and doubted, but he did not.

Humanity has the capacity to enjoy spiritual fellowship with its Creator or to reject this fellowship by seeking life on its own terms. Only by exercising this choice can people develop in the deepest spiritual sense. For John, a person's destiny is determined by belief or disbelief in Jesus, who not only has life within himself but who is also the bringer of eternal life to others. The arrival of Jesus heralded the time when the spiritually dead would be awakened. This is the potentiality for eternal life which Jesus offered to the cripple by healing his body and stimulating his will.

4. The Feeding of the Five Thousand, 6:1-16, 22-34:

This is the only incident which is included in all four gospels but John's treatment of and additional information to the Marcan story highlights his own particular approach. First, only John says that it occurs at Passover time, the second Passover of Jesus' ministry. The whole chapter, therefore, has to be seen against this fact. Second, as is typical of this gospel, it is not the disciples who take the initiative but Jesus, acting out of concern for the crowd. In practical terms, the disciples do not know what to do; the situation is beyond them. Third, it is the resourceful Andrew (1:40-42) who tells Jesus about the boy carrying five barley loaves and two fishes, even though he (Andrew) does not see how that can help much. Fourth, it is from John alone that we learn the crowd want to make Jesus king.

Jesus tells the disciples to make the crowd sit on the grass (cf Mark 6:39) for it is spring time. He takes the bread and says grace over it, as would be customary for any Jewish head of the household over a meal. He then distributes the food amongst the crowd. The same thing happens with the fish. The text implies that Jesus distributed everything personally, but if so it must have taken him some time! Perhaps John is deliberately emphasising the personal relationship which can exist between the giver and the recipient of the bread of life. The disciples are only required to gather up the leftovers so that nothing is wasted. The twelve each fill a basket with fragments but we are not told where the baskets come from.

John presents this story in a more miraculous way than Mark. It is possible to see Mark's version in terms of the crowd's change of heart; having been with Jesus all day and hearing him teach, they are prepared to share what they have with each other and thus all have enough. The crowd in John's gospel have followed Jesus because of his healing miracles and after the feeding they become very excited. They recall Moses' feeding the Israelites in the wilderness (Exodus 16:1-21, cf John 6:31,32) and believe that Jesus must be the Prophet whom Moses foretold (Deuteronomy 18:15). Jesus realises that the crowd's enthusiasm for him is reaching such fever pitch that they now want to make him king, so he withdraws into the hills to be on his own. According to Josephus, the Jewish historian, such Messianic movements to revolt were not uncommon in Galilee and were met with great harshness by the authorities.

Later in John's gospel (18:36) Jesus says very clearly that his kingdom is not a worldly one. He is concerned with the inner realm, the rebirth of the spirit, as he disclosed in his conversation with Nicodemus. But we also know from the Luke/Matthew story of the 'temptations' (4:1-11) that he had very real mental conflict about the proper use of power. One of the messianic alternatives which suggested itself to him was to be precisely what the crowds wanted, a rebel leader who would establish an earthly kingdom. But Jesus knew that the evil means of war and conflict always sullied the end product.

The symbolism of this third sign of Jesus as the direct giver of the bread of life, is more fully explained in the conversations at Capernaum. But the boy's gift to Jesus, a gift which is transformed into food for the huge crowd, is an attractive, even if difficult detail of the story. In the miracle at Cana, Jesus used what was available to transform water into wine. Here he does the same with the barley bread and salted fish, transforming earthly food into the abundant supply of spiritual life-giving sustenance. Unfortunately the crowd's basic self-interest leads it to misunderstand completely the nature of Jesus's gift.

Omitting for the present the disciples' encounter with Jesus by the shore (6:16-21 see p.22) we move on to Capernaum where the crowd meet Jesus again (6:22-34). They are intensely curious and observant. They know that there was only one boat at the landing stage, that Jesus did not go aboard with his disciples and yet during the night he had disappeared. Boats from Tiberias came ashore nearby so they take ship for Capernaum where they look for Jesus. When they find him, they ask him in effect how and when he got there!

Jesus does not answer them directly. He knows too well their motive in seeking him. They have not seen the feeding as a sign but simply as a resource for satisfying physical hunger. The body has its obvious needs but there are other basic necessities if a human being is to become a whole person. According to the Luke/Matthew 'temptation' stories, Jesus had himself worked through and discarded the not unnatural and popular expectation of a Messiah who would bring material plenty. The renewal of manna, (cf Exodus 16:12-31) would be the Messiah's gift in the new age. This particular choice must have been a hard one for Jesus to make, because his people were very poor and deprived. However he knew that humanity needs nourishment for the soul/spirit as well as the body (Luke 4:4). For Jesus, the important thing was to get the priorities right then the rest would follow.

This point is emphasised in John's Feeding story by Jesus saying to the crowd that they must work for the bread which gives eternal life. In fact this is the real food which the Son of Man gives, acting on the Father's authority. John's use of the title Son of Man is interesting here, especially in view of what follows. The crowd are willing to go thus far with Jesus and ask him what work of God they must undertake to obtain this spiritual bread. Jesus replies that they must believe in the one whom God has sent.

The crowd recognise that Jesus is claiming a relationship with God whose implications they cannot quite follow. They were ready to make him king after the feeding but he has disappointed them by his disappearance and his subsequent behaviour and conversation. What is he really up to? They ask him to substantiate his claim by a further remarkable sign and to clarify his own work. After all, according to the scriptures, Moses did a good job with their ancestors in the wilderness. If he is the one to succeed Moses, surely he can surpass the miracles recorded at that period?

Jesus retorts that it was not Moses who supplied the Israelites with bread but his Father (Psalm 78:24). Further, manna was and is perishable but the real bread which comes from God (i.e. 'heaven') is now available bringing life to the world. The Galileans respond by asking for a constant supply of this food as a means to satisfy their hunger.

The heightening of the miraculous element in this story serves to emphasise this gospel's use of symbolism to illustrate spiritual dynamics. The author could not possibly envisage a modern reader's problems in accepting miracles. For my own part, I can accept Mark's version much more readily because I recognise the power which Jesus had over other people, even if I cannot accept that he could or would multiply bread and fish. Nevertheless this fourth sign leads inexorably to the first I AM statement, which we will discuss later (see p.110).

5. The man born blind, 9:1-41:

This is a favourite story with many people, leaving the impression of a perfectly rounded drama full of human interest and dialogue. It follows on the most severe controversy yet encountered by Jesus in which he has said amongst other things, that he is the light of the world (8:12, see p.65), a claim which he repeats in the opening part of the story and which underlies both the outer and the inner reality of Jesus' vocation. John is describing two levels of being, the physical and the spiritual which, in Jewish thought, are never in opposition to each other, although unfortunately they became so in subsequent Christian tradition.

Background: The Evangelist would expect his readers to be aware of Jewish expectations about the Messiah. Isaiah 35 is a beautiful song of praise to the saving grace of God, similar in content and style to Second Isaiah and may well come from that period. While it expressed the longing of exiles for a re-established kingdom and the actual healing of the blind, the deaf, the lame and the dumb (35: 5,6), it came to be regarded as a prophecy of the Messianic Age.

In Mark's gospel, the people regard Jesus' healing of a deaf mute (7:31-37) as a fulfilment of prophecy. Mark also includes the healing of a blind man at Bethsaida (8:22-26) which, like the former story, is accomplished by outward signs and stages. He places the healing of the blind man after the incident where Jesus refuses to agree to the Pharisees' demand for a sign. The restoration of physical sight can therefore be taken to symbolise healing a state of inner blindness and the need for the growth of spiritual perception. In Luke (7:22,23), when John Baptist's disciples ask him on their master's behalf whether he is the Messiah or not, Jesus makes his answer by listing a whole range of cures which they have seen him do, as well as his preaching to the poor. So in this sense he did fulfil messianic expectations.

By asking Jesus whose sin caused the man's congenital blindness (9:2) the disciples expressed the Jewish traditional belief that illness and physical deformity were caused by sin, i.e. breaking the law of God. The Ten Commandments represent God as threatening to punish children for the sins of their parents to the third and fourth generation (Exodus 20:5, Deuteronomy 5:9). This gave rise to the proverb: 'Parents have eaten sour grapes and their children's teeth are set on edge' (Ezekiel 18:2), but was rightly rejected by the prophetic vision of Jeremiah (31:29) and Ezekiel (18:4) who knew that each individual person belonged to God and therefore must take responsibility for their own sin. Even so, we recognise that we inherit a tendency to certain strengths and weaknesses from our parents and may in fact inherit diseases. But we are not held culpable for that. On the other hand, we are responsible for what we do with our inheritance and, as parents, for how we support or weaken our children.

The question of sin in relation to the man himself, suggests the belief in reincarnation. Was his blindness the result of sinfulness in a previous life?

Comment: Jesus rejects all these associations between blindness and sin (cf. Luke 13:1-5, where he denies the connection between the death of eighteen people and their sinfulness). Superficially his statement that the man was born blind so that God's power will be more fully revealed through its cure, strikes a discordant note. He does not of course, mean that the purpose of suffering and its healing is to glorify God; given the fact of evil and suffering, he is pointing out what can be done about the situation through the power of faith and love.

Sometimes it is very right to ask who is responsible for a disaster, as in the case of a maritime oil spill and consequent widespread pollution of sea and land. At other times trying to apportion blame is a fruitless exercise especially when immediate relief and help are needed. As Jesus adds, collectively they must do what they can while daylight lasts for the time will come when no one can work, for it will be dark. While he is in the world, he is the light of the world. And John knows that when Jesus, the fully integrated human personality, becomes, through death and resurrection, the indwelling Christ, those who believe and experience him as such will walk in the light of the life they have in him.

Jesus acts immediately (9: 6), making a paste with his spittle (as in Mark 7:33, 8:23) to spread over the man's eyes before sending him to go and wash in the pool of Siloam, the source of water for the libations at the Feast of Tabernacles. Through obeying Jesus, the man is healed. What he experiences is more than mere restoration, for he was actually born blind and has never known sight, but now he is a new creature (cf. Paul in 2 Corinthians 5:17). He is so unlike his former self that his neighbours are confused about his identity. Some say he is the man they know and others that he is not, but looks like him. The man himself responds to the questioning by saying that he is indeed a person they have known to be blind. His reply "I am the man", can simply mean 'I am'. Although he is a particular man in a distinctive story, he also represents humanity. When questioned about his sight, the man simply gives an account of what has happened. He knows it is Jesus who has healed him but he does not know where Jesus is.

The man is brought before the Pharisees (9:13-34), partly because of people's astonishment at the healing, but also, from a Pharisaic point of view, because it happened on the Sabbath, when healing was forbidden unless it was a matter of life or death. In addition, since kneading was considered to be work, it could be construed that Jesus had twice offended Sabbath law. The Pharisees are divided in their opinions. Some stick rigidly to the letter of the law and therefore condemn Jesus as a Sabbath breaker. Others believe that such a miracle could not have been done by a sinful man. When questioned further about the one who had healed him, the man now states that he regards Jesus as a prophet, therefore a man inspired by God.

The authorities decide that they must check the fact of the man's original blindness so they call in his parents. Somewhat frightened by the occasion the parents admit that he is their son and was born blind, but say they do not know how he received his sight. They retreat behind the fact that the man is an adult and can answer for himself. John adds that the Pharisees have already threatened anyone who acknowledges Jesus as Messiah, with expulsion from the synagogue. To be cut off from all fellowship and support was an extremely severe punishment, second only to death.

For a second time, the man is summoned before the Pharisees and put under oath to speak the truth because they know a Sabbath breaker is a sinner. He sturdily refuses to go back upon the reality of his experience. He was blind, now he can see. When they ask him to repeat again the process of healing, he annoys them by resorting to sarcasm - do they also want to be Jesus' disciples? They become very angry with the healed man telling him they are disciples of Moses to whom God spoke but they do not know from where Jesus' power comes. The healed man retorts with biting courage. He himself is a transformed creature and their attitude is incomprehensible to him. No one who was not from God would have the power to perform this outstanding miracle. The Pharisees cannot stand what they regard as his insolence. Obviously he was born in sin, hence his former blindness, so he is not worth any more consideration. They forthwith excommunicate him from the synagogue.

When Jesus hears that the man has been turned out of the synagogue (9:35) he searches for and finds him, asking him if he believes in the Son of Man, another title for the Messiah. The man has already seen that Jesus was a prophet and then that he was 'from God'. Now that Jesus identifies himself with the Messiah, the man looks at him again and responds with a wonderful declaration of faith: 'Lord, I believe'. It is both to the Samaritan woman and to this man, that Jesus speaks the truth about himself. Strangely, for us perhaps, they are both nameless but this could mean they represent humanity. Both receive illumination and become vehicles for the Light of Life.

In effect, Jesus' answer to the question which the disciples asked at the beginning of this incident is a redirection of their thought. Innocent suffering is a profound mystery. Sometimes we simply have to accept the situation as it is and go on from there. We have to meet the challenge of what is and look for ways of changing it, if we can. The blind man was transformed by his encounter with love as personified in Jesus. He still had to face ostracism by his old community but he found fellowship in another, the community of those who believed. He received both an inner and an outer perception which made of him a new creation.

Jesus goes on to remark enigmatically (9:39-41) that his advent brings both sight and blindness. When the Pharisees ask if they too are blind, Jesus replies in effect that their lack of self-knowledge is the problem. While there are obvious reasons why some people lack perception, with the Pharisees it is otherwise. They are the accredited religious authority through their study of the scriptures but, if they were truly self-aware, they would recognise their own need for enlightenment in the profoundest sense. It is because they think they can 'see', ie. they are in the 'right', that they are guilty of spiritual pride and arrogance. The guilt lies in their lack of honesty and humility and in their failure to recognise that they need spiritual growth and change. It is the rigid assumption of always and only being 'in the right' which leads to intolerant fundamentalism. (For a synoptic parallel, see Mark 3:29).

6. The Raising of Lazarus, 11:1-57:

First: We have to consider the episode's relation to the Synoptic record. Here is a miracle of dramatic proportions and yet it has no place in either Mark or Matthew. Why is it not mentioned at all by them, if the incident actually occurred?. There is no mention of it either in Luke although we read there (Luke 10:38-42) of Jesus' visit to the home of two sisters, Martha and Mary, whose characters are sympathetically drawn by the Evangelist. Luke also includes a parable (16:19-31) about a very poor man called Lazarus whose plight is consistently ignored by the rich man at whose gate he lies. The rich man was probably a Sadducee who, not believing in life after death, spent his time in selfish pleasure. Tormented in hell after death, he can see, at a great distance, Lazarus with Abraham in bliss and begs that Lazarus be allowed to return from the dead to warn his five brothers of their fate if they do not mend their ways. Abraham replies that if his brothers did not heed either Moses or the prophets, they would still not pay attention even if someone returned from the dead. Luke is reminding us perhaps, of people's reactions to the resurrection of Jesus.

Second: John makes a further point in that he presents the Raising of Lazarus as the direct cause of the Sanhedrin's condemning Jesus to death. Some of those who witnessed this extraordinary event in Bethany went straight back to Jerusalem and reported what they had seen to the Pharisees, who in turn, decided to call in the Chief Priests. At a hastily convened meeting of the Sanhedrin, the fear was expressed that the populace would acclaim Jesus as Messiah and the resultant messianic uprising would all too quickly bring in the Romans, to the destruction of both nation and temple. Sentencing Jesus to death in his absence, they further authorised the immediate arrest of Jesus whenever and wherever he was found. Thus Jesus no longer went about openly and retired, for a time, to Ephraim, in desert hill country. (In Mark's gospel, it is the Cleansing of the Temple which convinces the Sanhedrin that they must dispose of him 11:18). In this gospel Jesus also makes clear that he knows of the leadership's intentions about him and warns them of the disastrous consequences of their action (12:8-12). Judas' betrayal hinged on where and when Jesus could be taken secretly for fear of a popular uprising on Jesus' behalf (14:1-2, 10, 43).

Various options are open to the New Testament reader. If the Synoptics are assumed to be written first then the Lazarus story is regarded as an addition to John's gospel. Some scholars feel the Lazarus material (John 11:1-46; 12:9-11) breaks the connection between chapter 10 and 12 and was either part of a second edition of the gospel or a 'Johannine construction' based on a Synoptic raising miracle (Mark 5:21-43; Luke 7:11-17) and the Lucan parable 16:19-31, see above). John Robinson, however, and others, would give John's gospel precedence. They believe the Fourth Gospel's chronology illuminates the Synoptics, explaining certain points, such as the need for extreme secrecy about the place of the Last Supper. Only if we accept the veracity of the Lazarus story can the decision of the Sanhedrin be satisfactorily explained. Robinson has argued that Mark's account of Jesus' public preaching in the Temple (Mark 11:27 -12:44) really belongs to an earlier period of his life when, according to the Fourth Gospel, Jesus was in Jerusalem.

A further option is to accept that the Lazarus story is valid but to argue that the two traditions do not necessarily conflict with each other apart from their timing. The Raising of Lazarus and the Cleansing of the Temple are both concerned with the challenge of spiritual renewal. The choice was between spiritual death or new life. Even Nicodemus was so fixed in his adherence to the sacred traditions of his people that he did not understand how he could be born again. The authorities could not accept the universalism of Jesus. This theory accepts the basic Marcan order of events, but adds that obviously Jesus would have visited Jerusalem more than once. It also accepts the additional material in John and his ordering of events as vital to his theological interpretation of the person of Jesus, the value of which to the reader is that it supplements and enriches the portrayal of the master by the other three gospels.

Problems: How far is this miracle a true happening? Did Jesus have power to raise from the dead? The Council of Nicea (AD 325), called by the Emperor Constantine to resolve serious disagreements amongst Christian leaders, finally asserted that Jesus Christ was of one substance with the Father. A later Conference, called by the Emperor Theodosius at Constantinople (AD 381), agreed to a credal statement which later became known as the Nicene Creed, in which the Trinity of Father, Son and Holy Spirit was established as an article of Christian faith. Therefore, if Jesus Christ was 'very God of very God' his power was limitless. He could indeed raise the dead. In consequence, believers who accept this doctrine have no problem with this story.

On the other hand some twentieth century scholars see the raising of Lazarus in symbolic terms rather than physical, as an inner experience of dying to self and raising to new life. Ravi Ravindra's commentary on John's gospel (*The Yoga of the Christ*, Element Books, 1990) presents an Indian perspective, referring to Hindu traditions and thus a mystical interpretation of the event.

The whole gospel of John concerns the person of Jesus the Christ, his purpose and his power. It is a challenge to individual seekers after spiritual truth to interpret as best they may. As this book demonstrates, I believe that Jesus by his own witness never equates himself with God. He is presented as both son of God and son of Man. Although he claims unity with the Father (10:30), he constantly states that his power is from the Father, not his own (8:28). This gospel presents Jesus as perfectly human. His parents are known (no virgin birth here), as is the name of his home town and his brothers. An actual conversation between them and Jesus is reported (7:1-9). It is because his contemporaries do know his origins that they cannot accept the tremendous claims he makes about himself, especially the 'I AM' statements and the expressed union with the Father. They accuse him of blasphemy, but nowhere does Jesus say he is equal to God (cf 10:36, p.67).

Further, in the Synoptics, Jesus is portrayed, par excellence, as the Servant of the Lord. This is confirmed both by the account of his mental conflict as to what kind of a Messiah he is to be (Luke 4:1-13; Matthew 4:1-11) and by his indirect references to Isaiah 53 (Mark 10:45; 14:21).

If Jesus was perfectly human he would not have the power to raise the clinically dead. His purpose was to raise the spiritually dead and to illuminate the profound complexity of the human situation, where people are largely unaware of their own need to realise the meaning of true life in all its richness, eternal life here and now. Since the basic experience of all humanity is that of mortality, I do not believe it helps us today to hear that someone two thousand years ago was credited with the supernatural power of raising a clinically dead person to life. This story is surely saying something much more important. The major theme of John's gospel is Jesus the Christ who is seen as the living water, the bread of life, the light of the world, the door, the good shepherd, the resurrection and the life, the way, the truth and the life and lastly as the vine. But those who believe in him are the branches of this vine. Through abiding in him they too can live in such a way that they experience eternal life here and now. As will be discussed later (see p.126) when studying the 'I AM' statements, this quality of spiritual vigour and indeed timelessness is not confined only to those who acknowledge Jesus as the Christ, for many others from different ages and cultures, walk the way of love without necessarily knowing or accepting anything about Jesus of Nazareth.

It is possible to rationalise the Lazarus story by saying Lazarus was in a deep coma, but not dead; we can explain the story's omission from Mark's gospel by saying that Peter (the accredited inspiration behind this gospel) was not present and perhaps was in Galilee at the time; but probably these are fruitless digressions to follow. The raising of Lazarus and the turning of the water into wine during the marriage feast at Cana (2:1-11) are in a similar category. Both incidents have a deeply symbolic significance in the gospel's structure. Thanks to the rich and vivid detail in both stories and the conversations between the participants, it is not difficult to credit that they were based on real events, the nature of which we cannot discover at this distance of time. To believe that Jesus did not (or could not) turn water into wine or actually raise to life a man four days dead, is not to deny the validity of the experience of those present nor to overlook the supreme lessons which are being taught. It is however important that we should question centuries-old assumptions based on a quite different worldview from our own and should ask, in the case of Lazarus, why was the story necessary to the gospel? According to John, the authorities determined to kill Lazarus as well as Jesus (12:10) for he was too great a witness to Jesus; perhaps they succeeded!

John's treatment of all the signs demonstrates clearly that it is their spiritual significance which is of paramount importance to the gospel presentation. When we study the last sign of all, Jesus' own death and resurrection, we shall see how it illuminates all the others.

Comment on the text:

a. 11:1-16   In chapter 10:40-42, Jesus withdraws to the region 'across Jordan', ie Peraea, to the place where it all began with the preaching of John Baptist. While he is here the two sisters in Bethany send Jesus news that their brother Lazarus is seriously ill. (In 11:2, the Evangelist associates Mary with the anointing story which he will recount in 12:1-13 (see p.47)).

On hearing of Lazarus' illness, Jesus makes two comments: first, that the illness will not end in death; second, that its purpose is the glorification of both Father and Son. This reply is reminiscent of his answer when the disciples asked whose sin was responsible for man being born blind (see p.37). On that occasion Jesus refuted the traditional belief that illness is always caused by sin and said that a healing would take place which would reveal God's power. So the question in both cases is not about sin and death, but about divinity, whose creative purposes are as yet scarcely understood. If we equate God with Love, we can say that both these stories are a further revelation of Love. 'Glory' and 'Power' in this context could mean further illumination as to the true nature of the creative will which can turn disaster into blessing.

Suffering and death are integral to human experience. They are places of change and can be opportunities for growth. This is not to say that this is their purpose. We do not know the reason for many things but have to accept the way life is and work to remedy injustice and suffering where we can. We agonise particularly about innocent suffering and often accuse the Creator of a basic flaw in creation which allows this to happen. But as we learn more about human nature and our planet earth, we realise that much suffering could be avoided if only human beings were more adult and responsible.

On the present occasion there are further considerations, for John tells us that, although Jesus loved the whole family, he delays going to Bethany for two days. When he does arrive outside the village, he is told that Lazarus has been dead four days, which means that Lazarus was already dead when Jesus received the message from the sisters. This is the fourth occasion in the gospel when Jesus resolutely follows his own sense of timing and apparently refuses to comply with others (with his mother, 2:4; with his disciples, 4:41-44; with his brothers, 7:8). He may, of course, have been contrary by temperament, but it is more likely that he rejected the easy option of placating those he was fond of in the mistaken idea that this was love. Perhaps the extra two days were necessary for the disciples themselves, in view of the horror which awaited them in Jerusalem.

By visiting Bethany, less than two miles distant from Jerusalem, Jesus probably knows he is going to his own death. The disciples realise the serious risk he is running. They warn him of previous attempts to stone him (10:31, 39; 8:50). Jesus answers them with a parable taken from the natural world. In the light of the sun a man may walk without stumbling, but when it is dark it is difficult to find the way. As in all Jesus' parables there are several levels of interpretation. On this occasion, he may have been referring to his own period of coming darkness so that it was important to do what he had to do while he still had the opportunity. Alternatively it may refer to the believer or unbeliever, as John often uses the symbols of light and darkness in his gospel to stand for sight and blindness, life and death, awareness and ignorance. Jesus has said he is the light of the world (cf. 8:12; 9:5). It is this inner illumination which sheds light on all our outward activity, as Paul says when he writes to his troublesome congregation at Corinth (2 Corinthians 3:4-6). Thomas (known as 'The Twin') speaks for all the disciples in resolving to go into Judaea with Jesus even if it ends in death (11:16).

The reader is challenged to explore deeper meanings both in the action and via the ambiguity of certain words and phrases. 'Fallen asleep'

(11:11-14) is taken by the disciples to be natural health-giving sleep but Jesus means 'death'. (cf. Paul, in 1 Thessalonians 4:13,14 who talks of 'sleep in death'). Jesus had already said earlier that Lazarus' illness would not end in death. On any count Jesus' views on life and death were different from those of his contemporaries.

When Jesus decides it is right to go to Bethany (11:11-15), he tells his disciples he knows Lazarus is dead but that he is glad for their sakes that he was not there. When he awakens Lazarus, they will be led to believe. What can this mean? All through the gospel Jesus has not been happy with the superficial faith of those who believed in him because of his miracles (2:24). The words cannot mean that he has now changed his mind. The author is writing with hindsight long after the actual event. He has experienced the terrible days when Jesus was arrested and crucified, but he sees them now in the perspective of the resurrection and the indwelling presence of the Christ. He has now come to believe Jesus is the new wine, the living water, the bread of life, the door, the good shepherd and now the resurrection and the life. These are all the realities of his experience. This endorses the view that the whole Lazarus story has to be seen in the context of Jesus' own death and resurrection. It serves both as a foretaste and as a contrast to the Seventh sign.

b. 11:17-43 It is typical of the Martha we know from Luke, that she gets up and goes to see Jesus, when she hears he is nearby. Perhaps she regrets not sending to Jesus earlier, yet she still trusts him. Martha believes in the traditional Pharisaic account of judgement on the last day. Lazarus will be raised then because of his righteous life on earth. But Jesus has something different to say. He is the resurrection and the life. Eternal life can be found in the here and now because it is awakening to the new life which he has come to bring. It is a present reality, when Love is the dominant factor in a person's life. It is clear from the Synoptic gospel record that Jesus does not believe that death is outright extinction, but this conviction is even more fully expressed here because it is the Evangelist's personal experience too.

Martha's response (11:27) to Jesus' question is remarkable. According to the story she knows that her brother is four days dead, and yet here is the Master saying that those who have faith in him never die. She glimpses that Jesus is talking about something other than physical death and makes her own statement of faith, which Jesus endorses. It is like, yet also unlike, Peter's declaration in Mark (8:29) but Martha does not make Peter's mistake; she does not allow her preconceptions about the Messiah to intrude into this conversation.

Martha runs back to Mary and tells her that Master has come and is asking for her. Jesus waits for Mary outside the village but her sympathetic friends go with her so that she has no time with him alone. When Mary sees Jesus she falls at his feet and repeats the same regretful words as Martha. Jesus is deeply distressed and asks where Lazarus has been laid - the tomb would be a cave with the entrance covered by a stone to keep out wild beasts.

Jesus' distress has been variously interpreted as indignation, anger or grief. But I believe it may be not only a combination of these emotions - for he truly loved Lazarus, Martha and Mary - but something else. There may have been real conflict in Jesus between his personal compassion and his awareness of the consequences of his actions. We are told many believed in him because of the miracle he performed, but he did not want that kind of belief. He knew it was too shallow. Belief has to come first, not as a result of a miracle. The miracle may confirm the belief, but not vice versa. We love because we love, not because of what the other does. We respond to something intrinsic in the other and this response usually results in action.

Jesus' tears impress the people present with the depth of his love for Lazarus but even Martha is appalled by his command to roll away the stone from the tomb. Jewish tradition held that after three days the person was really dead, the soul having left the body and corruption having set in; removing the stone would release the stench. Nevertheless Jesus is obeyed. He then prays aloud, wanting the onlookers to know that the source of his power is the Father, not himself. The whole act is for the glory of God. With a great cry, Jesus calls Lazarus by name to come out. Lazarus obeys, staggering out bound with the linen clothes customarily wrapped around a dead person. Jesus then orders that Lazarus should be loosened from the bandages, and set free to go home, which he does.

We have already asked the purpose of Lazarus' restoration to life in this world. According to 12:10, the chief priests will very shortly plan to put him to death; he is too remarkable a witness to the power inherent in Jesus. The gospel does not tell us anything at all about Lazarus' further life. This means we must look elsewhere for its meaning. The whole story is dramatically and vividly told and includes the kind of difficult intriguing dialogue which makes it even more memorable. Thus any analysis of the text or discussion about the validity of the sources, seems entirely secondary to the actual impact of the narrative. Its very authenticity means that it is worth endless struggle to discover for oneself the truths about living and dying that it reveals.

Jesus, and all that he represents as an authentic human being with fully realised potential, is the resurrection and the life. He is unique in this, being pre-eminently both the son of God and the son of man. The raising of Lazarus is both a symbol and a contrast with Jesus' own death and resurrection. It speaks of the new life here and now. The lifting of the stone can be seen as a graphic way of describing the moment of revelation when the truth about oneself and one's own motivation really becomes apparent. As so often, it is someone else, whether in person or through the written word, who 'speaks to our condition', striking home with the truth which sharpens our own inner voice and leads us forward.

Our particular culture is very bad at facing the terror of death. We tend to prolong life at all costs, regardless of the kind of existence the person may be enduring. The best preparation for death is living now in the fullest possible sense, living in an awareness of the centrality of the spirit.

We suffer psychological deaths in more ways than one. When someone we love dies, a part of us dies also. Yet in 'letting go' the possessiveness and self-regard which is found in even the best of human love, we learn a more selfless way of caring. Parents have to let go of their children in order to set them free to learn from their own mistakes. In some cases over-protectiveness can be as damaging as neglect. In any true relationship of love there has to be a letting go, otherwise jealousy, dominance and bitterness over failed expectations can take over.

We have to let go other props which we think necessary to life, props such as self-indulgence, over-anxiety, excessive self-denial for the wrong reasons, projection onto others of our own needs and faults. This is a very hard road to take but it can be full of joy, as well as pain, resurrection as well as death.

Self-knowledge is the key, but it is a search for self-knowledge in the conviction that change and development are not only possible but right.

7.   The Anointing at Bethany, 12:1-11:

Because this is a continuation of the Lazarus story, I have included it here. I feel we should compare this story with the one found in Mark (14:3-9) and perhaps Luke (7:36-50), although Luke's account has striking differences. I see Mark's story as a variant on John's.

Mark tells us that an unknown woman anoints Jesus' head with costly ointment at the house of Simon the Leper in Bethany. Some complain about the waste since the 'pure nard' would be valued at 300 denarii - a whole year's wages for a day-labourer. Rebuking her critics, Jesus praises the woman, saying her act of bountiful love will always be remembered. She has intuitively seen his approaching death and has anointed him for his burial. Why compare her generous single act with the need of the poor which is an always present reality? Mark places this incident after the Triumphal Entry into Jerusalem, the Cleansing of the Temple and continued controversy. He follows it with Judas' visit to the authorities to bargain with them over Jesus. Judas' betrayal is shown in sharp contrast with the woman's discerning love.

Luke places the story much earlier in Jesus' ministry and makes a quite different point from Mark and John. Jesus is in an unnamed city when he is invited to dinner by a Pharisee called Simon, who is frankly curious about him but who neglects the ordinary courtesies of a host to an honoured guest. The woman is a prostitute, who has probably heard Jesus' preaching on forgiveness. She washes Jesus' feet with her tears, wipes them with her hair, kisses them and anoints them with ointment. Simon is extremely critical of Jesus for allowing the woman even to touch him but Jesus, knowing Simon's thoughts, rebukes him. Publicly forgiving the woman her sins and praising her for her faith, he reinstates her in the community. The point of the story is the woman's response to Jesus. Her great love and gratitude are accepted by Jesus as true repentance and a changed way of life. The mention of Mary Magdalene in the following verses (Luke 8:3) has reinforced the tradition that she was the woman in question.

John's story is more vivid than Mark's and gives a different timing for the events. Six days before that last fateful Passover in Jesus' life and before the Triumphal Entry into Jerusalem, Jesus returns to Bethany. A supper is given in his honour, presumably in the house of Lazarus, although the narrative does not say so. John refers to Lazarus as one of the guests, but Martha is busy waiting at table and it is her sister Mary who anoints Jesus' feet with the precious perfume, wiping them with her hair. John adds that the whole house is full of the fragrance. This time it is Judas Iscariot who strongly protests at the waste. The Evangelist comments on the fact that Judas acted as treasurer to the band of disciples but was dishonest in his stewardship of their resources: this criticism, therefore was not based on concern for the poor, but his own interests. In words almost identical with Mark's account, Jesus describes Mary's act as foretelling his burial: this once and for all occasion cannot be compared with the constantly recurring needs of the poor.

We know from Luke's account of the two sisters (10:38-42) how conscious Mary was of Jesus' role. She was truly a disciple. She may have realised how much it would cost Jesus personally to restore Lazarus and how this miracle would further inflame his enemies. She apparently sensed the imminence of his forthcoming arrest and death. From the depth of her love she reached to share with Jesus this recognition of his approaching end. Her realisation met some understandable need in him.

John adds a further paragraph, concerning Lazarus, to the story. People were flocking to see the man who had been raised from the dead and were turning their allegiance to Jesus who had performed this miracle. This made the chief priests (Sanhedrin) determine to dispose of Lazarus as well as Jesus.

Why did Jesus come back into danger when he had previously been forewarned of the Sanhedrin's condemnation of him in his absence (see p.69, 11:53,57) We later read (see p.72, 12:23) that Jesus was now convinced that the climax of his ministry had arrived. The fact that Mary had also realised this, even if not in its fullest sense, must have moved him deeply.

As a final point, it is important not to minimise the significance John attributes to women in Jesus' life. Their role is highlighted in this gospel, particularly when we assess it in the light of the cultural and religious preconceptions about gender which were then current.

According to John it is four women, the Samaritan woman at the well, Martha, Mary of Bethany and Mary Magdalene, who evoke the most profound responses in Jesus.

CHAPTER 3 – CONFRONTATION AND CONTROVERSY

IN JERUSALEM

		Chapter	Page
1.	The Cleansing of the Temple,	2:13-22	51
2.	Opposition to Jesus after his Healing of the Cripple on a Sabbath and his Reply,	5:16-47	53
3.	Jesus at the Feast of Tabernacles,	7 & 8	57
	a. Jesus and his brothers	7:1-13	57
	b. Jesus in the Temple	7:14-24	59
	c. Further controversy	7:25-36	60
	d. The last day of the Feast	7:37-52	61
	e. Final disputation	8:21-59	62
4.	Controversy following the Healing on a Sabbath of the Man Born Blind	10:17-21	65
	and at the Feast of Dedication	10:22-42	67
5.	Repercussions to the Lazarus Miracle	11:47-57	69
6.	The Triumphal Entry	12:12-19	70
7.	Last Public Discourse in the Temple area	2:20-26	71
8.	Jesus' Hour of Inner Trial	12:27-36	74
9.	A note at the end of Jesus' public ministry	12:37-50	78

CHAPTER 3:

Confrontation and Controversy in Jerusalem

1.   The Cleansing of the Temple 2:13-22:

In John's gospel, the Cleansing of the Temple (2:13-22) is the first act of confrontation and takes place very early in Jesus' ministry. He tells us that after the marriage at Cana, Jesus goes to Capernaum with his mother, his brothers and his friends (2:.12). It is John's first mention of the town which in Mark's gospel figured not only as the home of Simon and Andrew (Mark 1:29) but also as the centre for Jesus' healing ministry and the beginning of his controversy with the Scribes and Pharisees (Mark 1:21-34, 2:1-12).

John, however, has a different story to tell, for after a few days in Capernaum, Jesus goes up to Jerusalem for the Feast of the Passover, the first of the three Passovers which this gospel records. While in the temple precincts he is outraged by the traffic in cattle, sheep, pigeons and money. Money changers were necessary because the authorities would only accept Jewish coin to pay the prescribed half-shekel of temple-tax. Jesus makes a whip of cords and drives out the animals, overturning the money-changers' tables. Naturally enough the authorities challenge his action. They ask for an authenticating sign of his authority. Jesus' reply was bound to lead to their misunderstanding him. He tells them that if they destroy this temple, he will raise it up again in three days time. They naturally assume he is talking of the actual building, begun by Herod the Great in 20/19 BC. They comment that (so far) it has been 46 years in process of being built (which puts the date for this incident at AD 27/28), so how could it be rebuilt in three days?

The disciples only realised after the resurrection that Jesus was talking about his own body, the shrine of his spirit, which according to their experience was raised on the third day. They also recalled Psalm 69:9, where the Psalmist suffered greatly for his devotion to the Temple, and they used the Psalmist's words as a prophecy of Jesus' passion (John 15:25, 19:38, Acts 1.20, Romans 15:3). John concludes his story by commenting that although Jesus gained many adherents during this time in Jerusalem, he placed no confidence in their belief realising that it was only superficial.

By contrast, Mark has condensed Jesus' time in Jerusalem to a single fateful week, but it is obvious from his narrative that Jesus has visited Jerusalem previously because he had friends there: he knew the man who lent his donkey, the owner of the house in which the Last Supper was held, and the allegiance of Joseph of Arimathea could not have happened overnight. So John no doubt is right to speak of three Passovers during Jesus' ministry and his gospel contributes much to our understanding of Jesus in Jerusalem and Judaea.

Mark sets his account of The Cleansing of the Temple (11:15-19) in the concluding phases of Jesus' life, representing it as an act of Messianic symbolism from the time when Jesus had decided that he must declare himself Messiah, however different from popular expectation. He therefore rides into Jerusalem on an ass, the symbol of peaceful intent, before leading the excited crowds into the Temple area, where they quietly disperse. Jesus then goes out to Bethany where he stays each night. His cleansing of the Temple next day is a protest against the corrupt practices of the temple authorities; they had turned God's house of prayer for all nations into a "den of thieves". When later questioned by the Sanhedrin about his right to take such violent action, Jesus refuses a direct answer but turns the question and instead asks the deputation their opinion of John Baptist. Knowing the people's devotion to the Baptist and the Baptist's view of Jesus they are unable to reply. Any acknowledgement or denial of John Baptist's God-given commission would have direct bearing on Jesus' own authority.

According to Mark, Jesus then tells the challenging story of the Wicked Tenants (12:1-12), infuriating his opponents further as they recognise that it is directly aimed at them. The parable's meaning is clear: because the Jewish religious leadership fail to recognise him as God's Messiah and son and because Jesus knows they intend to do away with him, God will terminate his covenant with them and give it to others. This is a solemn warning of the national disaster which fell upon the Palestinian Jews through the Jewish revolt. But, says Jesus, quoting from the Psalms (11:8-22) the rejected 'stone' will become the foundation of a new 'building', a new covenant or order. In the psalm, the despised cornerstone is Israel but Jesus applies the image to himself.

The importance of this passage to Jesus' disciples is illustrated by two later references to it. On trial before the Sanhedrin, Peter boldly declares 'This Jesus is the stone, rejected by you builders, which has become the cornerstone' (Acts 4:11) and in 1 Peter (2:4,5), possibly the work of Peter himself, that Jesus is the living stone of the spiritual temple. His readers, as believers in Jesus, are also living stones of the same spiritual structure and their priestly vocation is to offer spiritual sacrifices acceptable to God through Jesus Christ.

The Synoptic gospels portray Jesus' action in cleansing the Temple as leading ultimately to his arrest and trial, at which he was falsely accused of boasting that he would destroy the Temple and rebuild it in three days. As his accusers did not agree among themselves about his exact words (Mark 14:58,59), their evidence was invalid under Jewish law. But, as John adds, the disciples only came to understand the deeper import of Jesus' conversation with the authorities after the resurrection experience.

Scholars dispute which gospel gives the right timing for Jesus' action, but our present purpose is to try to understand John's reasons for including it at the opening stages of his gospel. He is concerned to establish the religious or theological truth of Jesus, not necessarily the chronological order of events. As far as he is able, he wishes to reveal the meaning of Jesus' ministry. He has come to appreciate the deep significance of Jesus' dramatic action in the context of his whole ministry and his resurrection. Even though he knows the Synoptic tradition, he puts the Cleansing at the beginning of his gospel so as to stress its direct connection to the first sign, when Jesus changed the water into wine at the wedding in Cana. Its symbolism is clear; it is the replacement of the old order by the new. Jesus' coming has rendered the sacrificial system and indeed the formal ritual of the temple practices obsolete. Therefore by a dramatic act he temporarily abolishes the means to carry out these rituals. Thus John sets the scene for further controversy.

The theme of sacred buildings is continued in the story of the Samaritan woman (see p.20). Although such buildings consecrated to God's glory have great beauty and sanctity of association, qualities which indeed can be very real aids to devotion, the essence of true worship lies within the individual and within the community which Jesus is creating. Outward ceremonial is meaningless unless it reflects inward spiritual vitality. This is the experience of the gospel writer and of those who follow Jesus in the power of the Spirit.

2.   **Opposition to Jesus and his reply, 5:16-47:**

We can divide this discourse into three sections.

a: Because Jesus healed the crippled man on a Sabbath (see p.32) and told him to get up and carry his bed, he was accused by the authorities of Sabbath breaking. In one sense, Jesus, by giving the man instructions to pick up his mat and walk with it, was deliberately provoking opposition.

b: Arising from this, Jesus states that he is God's son and therefore knows his Father's will better than his opponents do, a claim which the Jews somewhat naturally regard as blasphemy:

c: Jesus brings three witness to confirm his claim to be God's son.

a) and b) 5:16-30: In the Synoptics, Jesus encounters much hostility as a Sabbath breaker. Mark recounts criticism levelled at Jesus because he allows his disciples idly to pluck corn as they walk through the fields on the Sabbath (2:23-27). Jesus replies that the Sabbath was made for humanity, not vice versa. In any case the Son of Man (perhaps Jesus is referring to himself as the representative of humanity) is Lord of the Sabbath. In Jesus' view, humanity itself is more important than any institution. Matthew places a different emphasis on this incident (12:1-8). Jesus points out that by carrying out their Sabbath duties, the temple priests break the law yet it is not held against them; anyway, says Jesus, something greater than the Temple is in your midst. Luke's version (13:10-17; 14:1-6) is that Jesus argues that he must meet people's need on the Sabbath as on any other day. He accuses his listeners of hypocrisy, since they care for their valuable animals on the Sabbath and certainly would also rescue their sons or their oxen from disaster no matter what the day.

John has another different slant on the incident. Just as Jesus' Father continues to work on the Sabbath, so must he. According to the Law (Genesis 2:2,3) after God had finished his six days work of creation, he blessed the seventh day thus making it holy. Nevertheless, rabbis at the time of Jesus agreed that God continues to sustain the Universe on the seventh day. He is not idle. Obviously, for Jesus, the activity of love never ceases. This apparent direct contradiction of the literal meaning of Sabbath-keeping is in keeping with the light Jesus continually sheds on the inner meaning of scriptures.

Jesus' words (5:17), 'My Father.. and I...' would strike the Jews as arrogant in the extreme. Despite a few scriptural references to God being called the Father of his people (Deuteronomy 32:6;Isaiah 63:8) there is no direct evidence that God was usually so designated. Even in human relationships, Jewish tradition would argue that only the rebellious son would have the effrontery to claim equality with his father. But Jesus is not a rebel son. He is the obedient son par excellence and he strongly refutes that he claims equality with God (5:19). This refutation is repeated twice (5:30,31) with the addition (5:41) that he does not seek personal glory and honour.

Although his enemies may accuse Jesus of arrogance as well as blasphemy, he is humble in his selflessness. He states over and over again that as the son he does nothing by himself. It is his unity with the Father which enables him to do what he sees the Father doing. In other words if God is Love, which is the truth enshrined by Jesus, then Jesus acts always on the inspiration and example of perfect love. Thus Jesus is the means whereby humanity comes to know the source of its being. In this way life is given to the spiritually dead, as was illustrated and symbolised by the healing of the cripple at the pool.

In Mark (3:1-6) when Jesus is confronted by the hatred of the Pharisees in the synagogue on a Sabbath, he questions their motivation, asking them which is the better way of keeping the Sabbath, by doing good or evil, by saving life or killing. By implication he contrasts his desire to heal the crippled man and their desire to dispose of him. Jesus' mission was to make people whole in body, mind and spirit. John expresses this in terms of giving life. The 'greater deeds' (5:20) must refer to this whole restorative process, which continues to this day.

In the Fourth Gospel, Jesus is not represented as making himself equal with God. Jesus is always stating that he does not act upon his own initiative. On the other hand God as creator and giver of life, pure Spirit, acts through the Son and people are judged by their response to the one through whom God is revealed. It is even stated that Son and the Father are so in unity that to withhold honour to one is to withhold honour to the other (v.23). Luke's account of the old priest Simeon's words to Mary in the Temple is relevant here: (2:35) 'Many in Israel will stand or fall because of him; and so the secret thoughts of many will be laid bare'. The people we meet in John's gospel are judged by their acceptance or rejection of Jesus for he personifies the will of the Father.

From our own experience, however, we know there may be many extenuating circumstances preventing an honest seeker after God, the inner Spirit, from acknowledging the Christian church's representation of the Son of God. I believe it is Love who is the assessor. Infinite compassion has boundless understanding of human motivation and measures spiritual health by the individual's attitude to love, mercy and goodness.

In his capacity as Son of God, Jesus is also represented by John as judge over the living and the dead (5:27). This gospel makes a clear demarcation between those who have "done right" and therefore will rise to eternal life, and those who have "done wrong", who will consequently be judged (5:29). But Jesus does not act on his own initiative. He judges as he is bidden by the Father. In Mark (2:10) Jesus as Son of Man claimed the power and the right to forgive sins. In a later incident, (2:17) he says, in effect, that he has come to cure the sickness of sin. In John's gospel, John Baptist sees Jesus as the Lamb of God who has come to take away the sin of the world. All this must be taken into account when considering the role of judge which is attributed to Jesus in the above passage, especially as John refers to Jesus as Son of Man (5:27) whereas in 5:25 he has been called Son of God. It is surely by virtue of his very humanity that he both understands the true nature of sin and aims to cure it.

c) 5:31-45: Greek, Jewish and Roman courts prohibited anyone from acting as a witness in his own defence. Jewish law also stated (Deuteronomy 19:20) that a person could not be condemned on the testimony of a single witness; the charge had to be established on the evidence of two or three witnesses (cf Jesus' trial, Mark 14:55-59). Jesus acknowledges that personal testimony on his own behalf is invalid and gives three witnesses to refute the Jews' accusations against him. The first is John Baptist to whom the Jews themselves sent a delegation (1:19). The Baptist declared that Jesus was the Lamb of God (1:29, 36), the Chosen One on whom the Spirit descended (1:33), the Son of God (1:34). Jesus then describes John Baptist as 'a brightly burning lamp' (cf Matthew 11:7ff and Luke 7:22) saying 'for a time you were ready to exult in his light'. He was a man sent by God. People accepted him as a prophet and flocked to him yet the Jews ignored his witness to Jesus.

Jesus then passes on to the second witness, which is the evidence of their own eyes. They have seen what Jesus can do in his healing and preaching ministry and have witnessed the incorruptible quality of his own life. When Jesus warns his disciples against false prophets in Matthew (7:16,20) he says categorically that the way to assess the genuineness of a person is to measure his conduct against his words. The power manifested in Jesus comes from his own dependent relationship with the Father, a fact which the Synoptics depict by Jesus' acceptance of his role as the servant of the Lord whereas John expresses it in terms of the Father/Son relationship.

God is spirit, therefore humanity cannot hear his voice or see his form. The Jews diligently seek the scriptures and hope thereby to find eternal life. But it is misplaced devotion to focus on literal analysis of the text rather than seeking the spiritual perception to apply it to living. For, says Jesus (and this is his third witness) the scriptures do not in themselves hold the key but the scriptures point to himself as their fulfilment. The word of God has found no home in the Jews because they have rejected the one whom God has sent.

Jesus then turns the tables on his accusers. They cannot recognise his accreditation by God because they themselves rely too much on the praise of others (Matthew 6:1-18). Too much self love blinds them to the love of God in Jesus. At the final judgement, it is from Moses that their condemnation will come for Moses pointed to Jesus and prophesied his coming. In John's view, therefore, the scriptures are prophetic though not in themselves life-giving; central to them is the figure of Moses the great law-giver. Paul expresses a similar view when he tells the Galatians that the Law is our pedagogue whilst humanity remains in infancy and its job is to expose sin, for no one can keep the Law perfectly. It cannot however bring salvation; the true and spiritual vision of God is found in Jesus the Christ.

In looking at this discourse we have to acknowledge that much of it is not Jesus himself but clearly belongs to the Evangelist. The rabbinical style of argument reminds us of Paul's line of thought in Galatians. Jesus could and probably did argue with the Pharisees in a manner which twentieth century readers may find obscure and even tedious. But the Evangelist's purpose is not simply a reproduction of Jesus' teaching but the meaning intrinsic in his life.

3. Jesus in the Temple during the Feast of Tabernacles (chs 7 and 8):

These two chapters are a continuous whole and will be treated as such. (For the story of the woman taken in adultery, 7:53 - 8:11, see p.23).

The Feast of Tabernacles was the last of the three main festivals in the Jewish year, the other two being Passover and Pentecost. It was held in Jerusalem during September/October when all the harvests had been gathered in. Leviticus (23:33-36; 39-43) ordained that it was to be 'the Lord's pilgrim feast' when people must live in 'booths' or tabernacles i.e. tents in the open, for seven (23:33) or eight days (23:36); the latter duration was always used. The feast was held to remind the participants of Israel's long pilgrimage in the desert when, under Moses' leadership, the Lord brought them out of Egyptian bondage to the Promised Land. It was an occasion of great joy and celebration (Deuteronomy 16:13-15). During the feast water was bought from the Pool of Siloam in a golden vessel and offered as libations in the Temple. It was also a festival of light; the lighted candles set in four great candelabra in the Court of the Women, were said to be so bright as to illuminate the courtyards of Jerusalem.

a. JESUS AND HIS BROTHERS, 7:1-13

Despite the opposition recorded in John 6 (see p.118), Jesus apparently felt safer in Galilee than Judaea, where he knew his life was in actual danger. Nevertheless his brothers now urge him to go to Jerusalem for the very popular Feast of Tabernacles. According to Mark (6:3) their names are James, Joses, Simon and Jude. Their advice is worldlywise. If he wants to gain more followers he must demonstrate his ability to work wonders where there will be a maximum of publicity. Jesus rebuffs them with words reminiscent of his reply to his mother at Cana (2:4). The right time to go to Jerusalem is not yet. He will not go with them and the crowd of other pilgrims. He knows what reception he will get there from his enemies. His brothers know nothing of hatred and opposition, whereas his person and message are such that those who encounter him are forced to examine their own motivation and faith. The Evangelist has made clear that even the thoughtful, sincere Nicodemus was too rigidly traditional to understand that he had to begin again, (ie. 'be reborn') by opening himself to the activity and freedom of the Spirit (3:7,8). The Synoptists show that the majority of the Pharisees could not accept so radical a change of outlook as Jesus offered. In Mark (8:11ff) they demand from him an overwhelming sign which would release them from the personal responsibility of making their own decisions about his messiahship. Jesus of course refuses as he recognises it is totally non-productive to dazzle people into belief.

John's gospel makes no mention of virgin conception and Jesus' family is obviously well known.   At this point they do not understand the nature of Jesus' messiahship and Jesus does not trust himself to them. They were not his disciples, although they have some inkling of his strange power. Later, they came to believe in him (1 Corinthians 9: 5, 15:7, Acts 1:14).

Half way through the Festival, Jesus knows that he must go up to Jerusalem 'secretly'. He is not being contrary about this decision; his sole objective is to be faithful to his calling and this selfless fidelity gives him the inner authority to act when he feels it appropriate. The reasons for the Spirit's guidance may not be always apparent, but for Jesus the timing of events was all-important.

John tells his readers that the Jews (ie the official opposition) were expecting Jesus to be at the Festival and that the crowd held mixed opinions about him. Some thought he was a good man (Mark 10:17), others that he was leading people astray (Luke 22:2, 14, the accusation made against him to Pilate). Comments were not openly expressed because people were afraid of the authorities.

John's order of events is different from that of Mark, who records that Jesus went 'secretly' because he wanted time with his disciples (9:30). It did not work out quite like that; as he taught the crowds in Transjordan and after Jericho his procession became triumphal in character. John's account of Jesus in Judaea is much fuller. But he makes the point here that Jesus now left Galilee for the last time. Six months later he would be arrested and die.

b.   Jesus in the Temple, 7: 14-24:

Jesus arrives at the Temple half-way through the festival when tension about him is already high. He immediately assumes the role of prophetic teacher and the Jews are amazed at his authoritative power (cf. Mark 1:22). They know he has had no formal training as a rabbi, nor does he follow the familiar pattern of learned discourse by continual reference to other rabbinical sources. He further alienates them by his claim to have access to the highest wisdom of all, God himself. Time and again in this gospel Jesus reiterates (5:41-44) that he is not motivated by self-glory or arrogance; his teaching is not his own. His only motive is to reveal the true nature and glory of the Father. The proof will be that those who genuinely seek to do God's will can see the truth of his words (6:69).

Jesus reinforces his theme by appealing to scripture. The Jews claim the authority of Exodus (31:14,15; 35:2) to condemn him because they interpret his Sabbath healing as profaning the holy day. Yet in truth they are breaking Mosaic law by wanting to kill him. He admits he has healed once on the Sabbath (5:9-18), but they must look more deeply into their interpretation of the Law and act more justly. For example, take the case of Sabbath circumcision. According to Leviticus (12:3) a boy must be circumcised on the eighth day after birth. (This practice, originating from the time of Abraham, was an outward sign of the covenant relationship between God and his people.) If the due date of circumcision happens to fall on a Sabbath which rite takes precedence? The authorities themselves have ruled that it must be circumcision, presumably on the grounds that the rite furthers the true purpose of the Law and thus does not profane the holy day. Why then do they complain when Jesus makes a man whole again on the Sabbath?

On the actual occasion of the healing (5:1-18) Jesus answered his critics by arguing that he must follow his Father's example by continuing endlessly to work, the implication being that God's unceasing creative activity is necessary to maintain health and well-being and that if Jesus' identifies with the Father's work, he cannot possible profane the Sabbath. It is this certainty that he knows the Father's will, which makes the authorities accuse Jesus of blasphemy (5:16-18). When the matter is brought up again, Jesus answers his opponents in their own coin and debates points of the law with them (7:21-24).

It is interesting to compare John's treatment of the controversy over Sabbath regulations with the Synoptics. The point John consistently makes is that Jewish festival, liturgy, temple and ritual practices were all fulfilled in the person of Jesus the Christ and have therefore ceased to have meaning for believers in him. While the Synoptists bring out the central importance to Jesus of what is going on in a person's heart and mind, John leaves the ethical teaching implicit and always focuses explicitly on individual's or group's evaluation of the significance of Jesus the Christ.

Jesus' attitude towards Sabbath observance obviously formed part of the Sanhedrin's charges of 'subverting' the people and 'causing unrest' when they brought Jesus to Pilate (Luke 23:1-5). Pilate, however, was not at all interested or concerned with religious matters and may have understood these vague terms to refer to political subversion.

c. FURTHER CONTROVERSY, 7:25-36

The authority with which Jesus acts and speaks and the fact that he freely does so in the Temple, make the crowd wonder if their rulers have changed their minds about Jesus and have decided that he is the Messiah. The great stumbling block for them is the fact that his origins are known (Mark 6:3, 42). He is from Nazareth and has now come from Galilee (John 1:45,46; 2:12; 4:54; 7:3,10) whereas according to prophetic writing (Daniel 7:13; Malachi 2:1-3, a theme further developed in the Apocrypha, 2 Esdras 7:28, 13:32), the Messiah's origins will be shrouded in mystery. Jesus acknowledges that in one sense they do know where he has come from but in another they do not. He is not here by his own volition but has been sent by one who is true (or who truly IS) whom they do not know at all. As Jesus has previously claimed (7:16), that his teaching is a complete reflection of the one who sent him and is recognised as such by those who seek to do God's will, the implications of his words infuriate some of his listeners and there is an unsuccessful attempt to arrest him. The minds of these people are closed. They are incapable of seeing any fresh truth for they are circumscribed by tradition. Among the crowd, however, many are greatly impressed by Jesus and believe in him, but they demonstrate the superficiality of their faith when they speculate that even the Messiah, when he comes, may be unable to better Jesus' signs.

The Sanhedrin decide to take official action against Jesus and send off the temple guard to arrest him but these officials fail to do so. In John's gospel everything happens at the 'appointed' time. Reviewing Jesus' life many years later he portrays Jesus as being 'in control' of events because he is utterly obedient to the dictates of the Spirit. He is not arrested now because the time for that is not yet. Nevertheless the incident causes Jesus to comment on his forthcoming death, but in terms which wholly confuse the crowd. He will shortly leave them to return to the One who sent him. Even if they search for him, they will not find him, for where he is (not 'will be'), they cannot come. Jesus' eternal, indwelling unity with the Father is a present state of being. It is not a temporal place at all. This is the secret of his spiritual power and authority. The phrase 'searching but not finding the Lord' echoes the words of Hosea (5:6) where the search is fruitless because the motivation is wrong. But Jesus may also be thinking of Isaiah's promise (55:6) of the Lord being present among his people; by real faith he can and will be found.

The crowd discuss Jesus' words in terms of possible geographical destinations; did he mean that he might go to the dispersed Jews around the Empire and even teach the Gentiles? This, of course, was what Jesus sent his disciples out to do (Matthew 28:19) and is the theme of Acts. By repeating Jesus' words (7:34 and 7:36) the Evangelist emphasises their importance and highlights his profound concentration on who and what Jesus is. The implications for his readers are likewise beginning to emerge. The key to our behaviour lies in what we increasingly are. Jesus' emphasis on inner motivation as found in the Synoptics (Matthew 5:21-6:18), is pared down by John to the essential core: it is being which leads to doing.

d. THE LAST DAY OF THE FEAST, 7:37-52

Many commentators link the libations of water, which they assume took place on this day, with the symbolism of Jesus' words. Jesus certainly uses a free translation of the scriptural passage (Zechariah 13:3; 14:8) appointed for that time, one which spoke of an abundance of water which would come with the Messianic Age. For John, however, Jesus' declaration that he is the water of life for those who believe, is a public and more specific endorsement of what he had said privately to the Samaritan woman (4:14,15). The Evangelist adds the comment that Jesus was talking about the gift of the Spirit which was to come upon his disciples after he had been glorified, ie. after Jesus' death and resurrection (20:22). Of course, it would be totally against this gospel's teaching to suppose that John believed the Spirit only came into existence after Jesus' glorification. The Prologue shows the writer's awareness of scriptural testimony that God's spirit was active from the beginning of all things (Genesis 1:2). But the Evangelist's own experience had been that particular manifestation of

God's spirit which was the fulfilment of Jesus' promise to his disciples (14:16,17) so it was inextricably linked to faith in Jesus as the Christ.

The crowd react to Jesus in three ways, some saying that he is surely the prophet (Deuteronomy 18:15, cf John 6:14), others that he is the Messiah, while the third group say he cannot possibly be the Messiah because he comes from Nazareth. They are thinking of the prophecy that the Messiah would be of David's line and born in Bethlehem (1 Samuel 16:1,12; 2 Samuel 7:12f; Isaiah 11:1; Micah 5:2; cf. Matthew 2:1); if we are right in assuming that John's readers were already familiar with the Synoptic tradition, then this passage is another example of John's irony.

The temple police return empty-handed with the excuse that they were abashed by the power of Jesus' words. They are strongly criticised by their masters for thinking themselves competent to make such a judgement when it is the considered opinion of the Sanhedrin that this man should be arrested. The rulers contemptuously class the crowd as 'the rabble' and curse them for wilful ignorance of the law.

With some courage, Nicodemus (3:1) attempts to divert the Sanhedrin's wrath by drawing their attention to a matter of principle: the law specifically says that judges in Israel should hear both sides of the dispute and be impartial (Deuteronomy 1:16,17; et al) in their judgement. Surely the law does not allow judgement without the accused saying a word in self-defence? Nicodemus is scornfully ridiculed for having a false loyalty in the case. Is he too a Galilean? Why else should he support this man when it is clear from the scriptures that no prophet ever came out of Galilee? (This was not strictly true, since Jonah was Galilean (2 Kings 14:25) but in Jesus' day 'Galilee of the Gentiles' was considered beyond the pale by any strictly conservative Jew.)

    e.   FINAL DISPUTATION, 8:21-59

Jesus has already declared he is the light of the world (cf. 8:1-20, see p.118). This is central to the whole debate, as is also the phrase "I am what I am" which occurs twice in 8:24,28. and "I am " in 8:58 We may divide the last part of this bitter controversy into four sections;

(i)   *8: 21-30*

The pilgrims are perhaps thinking of going home after the festival. Jesus seems to refer harshly to his own homecoming, but where he is going they cannot follow. His listeners wonder if he thinking of suicide, but in fact, they cannot follow him because they do not belong to his state of being. They interpret the words 'above' and 'below' literally.

The Evangelist draws a clear distinction between Jesus' spiritual awareness, his oneness with the Father - and the 'Jews', the opposition, who misunderstand and do not recognise him. To ask Jesus yet again who he is when they have seen and heard him in action, seems to John almost wilful ignorance; to 'die in one's sin' is to die unawakened to the possibilities of spiritual growth. Jesus personifies the truth about humanity and its Creator: as such he personifies love and truth, rejection of which is spiritual death.

Although there is an apparent threat in the words - if you do not believe ... you will die in your sins - I do not believe that threat is part of the divine/human relationship. Fear of hell fire (or of escalating retribution for sin in reincarnate lives) never works. Threats always create wrong motivation. On the other hand, the facts of experience cannot be denied. There is a creative approach to living the truly human life but there is also a destructive way of living which is in the long run abortive; this is how things are. The Evangelist is stating the facts as he sees them when he considers both the mystery of unbelief and the mystery of Jesus' sacrifice. He goes on to comment that many believe Jesus' claim to be in unity with the Father.

(ii)   8: 31-36

This passage contains an important saying about freedom. When Jesus' true disciples abide in the revelation he has brought they can know the truth and the truth can set them free.

The Jews believed that the Law of God, the Torah, was the Truth. As Abraham's descendants they were free men, not slaves, although as a nation, they knew a great deal about servitude to a foreign power. They were at that moment subject to the might of Rome. Jesus however explains that they are slaves to sin. His hearers are ignorant of their bondage, of their motivation, of themselves.

In Mark's gospel, Jesus states that he has come to cure the sickness of sin (Mark 2:13-17), later declaring that he has come to give his life as a ransom for many (10:45). In Jesus' day a ransom was the purchase price for those condemned to slavery. A superficial reading of Mark might suggest the concept of a God who demanded the price of Jesus' life as a restitution for other people's sin. This abhorrent idea is totally at odds with Jesus' own concept of God as Love, so we need to think carefully what Jesus meant by this 'ransom' phrase.

The argument in John is based on a different premises and here again, I believe, the Fourth Evangelist shows that although he is aware of the

Synoptic tradition, he has something further to add. A slave in the household has no rights, but a son has a secure and loved position. As the Son of God, Jesus effectively has the power to free the slaves, an image which, Paul uses in his letter to the Galatians (5:1).

The Jew defined sin as breaking God's law (as found in the Torah). Jesus, as we have seen, summarised the whole law in terms of love. Therefore for him, sin was the unloving thought, word and action. In this sense, of course, we are all sinners and can only break free when we come to understand our motivation, our impulses. 'Sin' in this context is that which prevents us from fulfilling our potential as human beings. It destroys relationships and hinders our progress into adulthood. Knowing the truth about ourselves can bring freedom from self, if we are loved enough to face the truth. I see Jesus as the supreme liberator, both in his own experience and as example and witness. As the indwelling Christ, the Spirit of truth and love can bring us to maturity.

For George Fox, it was the illumination brought about by the Inner Teacher, Christ Jesus, endorsed by scripture, which was the truth and which brought freedom from sin. We need to evaluate clearly what we mean by freedom and the responsibilities it brings. In Paul's day and our own, people have mistaken freedom for licence to do as they please. This form of self-indulgence only leads to greater slavery.

(iii)   8: 37-47

In this biting exchange of insults, Jesus says that the Jews, although the physical descendants of Abraham, are really children of the devil. Their desire to kill one who has been sent by God proves their inability to grasp God's truth. Abraham was God's friend (Genesis 18:1-8), but their rejection of Jesus proves what their parentage is! The Jews retort that they are not base-born, by implication unlike Jesus. God is their father. But, says Jesus if you were really God's children you would recognise and love me because 'God is the source of my being'. In the Genesis myths Satan is portrayed as the great liar (Genesis 2:17; 3:19) who, through his deceitful temptation, brought death to Eve and Adam and mortality to humanity. Jesus then offers his listeners a challenge. If they can prove him false, they will have won the day. Since they cannot fault his integrity, why do they not listen to him and accept the truth he utters if they are truly God's children. Their unreceptiveness proves their parentage.

(iv)   8: 48-59

The Jews cannot prove anything against Jesus (apparently the charge of being a Sabbath breaker has been dropped) but they doubt his origins;

surely he is a Samaritan - a half-caste and not a true Jew at all. Furthermore he is apparently mad, or possessed (cf. Mark 3:21, 22). Jesus refutes this claim and denies that he is seeking fame. All he wants is that people should honour his Father. This I believe, is the basis, of the I AM statements. He is completely the vehicle of the glory of God/Love. He then makes an astonishing claim. Those who accept his teaching will never die. Not unnaturally, the Jews come back in triumph; now they know that he is mad for Abraham and all the prophets are dead. Is he claiming to be greater than their deceased great ancestors?

Jesus' reply that Abraham rejoiced to see his day may refer to the rabbinical tradition that God allowed Abraham to glimpse the future fulfilment of the divine promise to him and the dawn of Messianic Age (2 Esdras 3:13,14). The implication, therefore, is that Jesus is the Messiah. But this is not the only thing which incites the Jews to violence.

Jesus, of course, is not talking about physical death and life, but spiritual vitality, which is the stuff of eternity. Self-glory is worthless. It is only the Father who glorifies him. He existed with the Father before Abraham was born; he already existed when time was not a meaningful dimension. This reflects the idea expressed in the Prologue (1:1). In the sense that we also believe there is that of God within us, we too have within us the Spirit, which is out of time.

When Jesus concludes by using the sacred name for God, I AM, it is the last straw for his audience. The Temple was still in the process of being built so the Jews could readily pick up missiles and attempt to kill him by stoning, the traditional penalty for blasphemy. Jesus, however, mysteriously escapes.

Comment: I do not find this last controversy easy. Perhaps we may say that Jesus had the courage to 'speak truth to power'. He certainly seems to incite his hearers to hatred by deliberate provocation. Unlike the synoptists, the Fourth Gospel does not present the authorities as being offended by his acts of mercy or his ethical teaching, but only by the claims he makes about himself. Maybe this reflects more of the gospel writer's own later experience, rather than the time of Jesus himself.

4. Controversy following the healing of the man born blind and at the Feast of Dedication, 10:17-42

The healing of the man born blind, the fifth sign (see p.36), ended with a discussion between Jesus and some Pharisees about 'blindness' in which it was clear that Jesus was talking about their lack of spiritual perception.

The conversation is presumably continued in John 10, although the Evangelist does not say where it takes place. The theme of 10:1-16 has been dealt with under the heading of the I AM sayings as it contains the third and fourth statements (see p.121). Jesus is the Door of the Sheepfold and also the Good Shepherd. This is in striking contrast to the Pharisees, false leaders unworthy of the trust placed upon them.

Comment on 10:17-21: Verses 17 and 18 are difficult. We think of true love as unconditional and know how rare a quality this can be. Yet here is Jesus saying that he is loved by the Father conditionally: he is loved because he lays down his life. On a deeper level this does speak truth about the human condition. Love is reciprocal: we give and we receive. We have to be willing to take the initiative. Love is never passive. It is always regenerating itself. The more we love, the more we are enabled to love, but it is never easy. The recognition that we are loved by God, the divine spirit of love itself, empowers us to have a proper sense of self-worth. Although real love gives itself unconditionally we cannot grow unless we recognise and respond to this gift, nor can the relationship ever develop until it is reciprocal though not necessarily equal.

Jesus sees the reciprocity of love between Father and Son as paramount. He therefore stresses that the offering of his life is a matter of personal decision, based on what he understands to be the dictates of Love itself, personified as the divine Father. He has the power (ie the freedom of choice with all that this means) to withhold or to give, to lay down his life or 'to take it again', ie, to withdraw the gift. It is obvious from the gospel story that Jesus could have avoided arrest if he had been prepared to 'lie low' and save his life. He rather chose to dedicate himself to speaking truth about the human condition as long as he had breath in his body.

Whether Jesus actually said these words or not is immaterial. What we have here is the Evangelist's mature and considered understanding of the validity of his master's death and resurrection. In no way was the death of Jesus the end of the story. In some way beyond mortal comprehension, the essential Jesus went through the experience of death to the other side. By his fidelity to the utmost demand of Love, he was liberated 'to take up' his life, his true self, to be again. This too, is our hope and our promise. When the false egocentric self is laid aside, the true self which is endowed by the Spirit of Love has a chance to grow and develop. Jesus let go of his lesser self so that he was filled with the power of Love, of God, to such an extent that he could say with total lack of arrogance and pride, I AM ..the bread of life (6:35), the light of the world (8:12), the door (10:9,10), the good shepherd (10:11,14-16).

It is no wonder that the Jews did not understand him or that they were confused. John tells us that some of his audience thought him devil-possessed and therefore not worthy of any more attention, but others could not reconcile the power to do good which Jesus actually possessed, with evil. How could an evil spirit actually open a blind man's eyes?

The Feast of Dedication, 10:22-39:

In chapter 7, it was the Feast of Tabernacles. Now, with the mention of the Dedication festival, time has moved on three months later, to December. In 164 BC. Judas Maccabee restored the Sanctuary of the Temple, desecrated three years earlier by Antiochus Epiphanes (1 Maccabees 4:52-59). Jesus would be teaching under the shelter of Solomon's portico. The site is unknown today but it is mentioned in Acts (3:11, 5:12) and also by Josephus. Solomon, of course, built the Temple originally planned by his father, David (1 Kings 8:17ff). It is John's intention to link Jesus specifically to certain important Jewish festivals to show how he has superseded them.

The Jews gather round Jesus and ask him once and for all if he is or is not the Messiah. Jesus has never made this kind of public declaration nor does he do so now. Twice before in this gospel he has responded privately to a particular person, acknowledging he was the Christ to the Samaritan woman at the well (4:26) and admitting to being the Son of Man when speaking to the restored blind man (9:37). Faced with the Jews, he retorts that surely his deeds proclaim who he is. He may be angry, for he certainly speaks in very harsh either/or terms. Those who believe in him and become his followers (his sheep) are given eternal life and will not perish because they are the gift of the Father to the Son, between whom there is complete unity, 'I and the Father are one'. The neuter word 'one' is appropriate because God is beyond gender, even though Jesus, as became his origins and period, called God, Father.

Eternal life begins here and now. It is the attitude of mind and heart that attaches central importance to nurturing the spirit within. Jesus' promise of security does not necessarily relate to physical life but indicates inward serenity and continuance against all odds, even in the face of death itself.

In Mark's gospel (3:20-30) direct confrontation between Jerusalem lawyers and Jesus occurs when they accuse him of casting out devils by the power of Satan himself. Jesus replies by appealing to common sense but he also condemns the state of mind which attributes acts of compassion and love to evil.

As love is reciprocal, so is forgiveness. We cannot actually receive forgiveness until we are conscious of our need of it. However willing to give, Love cannot force itself upon another. Even if it were possible, it would rob the other of the dignity of willing response. It is extreme perversity to call good, evil. The situation can only be resolved when the person recognises something deeply wrong in his/her own psyche and experiences the desire to put it right. Until that moment of truth, those who remain outside the sheepfold do so at their own choice. The statement that Jesus' sheep are his Father's gift to him, hints at predetermination, but again it is simply stating facts about the nature of Love. Those who are open, who are seeking spiritual growth and understanding, recognise Jesus as the revealer of truth, the way to the Father, to ultimate reality. They thus become the gift of Love to the person who has awoken this love within them; hence the reciprocity of all true relationships.

Once again Jesus' claim to be one with the Father infuriates the Jews into picking up stones to kill him (cf. 8:59). Fearlessly, Jesus continues to confront them demanding to know the precise good deed which has aroused their hostility. They reply that it is not his deeds but his blasphemous words which condemn him. In true rabbinical fashion Jesus answers by an appeal to scripture, whose authority everyone would accept. In Psalm 82:6, when God utters his judgement on the negligent and corrupt leaders of his people, he calls them 'gods' and 'sons of the Most High'. Even though they were mortal and died, God acknowledged these inadequate and sinful leaders as 'gods' because of the divine spark within them. That being so, how much more right has someone to call himself Son of God, if he has been consecrated and commissioned by God?

Once again Jesus appeals to the validity of his actions to support his unity with the Father, but the Jews attempt an unsuccessful arrest. He retires again across the Jordan to Peraea, where the Baptist had ministered, and many people come to believe in him, (10: 39-42).

We see from the Synoptic accounts of his mental conflict before beginning his ministry (cf. Matthew 4:1-11, Luke 4:1-13) that Jesus' idea of Messiahship was totally different from that of his fellow countrymen. However much his good deeds proclaimed who he was, they could not possibly make the mental leap to accept him as the Messiah. In Luke 7:17-23 he answers John Baptist's disciples by saying 'Go and tell John what you have seen and heard' and then he lists the healing of the blind, the lame, the lepers, the deaf, the raising of the dead and preaching good news to the poor.

John has given us the healing of the official's son at Capernaum, the healing of the crippled man, on a Sabbath, at the pool of Bethesda, the feeding of the five thousand and the healing of the man born blind. So there is quite sufficient evidence of the power of compassionate love in Jesus to signify that his relationship with God is genuine. There is, however equally bitter controversy arising from the claims Jesus makes about his relationship. Despite the Old Testament vision of humanity's origins created in the image of God, (Genesis 1:27) and receiving the breath of God, (Genesis 2:7), the Jewish tradition also proclaimed an unbridgeable gap between God and his creation, thanks to the concept of the omnipotent all-seeing, all-wise Ruler.

Jesus' mission was to bridge this gap by illuminating our ideas about divinity and by awakening the latent spiritual perception and possibilities within each human being. This emphasis is important, because, I believe, Jesus is a human being, whose parents, family and place of origin are well known by his contemporaries. It is because of this familiarity with Jesus and his circumstances, that his opponents cannot stomach the extra dimension which surrounds him. Here is the mystery with which we must come to terms, a mystery that relates to the potential within any human being who is open to the full impact of the divine Spirit. The complete indwelling of the Father and Son is a foretaste of the Spirit's indwelling in us (cf John 17:21-23). The mystics of all faiths have experienced and expressed this sense of union, each in their own terms.

5.   Repercussions of the Lazarus miracle 11:45-57:

The crowd reacts to the extraordinary resuscitation of Lazarus (see p.40) in two ways, as John has recounted already (7:12; 10:20f) and will do so again (12:29). While some believe, others go straight back to Jerusalem to report the matter to the Pharisees who call in the Chief Priests. A meeting of the Sanhedrin is hastily convened. Jesus is condemned in his absence and an order goes out that he is to be arrested on sight. The High Priest at that time was Caiaphas, who held office from AD 18-36. According to Jewish tradition, the very office could enable its holder to speak prophetically so what might appear to be the wisdom of expediency on Caiaphas's part - one man dying for the sake of the nation - is turned by John into an echo of Jesus' own words recorded earlier, 'God so loved the world that he gave his only son' (3:16). The Chief Priests had particular reason to fear any Messianic uprising, for they held office through Roman patronage. They could not be expected to know or to credit that Jesus had already rejected a worldly concept of Messiahship (6:15).

John's irony is clear. If the gospel was written after AD 70, the Evangelist would know of the fall and total destruction of the city and the Temple. The nation was without a homeland for centuries, yet faith in Jesus the Christ could become the source of life for many millions.

Jesus obviously had inside information about the Sanhedrin's intentions. We have already read of Nicodemus' previous protest (7:50ff). Clearly he would be ready to help Jesus if he could and he later risked much, with Joseph of Arimathea, to bury Jesus (19:9). Therefore Jesus may perhaps be acting on Nicodemus' advice, when he returns with his disciples to Ephraim, a village in the desert hill country (now thought to be the modern El-Taiyibeh).

The Feast of the Passover is due in Jerusalem (11:55-57), so we read of the time allotted to the necessary ritual purifications. Once more the crowd is agog with curiosity as to whether or not Jesus will appear at the festival.

6. The Triumphal Entry, 12:12-19:

I have included this incident here, because John seems to present Jesus' action as deliberately confrontational, in view of his knowledge that the Sanhedrin had already condemned him (11:53,57). By contrast the Synoptics state that the authorities finally make up their minds to dispose of Jesus after the Cleansing of the Temple.

All four gospels include this story and it can be useful to compare the synoptic accounts with John. In Mark (11:1-10) Jesus makes arrangements on the first day of the week to obtain a colt from a nearby village where he obviously has some friends, and he rides into Jerusalem on the donkey. The pilgrims accompanying him are wildly enthusiastic, some spreading their clothing on the road, others cutting leafy branches to scatter, all of them crying 'Hosanna' and seeing in Jesus the possible restoration of David's throne. Jesus handles the crowd very astutely, especially in view of the fact that the extra strong Roman garrison in the Castle of Antonia, overlooking the temple precincts, would be on the lookout for trouble at Passover time. By leading them into the temple area, he ensures they will quietly disperse while he himself goes out to Bethany for the night with his disciples. According to Mark, there is some mystery about the colt, which had never been ridden on before, but the point the gospel is making is that Jesus has now decided the time has come for him to declare himself as Messiah, but that his concept of Messiahship is wholly different from Jewish expectations. The Cleansing of the Temple on the next day dramatically illustrates the revolution in outlook which Jesus is initiating.

Luke (19:29-44) basically follows Mark although he changes the nature of the story by several additions. As the pilgrims look across the Kidron valley to Jerusalem they cry out with a great song of praise, acknowledging Jesus as their messianic King (19:37,38). When some of the Pharisees in the party suggest to Jesus that he should rebuke his disciples' enthusiasm, he refuses to do so. He weeps over the city (19: 39-44), predicting that because its people reject the way of peace and reconciliation which he offers, the city will ultimately be destroyed.

Although Matthew's gospel (2:1-9) follows Mark, the author adds, as usual, that Jesus acted as he did in order to fulfil the scriptures, in this case Zechariah's prophecy (9:9). He also mistakenly places Jesus' Cleansing of the Temple immediately after the Triumphal Entry; such a chain of events would certainly have caused a riot.

John's account is simpler yet perhaps more profound. Jesus himself finds a donkey and mounts it. The pilgrims within the city, who had been on the lookout for Jesus, especially since the raising of Lazarus (11:56), now come out to greet him with palm branches - a sign of homage - and acclaim him King of Israel. This is precisely what the Galilean crowd wanted to do after the feeding of the five thousand (6:15) but on that occasion Jesus withdrew from them into the hills. Now he demonstrates what kind of a Messianic king he is by riding into the city on a donkey's colt. He knows the final conflict with the authorities is at hand (cf. v.23). John wisely adds that the disciples did not realise the symbolism of Jesus' action at the time. Only later, when their Master 'has been glorified', did they understand its full meaning and recall the prophecy of Zechariah (9:9,10); John quotes only the first verse, but it is worth reading the second one as well.

The Evangelist's final note is ironic. The Pharisees say to each other that the case against Jesus seems hopeless for 'all the world has gone after him' (12:19) meaning in their terms, 'the rabble'. But for John their idle words were as truly prophetic as those of Caiaphas (11:50-52). The peaceable kingdom of the reign of love which Jesus was inaugurating could and would be found within each person who believed in his way. It was the kingdom which would continue to have significance until the end of time.

7. **Last public discourse in the Temple, 12:20-26:**

John follows the story of the triumphal entry into Jerusalem by introducing a group of Gentile worshippers who have come to the Temple for the festival. These men approach Philip; coming from Bethsaida in Galilee, Philip had a Greek name and was probably Greek-speaking. The Gentiles ask to see Jesus but Philip first consults Andrew (whose name is also Greek in origin) and together they go to Jesus with the Gentiles' request. This seemingly simple incident causes a profound response in Jesus; he now knows beyond any doubt that his hour is upon him. The gospel's words 'The hour has come for the Son of Man to be glorified' illustrate how, for the Evangelist, Jesus' death, resurrection and subsequent gift of the indwelling spirit are best described in terms of glorification. They all clearly manifest the reality of Jesus' relationship with the Father, whose vessel of glory he is.

Jesus prefaces his next words with 'In very truth' (Revised English Bible) or 'verily, verily' (Authorised Version), a phrase used frequently in John's gospel to emphasise the importance of what follows (cf. 1:51 et al). In this instance it introduces what can be described as the heart of his teaching. Jesus first speaks of the natural life cycle of a grain of wheat which falls to the ground, dies and then bears a rich harvest. He interprets the cosmic law of life through death not only in physical but also in spiritual terms. His very choice of the symbol of a seed illuminates his meaning. The seed falls to the ground, and in due time its husk breaks open. The seed itself ceases to be (ie 'dies') but the life-force within produces roots and shoots and finally an ear of corn in which are forty seeds. The seed that does not germinate or 'die' in this sense, stays within its husk and eventually crumbles into dust. Jesus applies this process to spiritual development. There is a wrong kind of self-regard or self-protectiveness which destroys a person's essential being. This false self must be given up or broken open, for it encases the true self with its outer cover of superficial values (in John's terms 'worldliness'). Only through this process of 'breaking open' can the true spiritual essence grow and be equipped for eternal life (cf. Mark 8:55). The use of the words 'love' and 'hate' in this context are difficult because Jesus has also taught that there is a place for proper self-love (Mark 12:31). Self-knowledge is the key. Those who wish to be Jesus' disciples must follow his way of true love; then he will dwell in them and they too will become vehicles of the light and glory of the Father.

We tend to confuse the right kind of self-love, which has its place alongside love for others, with self-preoccupation, vanity, arrogance. Jesus said, 'treat others as you would like to be treated yourself'. There is something unresolved in us if we demand adulation and constant praise from others. Our real need is to be loved despite all our failings and shortcomings, to be loved even when the truth about us is known. We gain confidence when we are accepted simply as we are and when we accept ourselves.

We are not told whether in fact Jesus ever met these Greeks. They are presented in the gospel almost in symbolic terms for Jesus himself could have met only a few thousand people in his lifetime, yet he has been experienced as an indwelling reality by millions upon millions down the ages to this day. Even in the latter half of the first century at the time of the gospel's writing, there were probably more gentile followers of Jesus than Jews. But Jesus in this gospel, speaks of being the Good Shepherd (10:16) to others, i.e Gentiles, who were not of 'this fold' i.e Jewish. Further the resurrected Jesus says to Thomas 'Because you have seen me you have found faith. Happy are they who find faith without seeing me' (20:29). The incident of the Greeks, therefore, is used by the Evangelist to prefigure the worldwide church which could only be accomplished after Jesus' death and resurrection, when the historical Jesus stepped out of time and became the indwelling Christ. This literally could happen only though Jesus' death. Thus he personally fulfils the cosmic law that through death comes life.

According to Mark (11:15-19) the day after the triumphal entry, Jesus takes decisive action against corruption and racial religious discrimination. He clears traders from the Temple's Court of the Gentiles and stops it being used as a thoroughfare. Quoting from Isaiah (56:7) he declares that what should be a house of prayer for all nations, has become a 'bandit's cave' (Jeremiah 7:11). Mark here emphasises the universal significance and purpose of Jesus' ministry.

Although John includes the Cleansing of the Temple much earlier in his gospel (2:12-22) and adds a different dimension to the story (see p.51), he also shows that he is aware of the synoptic tradition by making the request of the Greeks - which holds the promise of a universal church - the moment of truth for Jesus himself.

When the wine ran out in Cana, Jesus said to Mary that his hour had not yet come (2:4). At the Feeding of the Five Thousand, in which Philip and Andrew had also played a part, he had avoided kingship; later he declared in Capernaum that he was the bread of life (6:35) and that his own flesh would be given for the life of the world (6:51). By this he meant the total offering of himself even unto death, from which would come the birth of the indwelling spirit.

The Evangelist, of course, does not present Jesus' physical death as a defeat of his cause, rather he sees it in terms of victory. But it is the manner in which Jesus lived and died which showed forth the glory of his relationship with the Father. Jesus was utterly faithful to the bitter end, even through those terrible moments when agony robbed him of his closeness to God (Mark 15:34). He did not run away. He did not retaliate. He did not misuse his power. He personally broke out of the horrendously recurring cycle of hatred, recrimination and revenge. He forgave his tormentors (Luke 23:34). On the point of death, he was even able to reach out to his fellow sufferer (Luke 23:43) and to provide for his mother (John 19:26,27). Because he lived the way of absolute love - the way of the Father - he had died to his lesser self many times to rise again as a more perfected vessel. Thus he transformed personal human death into a gateway which could lead to a richer state of being. Those who accept his analysis of the human condition and learn to die and rise again in their daily living, can experience even now the joy, peace and fulfilment of the life of the spirit.

Paul affirms his belief not only in the resurrected Jesus whom he believed he had personally encountered, but in a general resurrection from the dead. He writes to his Corinthian friends 'If it is for this life only that Christ has given us hope, we of all people are most to be pitied' (1 Corinthians 15:19). He then goes on to use Jesus' symbol of the seed which is transformed into something more splendid by its 'death' to show how this same kind of change will take place for us. 'What is sown as a perishable thing is raised imperishable. Sown in humiliation, it is raised in glory; sown in weakness it is raised in power...(15:42,43).

Jesus' death and resurrection was not a magical rite which bestowed on the believer eternal life, nor was it in the same category as an initiation ceremony, as practised by the ancient mystery religions, to give the initiated the chance of immortaity. By giving himself totally, Jesus opened a new direction for all humanity. Through his action, there is the opportunity for others to follow and they do not walk alone. We must be clear, however, that self-denial for its own sake is not life-enhancing. The whole thrust of Jesus' ethical teaching was the importance of inner motivation, and this demands searching self-honesty and knowledge. Seeking for spiritual growth and development is too costly a process unless we are inspired by a passionate commitment to love itself in all its many forms.

8.   Jesus' hour of inner trial, 12: 27-36

John has no account of the agony in the Garden of Gethsemane but the opening words of this passage are very similar to those given in Mark's account (14:33-36). They reveal the depth of Jesus' own conflict and fidelity. Even as he considers his natural desire for a more peaceful resolution to his precarious situation, he knows there is no other way for him to go if he is to bear witness to the truth which is in him. His whole purpose is to glorify the name of the Father (cf. Matthew 6:9 - the opening of the Lord's prayer). We might express this phrase in terms of understanding the nature of Ultimate Reality and our role as human beings in creation. Jesus, I believe, opened the window of our spirits to reawaken us to the endless possibilities of creative living.

John recalls that when Jesus prays aloud in this manner, he receives an answer variously interpreted by the crowd as thunder or the voice of an angel. Jesus is given absolute confirmation that what he has done and will do is in accordance with the Father's will and thus will reveal God further to humanity. Jesus then addresses the crowd for the last time.

The external sign - thunder, an angel's voice, the voice of God - has been given for the sake of the crowd only. What it means is that the crisis of judgement is upon them all, when evil will be overcome and shown up for what it is. For the Evangelist 'when I am lifted up' means that at the point of crucifixion, Jesus is exalted and will draw all humanity to him. This extraordinary vision needs restating and clarifying for our time. The crucified figure is an offence to some, as Paul knew it would be. To others it is a symbol of what is done for them as celebrated in the Mass, the Eucharist and other services.

George Fox disputed the validity of this kind of commemoration - 'You must have fellowship with Christ in his sufferings. If ye will reign with Him, you must suffer with Him; if you will live with Him, ye must die with Him, and if ye die with Him, you must be buried with Him. And being buried with Him in the true baptism, ye will also rise with Him. (*George Fox and the Children of Light*, p.120; edited Jonathan Fryer, pub. Kyle Cathie Ltd 1991). In other words we have to understand in spiritual terms the cosmic law which Jesus is demonstrating and the truth about the Creator which he is revealing and apply it to our lives with the inspiration, insight and power which the indwelling Christ will unfold to us.

The crowd expect that the Messiah will always be with them and that his kingdom will never end (Isaiah 9:7; Ezekiel 37:25; Psalm 110:4; Daniel 7:13f). They do not understand what Jesus means by the term 'lifted up' but if he is talking about dying, going away or even ascending to the heavens, then he cannot be their Messiah. Jesus does not answer their questions. He talks about the necessity of making a journey in the daylight because when darkness falls it is impossible to know where one is going. He uses the image of physical light and darkness to symbolise the illumination of the spirit within. He has, of course, declared that he is the light of the world (8:12).

In John's experience the risen Jesus the Christ has become the inward light (cf. 1:4-14) and all who accept him as their Lord and Saviour become themselves children of light. This phrase, much used by George Fox, at one time became a title for his followers. To be a 'child of the Light' was part of the challenge to which Margaret Fell responded when she first heard George Fox preach at Ulverston church.

'Trust to the light while you have it' may refer to the fact that Jesus' time on earth is now very limited, so make the most of him while he is still there. On the other hand, I think it more probable that he is talking about the life of the Spirit potentially present in each human being. It has to be recognised and developed lest it become so shrouded by other things as to be almost non-existent. Perhaps we can paraphrase his words - make the most of what illumination you still have - the glimpses of truth and reality that are your own now; work on them and give them a chance to grow, otherwise even the light you now have will disappear (cf Mark 4:25).

How can we interpret that moment of crisis, of judgement, not only for the Jerusalem crowd but indeed, Jesus claimed, for the whole world when the 'prince of this world' would be driven out? Obviously evil is still rampant at all levels of societies and cultures. It knows no boundaries anywhere. There is no need to list its countless manifestations. We see enough of this daily on our television screens. However, Jesus for me, is the supreme liberator for humanity. This is not to belittle the great religious leaders of other faiths or the heroic witness of countless others in various cultures. But Jesus has shown us the way of creative love, that God is love, and that the path forward for humanity must lie in developing the life of the Spirit which manifests itself through the whole person in a passionate concern for justice, peace and truth. To crucify the prince of peace and love was a terrible indictment of those who committed this crime, even if it was done in partial ignorance. As Jesus made clear in the healing of the blind man, people are judged by their response to acts of compassion and justice. They reveal themselves by their reactions. We see how deeply an individual or group can injure its humanity by perpetrating terrible acts of violence and injustice on the innocent. By such deeds people become hardened, callous and less human. In the end such actions can totally corrupt the human personality.

The New Testament writers believed that the old order had come to an end and a new age had begun with the coming of their Master. Paul expresses his view of how far humanity has strayed from its potential by describing people as being under the dominion of 'the god of this age' (2 Corinthians 4:4). The writer of Ephesians speaks of 'the commander of the spiritual powers of the air, the spirit now at work among God's rebel subjects' (Ephesians 2:2). Where fear, despotic rule, corruption, deceit and cruelty are dominant, it seems evil has sway. In New Testament and medieval times and even to this day, people personify these evil forces as Satan or the devil. Jesus described his own mental conflict about messiahship (Luke 4:1-13) in this parabolic form and in the second temptation Satan supposedly has lordship over the pagan kingdoms of the world. This would be a typical Jewish assessment of the situation. Behind the imagery, Jesus is actually facing up to the temptation to take a short cut - to use evil means to accomplish a good end - a course which he totally rejects. According to Luke's gospel (10:18), after the seventy-two disciples return from their successful mission, Jesus describes his own vision of 'Satan falling like lightning from heaven.' John's gospel makes two further references to the 'prince of this world' (14:30; 16:11) who has no power over Jesus and who stands condemned. Paul was totally convinced that Jesus Christ had disarmed these 'cosmic powers and authorities' (Colossians 2:15). The power of evil had been broken in one life whose victory had cosmic significance.

Even though we have a totally different view of the world in which we live, we must accept the way first century people thought about the mysterious and terrifying universe which they inhabited. They had the same experiences as we do in encountering evil and attempting to overcome it in themselves. We too may recognise evil as a spiritual force, even if we do not personify it, and we have seen its unbridled horror in this century, perhaps as never before.

As a first century man, Jesus himself could have used the expression 'the prince of this world' to describe the forces arrayed against him. This makes his resistance to them and his freedom from their tyranny all the more remarkable. Without expressing our own beliefs in terms like this, we may yet respond to Jesus' witness and the validity of his life, death and resurrection, by coming to understand that Love is the active energy in Creation and in human history. Thus we can have hope. Despite the grievous faults of the Christian church, especially in its literalism and its external interpretation of the crucifixion, it has within its founder the seeds of a new world order. Even though most of the signs are contrary, I do believe there is a good chance that we will grow up spiritually in time to save our species and our planet. Everywhere there are pockets of resilient, truly creative lives and there is growing awareness of what needs to be done.

On a personal level too the moment of self-realisation when we recognise our failure to love, comes as a self-judgement so that we experience the need for change. The lesser good or the evil in us, can be weakened and overcome by the greater good.

9. The end of the public ministry, 12:37-50:

This falls into two sections - the first of which (12:37-43) deals with people's reactions to Jesus. Despite his works of power, they do not believe and cannot trust him. To the Evangelist, this is the fulfilment of Isaiah's prophetic words (Isaiah 53:1) and he recalls a further saying of Isaiah (6:10) which explains the nature of unbelief. God commands the prophet to go and tell the people that their wits are dulled. They have stopped their ears and shut their eyes so that they will not turn and be healed. It is a prophecy of the judgement and doom that will fall upon them because of their unresponsiveness.

Jesus himself quotes this passage (Mark 4:12) in a private conversation with his disciples to contrast their willingness to listen and absorb his message with those who doubt Jesus himself and therefore can get very little from him. But his parabolic form of teaching could and did reach them on different levels; maybe one day they would see further. Jesus' words have been misinterpreted to suggest an elitist attitude, but it goes against all we know of him to believe that he was deliberately obscure. He was, however, a realist. He knew the complexity of human nature and recognised that people were at different stages of spiritual development.

In the parable of the sower (Mark 4:3-9) he assessed that approximately one in four of those who heard him preach would respond to his message in such a way that they themselves would bear 'a rich harvest'. This very high percentage of people in themselves would be spiritually fruitful and was enough to ensure real spiritual progress. Jesus had a deep love for the natural world. Very likely he understood that opposition is essential to growth and therefore could accept disaster, disease, disbelief and calamity as a challenge to the creative Love whose channel he wished to be.

We have first to acknowledge and accept the way things are and then work to change that which can be transformed within ourselves. When we also become vehicles of Love, amazing things happen all around us. The writer of the Fourth Gospel slightly alters the original Isaiah passage to say that it is God who blinds and dulls the people so that they are not able to 'turn to me and be healed'. The dilemma which runs throughout the Old Testament is how to square evil and suffering with the concept of an almighty, omnipotent creator God with everything under his control, even disbelief. Such a concept makes a nonsense of human free will and the possibility of entering into a reciprocal and developing relationship between creature and Creator. John finds unbelief so astonishing that he seems to revert to Old Testament theology to explain it. In fact, however, this view does not fit with Jesus' concept of God, a concept which we still do not fully understand. There is great mystery about the human condition and the world in which we live, neither of which can be described in black and white, either/or terms. I believe we are assessed on what we have made or done with what we have been given. Neither more nor less is required of us.

John adds a final note to this passage by recording that many did believe in Jesus but were afraid of the consequences if they declared their allegiance openly.

The second part (12:44-50) contains a summary of Jesus' message, the most dominant theme being Jesus' reiterated claim that he is the vessel through whom God speaks. 'To believe in me is not to believe in me but in him who sent me' (12:44). He is so clear and transparent a vehicle that to see him is to see 'the one who sent' him. In this sense he is the light of the world and the purpose of his coming is not judgement, but salvation. On the other hand to reject what Jesus has to offer is self-damnation, for he is the channel of eternal life. He has remained utterly faithful to his commission from the Father.

CHAPTER FOUR – THE FINAL DISCOURSES AND JESUS' PRAYER

	Chapter	Page
1. The Last Supper;		
a) Jesus washes the Disciples' Feet,	13:1-20	81
b) Comment on the text		85
c) Judas Departs,	13:21-30	88
d) The New Commandment,	13:31-38	90
2. John 14		
a) Present Reassurance and Future Promise,	14:1-14	91
b) The Spirit of Truth,	14:15-26	95
c) The Gift of Peace,	14:27-31	96
3. John 15		
a) Jesus as the Vine,	15:1-10	97
b) Loyalty to Jesus means Attaining Heavenly Joy,	15:11-17	98
c) Hatred of the World,	15:18-27	100
4. John 16		
a) Judgement by the Spirit,	16:1-15	101
b) Jesus' Final Words to the Disciples,	16:16-33	102
5. Jesus' Prayer, 17:1-26		
a) The Son's Relationship with the Father,	17:1-8	107
b) Prayer for the Disciples,	17:9-19	107
c) Prayer for the Unity of All who Believe,	17:20-26	107
d) Difficulties		108

CHAPTER 4:

The final discourses and Jesus' prayer

Jesus' public ministry is now over. John moves into the second part of his gospel in which his interpretation of his Master's purpose and person is further clarified. In the preceding chapters the reader has been able to see how a pattern has been unfolding. After confrontation and controversy the Jewish authorities have finally decided that Jesus must be arrested and killed. They have rejected his claims about himself and shut their eyes to the witness of his living integrity. The six signs have all been significant in themselves but have also been leading up to the final conflict which embraces the seventh sign, Jesus' own death and resurrection (see p.130). In the chapters under present discussion, Jesus now concentrates upon his disciples. We have no further encounters with others outside the immediate circle. Jesus is portrayed by the Evangelist as talking deeply and freely to his disciples in the intimacy of the last supper together, preparing them for what lies ahead (John 13-16). He is also represented as praying aloud to the Father (John 17). He is finally arrested, tried, crucified and resurrected (John 18-21).

1 A) THE LAST SUPPER, JESUS' WASHES THE DISCIPLES' FEET, 13:1-20:

First, we need to compare John's account of the last supper with that found in the Synoptic gospels (Mark 14:17-25; Luke 22:14-38; Matthew 26:20-29). Mark tells us it was the first day of Unleavened Bread, when the lamb was sacrificed in the temple precincts. The meal was therefore held after six pm on the Thursday evening as a Passover festival. Luke adds that Jesus speaks of longing to eat this last Passover with them (22:15). The Synoptics record that, to use Christian theological terms, Jesus here 'institutes' the sacred rite known variously as the Mass, the Eucharist, Holy Communion and the Lord's Supper. In Mark, Jesus takes the bread, blesses and breaks it and tells his friends to take, as it is his body. He also refers to the wine as the blood of the covenant giving thanks for it and then passing it round in a single vessel. These words are endorsed by Paul, when writing to the Corinthians (1 Cor. 11:23-25) as having been received by him 'from the Lord' by which he presumably means he has known of it both by that which has been passed on to him from those who were present at the time and through his own intuitive personal experience. I believe, therefore, that we can assume Jesus said something of this nature to his friends and I would consider Mark's actual reported words, given that his is the earliest gospel, as being relatively accurate.

The earliest Old Testament reference to the institution of the Passover is in Exodus (12:1-28) where we can see how the Feast of Unleavened Bread came to be associated with the Passover. The two feasts were celebrated during the eight days from the 14th - 21st Nisan (the name of the first month according to the Jewish calendar The Jews had a lunar calendar and the first day of a month would be calculated when the new moon was seen).

John, however, places the supper before the Passover festival (13:1). He agrees that it took place on the Thursday evening and that Jesus was crucified on the Friday, the eve of the Sabbath (19:31). That year the Sabbath was the first day of the Passover festival (18:28). John omits Jesus' reference to the bread and wine as his body and blood. Instead he shows Jesus washing the disciples' feet, including those of Judas. A hint as to why Jesus should take this action is provided by Luke who says the dispute as to who was the greatest amongst the disciples happened at the last supper (22:24-30). Mark (who places the episode earlier) gives much more detail about this argument, telling us it arose from a request by James and John (10:35-45) for positions of glory in the Kingdom. Saddened by their misunderstanding, Jesus makes clear his belief that true greatness lies in service to others and he goes on to give a reason why he must die: to give his life as a ransom for many (10:45).

The reader can legitimately ask three questions. John's gospel is traditionally attributed to the Apostle who was also the beloved disciple, sitting beside Jesus at the meal. Why does this gospel above all others not include Jesus' words about his body and blood? Secondly, why do the Synoptics omit the feet washing incident, in which Peter played a rather prominent part? Thirdly, was it or was it not a Passover meal?

Many orthodox scholars, who take the Synoptic tradition as the most authentic, would argue that John simply arranges matters to suit his own theological purposes and that he has already dealt with Jesus as 'the bread of life' on a previous occasion (6:48, 51, 54-56). Others speculate that John omitted it because early Christians held the rite of breaking bread too sacred to be mentioned in the larger context of the then pagan world. It is true, of course, that this rite, as it later developed, was very much misunderstood by the pagan world as a whole. There is evidence to suggest that the population of Rome disliked Roman Christians so intensely that Nero was able to blame them for the fire of Rome with impunity, leading to great persecution.

If we base our interpretation on the assumption that John's readers knew the Synoptics, we see that the author of John now sets out to deepen their appreciation of the mystery surrounding the man Jesus. Presumably he knew of Jesus' words at the Last Supper but he deliberately puts them in the more universal context of Jesus' mission. Recognising the deeply spiritual significance of what Jesus was saying, he shows Jesus speaking about his self-offering not to the select few in the highly charged atmosphere of a farewell supper, but to the many in the Capernaum synagogue after the Feeding of the Five Thousand (p.111). Here Jesus compares his body as the living bread of life come from heaven with the manna eaten by their ancestors in the desert (6:49). The spiritual bread which Jesus gives is his flesh, that is, his life. Whoever identifies with him in his self-offering has eternal life (6:54). The manna their ancestors ate simply sustained temporal, physical life. Thus the Evangelist has spiritualised the whole concept and removed it from any specific symbolic gesture.

I do not know whether Jesus actually spoke these words or not in Capernaum but he could have done. Certainly John's account of people's hostile reactions to Jesus is very graphic. The meaning of the fourth sign, which contains the first of the I AM sayings, is perfectly clear. In accepting Jesus' total self-offering and all that this means in holistic living, the believer will experience the indwelling Christ in the deepest part of her/his being. It is the indwelling which is all important. This essential inner experience is expressed in terms which could be alien to us, nevertheless I believe we have to surmount the cultural difficulties and concentrate on the essence.

Our second question relates to the fact that Mark omits the feet washing incident from his gospel. We can readily deduce from a detailed reading of the text that Peter at that time has little self-knowledge. First he cannot bear his Master to perform the menial job of a slave in washing his feet but when Jesus explains its significance he swings to the opposite extreme and wants to be washed all over! He strongly protests that he is willing to die for Jesus and does in fact try to fight at Jesus' arrest (18:10), but when he is put under pressure in the High Priest's courtyard, Peter denies that he is a disciple of Jesus. Earlier in Mark's gospel, Peter has shown how little he understands Jesus by attempting to rebuke him on his interpretation of Messiahship (8:32) and he fails his Master by falling asleep in the garden of Gethsemane.

However, Peter is forgiven and reinstated by Jesus after the resurrection. According to Acts he is, for a time, the leader of the new community in

Jerusalem. He is brave, forthright and wise, the spokesman for the disciples and recognised by Paul as having great authority. Oscar Cullmann (*Peter: Disciple, Apostle, Martyr*, SCM Press, 1962) suggests that we owe to Peter the concept of Jesus as servant of God. This title occurs four times in Acts (3:14,23; 4:27,30) twice in a speech by Peter and twice in a prayer that Peter could have uttered - certainly on an occasion when he was present. In the First Letter of Peter, a document which may bear his authority even if Silas actually wrote it, the author movingly cites Jesus' own bearing through his sufferings as an example for Christian household slaves and servants to follow. It would seem, therefore, that Peter absorbed the meaning of Jesus' act at the last supper and afterwards presented it clearly (according to Luke in Acts) in his teaching about Jesus, even if the incident itself was omitted from Mark's gospel.

The third question is the seemingly unimportant issue as to whether or not it was a Passover meal. Only Mark and Luke (obviously following Mark) mention the Passover lamb being sacrificed (Mark 14:12, Luke 22:7) on the day of preparation, which means that the evening meal would be the first day of the Feast. Strangely Matthew does not mention the Passover lambs at all and no gospel mentions a lamb being eaten.

There are two reasons for considering that John's timing is the right one. It is unlikely that Jesus was actually crucified on a feast day, which would merit the same strict solemnity as a Sabbath. John Robinson (*The Priority of John*, pages 147-156, SCM Press Ltd, 1985) points out that on Nisan 15, the first day of the feast, all work was prohibited (Leviticus 23:6f). The Fourth Evangelist says that the crucifixion took place about noon on the day of Preparation for the Passover. He never in so many words associates Jesus' death with the sacrificial lambs, although this idea has been attributed to him as a cause for his timing. His sole reference to Jesus as Lamb of God occurs right at the beginning when John Baptist (1:36) calls him this.

All four gospels agree that after the supper Jesus was arrested, tried and crucified on the following day, the eve of the Sabbath. Assuming the Fourth Gospel gives the correct timing of events, John Robinson has discussed (see above) the possibility of actually dating Jesus' death. Given the margins of AD27-34, there are only three dates possible. If Nisan 15 fell on a Friday then the date is AD27; if on the Sabbath, which is what John's gospel says, then AD 30; if for some reason an extra month had been intercalated then AD33 is the date. If Nisan 1 was calculated a day late because the sighting of the new moon had been missed (!), then Nisan 15 could have been celebrated on AD28 or 31.

We know from Matthew and Luke's gospels that Jesus must have been born before Herod the Great died, which date is now assessed at 4BC. If he was born that year then Luke confirms that he was about thirty years old when he began his ministry (3:23) in AD27/28. He would then be 33/34 when he died in AD 30.

The reason for this digression into dates is to affirm that John's gospel has another kind of authenticity beyond that of a great meditation upon Jesus the Christ. It would seem that this gospel does contain vivid glimpses of 'how it was' during the period of Jesus' ministry on earth. Above all else, the author believes that the indwelling spirit of Christ illuminates the purpose and person of Jesus in a way the disciples were incapable of grasping during his lifetime (2:22; 12:16; 13:19).

b)   COMMENT ON THE TEXT:

John introduces the supper by an intimate glimpse into the mind of Jesus. Realising that the crisis is imminent he tries to prepare his disciples for the fact that he is physically going to leave them through death. He believes he is going to the Father. As always Jesus is motivated entirely by love. John movingly expresses this by his awareness of Jesus' steadfast love for them all to the end of time and beyond.

John interprets Judas' betrayal as diabolically inspired. We will discuss Judas' possible motivation later. It is inconceivable that Jesus, with his wonderfully penetrating insight into human personality had not seen Judas' potential weaknesses. John stresses that it is during the meal, not before or after, that Jesus gets up, lays aside his robe and takes a towel to give to his friends the services of a slave, so perhaps Luke is right to say that the mealtime dispute as to who was the greatest actually sparked off this act of Jesus. It could be argued on the other hand that if the washing was the central experience of their last meal together with Jesus, it is understandable that Luke should attach the story of the dispute to his account. He does however alter Mark's words (Mark 10:42-45, cf. Luke 22:24-30) and he does comment elsewhere on the theme of exaltation and humility, (14:11; 18:14).

Many commentators consider Jesus' action symbolises the believer being cleansed from sin by Jesus' atoning death. John uses precisely the same words for Jesus taking off his outer garment and then putting it on again after the washing (13: 3,12) as he did to describe Jesus' role as the Good Shepherd (10:11, 15,17f) prepared to lay down his life for his sheep and then receive it back again. Other commentators compare the water of the foot washing with the sacrament of Christian baptism and its teaching that the baptised person is cleansed from sin and enters into the benefits of Christ's death and resurrection.

For me the action speaks of the reciprocal nature of love and gives a further insight into the mission and purpose of Jesus. He demonstrates to his friends that as their Master he is also their servant. By undertaking the most menial of tasks for them, he shows them that true greatness does not lie in hierarchical structures (Mark 10:43-45) but in our concern for one another. Peter cannot bear that his beloved Master should stoop to him and protests, which calls forth Jesus' response that if he will not be washed, he has no part in Jesus. How are we to interpret this? We have to be willing to receive as well as to give. To accept the vulnerability which is involved in loving, to accept the truth of the fundamental message of Jesus, is not at all easy. He has shown that it is through the death of the false self that the true self will awaken and live. Not yet understanding, Peter asks for his head and his hands to be washed as well. Although he is surely talking about inner motivation, Jesus answers Peter in his own terms; Peter's devotion to Jesus makes him 'clean all over' although he does not yet have true self-knowledge. When tested he will fail (13:38) but that will not be the final word about him.

Yet there is one present who also has his feet washed but is 'not clean'. Although Jesus knew and loved Judas, he could not save him because Judas could not accept the truth that was in Jesus. Judas made his own choice and was left free to do so because this is of the very nature of love.

When Jesus again sits down he asks his disciples if they fully understand what he has done. He acknowledges that he is their Teacher and Lord yet he has acted as their humble servant or slave. So ought they to treat each other, for they could claim no greater status than being both his servant and each other's. This is why this passage is of such importance in the whole structure of the gospel. Jesus shows by his actions the purpose of his mission. As he says at the end of the discussion of true greatness in Mark, he has come not to be served but to serve and to give his life as a ransom for many (Mark 10:45). We have not yet absorbed this lesson. Humanity is riddled with false power structures because we are obsessed with trying to find purpose and fulfilment by possessing and wielding power. But power corrupts unless it is used in the service of others, in the service of Love itself.

I doubt whether we have yet fully explored the authority which comes from voluntary powerlessness. Jesus personified this condition because, as God's representative, he used no other means of persuasion than the spirit of truth and love. It is indeed far more comfortable to postulate an almighty God who controls everything, than the one Jesus actually portrays.

We may deduce from Jesus that happiness will not be found or experienced through power structures. Happiness lies in loving and being loved, in accepting the vulnerability and strength of reciprocal relationships in which we serve and are served. There is no inner weakness in this way of life because it accords with the fundamental moral law on which the whole of creation rests.

Speaking indirectly of Judas (13:18), Jesus next refers to a passage from Psalms (41:9) about the disloyalty of a friend 'who ate bread with me'. When they later realised that one of them had betrayed their Master it must have been a horrifying revelation to the disciples and must have taken a long time to accept. The Evangelist, of course, is writing of Judas' betrayal with hindsight, but it is apparent from Mark's gospel that Jesus did know what was in Judas' mind and warned Judas of the consequences of his action; he would regret ever having been born (Mark 14:21).

Jesus left Judas free to make his own decisions and go his own way. I do not share the Evangelist's belief that these things were a fulfilment of Old Testament prophecy and therefore perhaps in some way predetermined. To understand Jesus' alleged quotation of the Psalm we need to appreciate that Jesus knew there was one disciple who did not fully accept his truth and would therefore take action against the principles which Jesus taught. Jesus would realise that when the eleven other disciples later recollected their last evening together it would be important for them to recall that Jesus had seen what was in Judas' mind and that the only constraint he put upon Judas was that of love. This is the cost that true Love accepts by not stooping to compulsion. It knows the risk it is taking and bears the total consequences. As adults we have to face the fact that certain courses of action are completely self-destructive, as well as destructive for others.

Jesus' ministry demonstrates time and again his marvellous capacity to penetrate people's hearts and minds; why then did he choose Judas? I believe that he took a chance with him. He saw Judas' potential and gave him the opportunity to develop and grow in the life of the spirit. We do not know much about the characters of the other disciples, Peter excepted, but I suspect they were a very diverse group, often inadequate and therefore representative of human nature. We may suppose that they were transformed to a greater or lesser degree by their encounter with Jesus. That one out of the twelve would actually betray him is something we all can recognise, confirmed by the history of humanity and perhaps in our own experience. Judas' act of betrayal was primarily a tragedy for Judas himself, as Jesus knew well. If Jesus had prevented Judas in some way, it would have made little difference to the final outcome because the

Sanhedrin had given judgement in advance. Jesus was already doomed unless he fled to the desert or some far away place. What the Sanhedrin wanted of him was silence and absence. Jesus was not prepared to abandon his declaration of the truth as he understood it. Nor did he abandon Judas (what action might the disciples have taken if he had told them Judas was the betrayer?); he made every effort to reach the depth of Judas' being but left him the freedom of his own choice.

The passage ends with words (13:20) familiar from the Synoptic tradition (Mark 9:37; Luke 10:16; Matthew 10:40). Jesus' union with the one who has sent him is to be continued through his disciples. If they are one with him, people who encounter them will also encounter God, Love itself.

c.   JUDAS DEPARTS, (13: 21-30)

John recounts that Jesus is in deep distress as he exclaims that one of his disciples will betray him. The Evangelist uses the same phrase to describe Jesus' anguish when he sees Mary's grief (11:33) for her brother, Lazarus. It is natural to suppose that Jesus was deeply wounded by the thought of a close friend's treachery, but I would suggest that the depth of his feelings is evidence of profound inner tension over his interpretation of Messiahship.

He experienced conflict before the raising of his friend Lazarus because he knew the inevitable result of such a miracle. People would believe in him for the wrong reasons and the end result would be the Sanhedrin's death sentence because they would argue that he was 'leading the people astray' and 'perverting the nation' (Luke 23:2). Jesus' fate as a public figure had been sealed by the raising of Lazarus whether Judas betrayed him or not, so the point at issue for Jesus here is how should he deal with Judas; in what way should Love be truly manifest? Although it was a particular case, it exemplifies how God/Love deals generally with humanity.

Most of the disciples react in bewilderment to Jesus' statement but Peter tries to find out who is the traitor, perhaps to prevent the betrayal by violence; he has with him the sword which he tried to use at Jesus' arrest (18:10). The 'disciple whom Jesus loved' discovers the identity of the betrayer but does not pass on this information to Peter. He too (the unnamed disciple) does not understand what is going on, but his love and trust for the Master is such that he remains silent, letting the others suppose Judas had left them at Jesus' word, because he had other things to do. Only Matthew's gospel states that Jesus openly confirms that he knows

Judas' intentions (Matthew 26:25) and narrates the story of Judas' death (Matthew 27:3-10), although Acts also records it (Acts 1:18-10).

John specifically attributes Judas' action to Satan (13:27), saying he 'entered' into Judas after Jesus had given him the mark of special favour, the chief place at supper. John has previously called Judas a thief (12:6) accusing him, as treasurer of their common fund, of pilfering their money. The accusation of avarice surfaces in the Synoptic tradition, where Matthew tells us that the Sanhedrin paid Judas thirty silver pence, the possible price of a slave (Matthew 26:14-16). He probably undertook to tell them where and when Jesus might be taken secretly, since the Council were afraid of Jesus' popularity and possible rioting if his arrest were public.

Luke agrees with John that Judas' betrayal was due to Satanic possession (Luke 22:3-6) but Mark does not attempt to explain Judas' motives and whatever our speculation about the matter, in actuality we can not know what they were. The most plausible ideas are either that Judas was disillusioned because Jesus was not turning out to be the Messianic leader he had hoped for, or that he tried to manipulate Jesus into following the course of action which he (and not Jesus) deemed right. If he was critical because Jesus was not ardent enough in keeping the law or did not declare himself a rebel leader, it would suggest that Judas himself may have ben a Zealot. If so it was not common knowledge, whereas one disciple was actually named Simon the Zealot (Mark 3:18) and obviously was known to have previously espoused the cause of armed revolt against Rome. It is possible that Judas took money from the communal purse not for his own gain, but to further his idea that the proper messianic cause was outward rebellion against the occupying power. He may have hoped to bring about a direct confrontation between Jesus and the authorities, expecting that Jesus would then declare himself and take decisive action. If this supposition is correct, then Judas did not intend Jesus to die and therefore tried to 'buy Jesus back' when his plan failed, as recorded by Matthew (27:3-10). Judas was the only non-Galilean member of the twelve so he may have felt an outsider. Possibly he was simply so disappointed or jealous that he decided to take steps to provide for himself, though this is hardly likely.

It has been suggested that Judas was fated or predetermined to betray Jesus, but this is a terrible concept, totally unacceptable and irreconcilable with the belief in a God who is love and who gives human beings free choice in order that they might grow into adulthood. One commentator has even argued that Jesus commanded Judas, as his favourite disciple, to hand him over to the authorities so that he could help fulfil God's demand that his Son should die for the sins of the world. I find this idea just as repulsive as the predestination theory.

The complexities of Judas' character are unknowable. The important thing now for us is to reflect on Jesus' treatment of Judas. Three times in this chapter Jesus warns Judas (13:10ff, 18,21) that he knows of his intentions. Even while he is making a last appeal of love to Judas by offering him the piece of bread dipped in the dish, it is clear from his comment to the beloved disciple that he feels Judas will not change his resolve. The moment when 'Satan' enters into Judas, may be the Evangelist's description of the way in which Judas' face hardened in response; in any case it would be impossible for John to think of Judas' action in any other way than Satanic possession. Jesus then bids Judas get on with what he has to do (13:27). It is this verse which causes such controversy because literally speaking Jesus is commanding Judas to betray him. There are several points to clarify here. Did Judas need Jesus' permission to leave the room? For the Evangelist, Satan's agent could not act unless Jesus permitted it. We might express it differently. Jesus went through great anguish, conflict and suffering but proved himself incorruptible. In that sense, the power of the Spirit within him as a vehicle of God/Love, was greater than any evil impulse. Also, being essentially a realist with proven insight into people's inner motivation, Jesus would judge correctly Judas' state of mind. If as we have suggested, Judas was sure he was right and Jesus wrong, Jesus would feel bound by love to let him find out the truth for himself, whatever the cost to Jesus personally. In saying this, I wish to emphasise that we are discussing relationships between individuals not matters of law and society.

d. THE NEW COMMANDMENT, 13:31-38

Judas has now gone out into the night - a deeply symbolic word for the Evangelist. How would I have treated Judas if I had been Jesus? An impossible question to which I do not know the answer for I have not Jesus' utter compassion. Jesus truly loved Judas. He had seen Judas's potential greatness and his weakness. He had warned Judas of the desolation he would experience if he persisted in this course of action, yet he left him free to pursue it. Therefore, I believe at this moment in time, Jesus reveals to us the nature of the divine. As Jesus treated Judas, so God treats us: hence Jesus' words about glorification both of the Son and the Father. Commentators consider that reference to glorification must be associated with Jesus' passion, which has yet to come (see p.131). Here, however, Jesus uses the present tense, so I think we are free to look for a further meaning as discussed above. I prefer to use 'glorification' in the sense of praising and honouring the true nature of God, which Jesus at that moment reveals.

Jesus now warns his friends that he will be leaving them shortly but he gives them a new commandment to love each other as he has loved them. This strong compassionate love amongst them will lead others to recognise that they are Jesus' disciples. The Synoptic gospels have given us Jesus' summary of the whole law in terms of love (Mark 12:28-34), the command to love our enemies (Matthew 5:43-48, Luke 6:27-28, 32-36) and the golden rule of treating others as we would like to be treated ourselves (Matthew 7:12, Luke 6:31). The Fourth Gospel is here both more specific and illuminating because it gives us the example and the power of Jesus himself in his total capacity to love. If we can understand and cultivate the 'abiding' relationship as far as we are able, we may find ourselves empowered by his spirit to see others as he saw them. Our whole spiritual journey is about the further knowledge of love. We have to learn to love from Love itself. It is Love in its many manifestations which awakens the seed of God within us. We have to discover the mutuality of all relationships. I cannot, therefore, believe this command of Jesus was meant to be exclusive, ie. that we should love only our 'brethren', fellow-followers of Jesus, Christians or members of our particular denomination or religion. This would make a nonsense of the whole of Jesus' ministry. When reading 1 John 2:7-11, in which the writer recalls this passage in the gospel, I would again interpret 'brother' as fellow human being. I base my reading on Jesus' own witness to love regardless of gender, race or religious affiliations. We have to interpret these passages for our own time, believing they contain the truth of human experience. If we can see some facets of Jesus the gospel writer could not conceive, then that only endorses and vindicates Jesus' timeless relevance.

Peter asks Jesus where he is going (13:36) because he does not understand that Jesus is talking about dying. The same mistake occurred in Jesus' conversation with 'the Jews' (7:34, 8:21). Death is a complete physical parting and we cannot follow; we can however learn to internalise the relationship, which is what happened to the disciples when they realised the indwelling Christ. Peter protests that he is ready to die for his master and indeed he does start to fight when Jesus is arrested (18:10), but Jesus warns Peter that another kind of trial awaits him. Although he is not prepared for it, he will learn a great deal about himself from the experience.

2. **John 14**

a) PRESENT REASSURANCE AND FUTURE PROMISE, 14:1-14:

Jesus has been through a profound crisis. Now he is at peace within himself and able to reassure his friends. The Marcan account of Jesus' agony of heart and mind as he is wrestling with his fears in the Garden of

Gethsemane (Mark 14:32-42) probably describes what literally did happen. Although John never mentions this event he shows that he also is aware of the great conflict and tension portrayed by Mark's poignant passage. On three occasions he speaks of Jesus' state of mind; at the raising of Lazarus (11:33, p.46), at the request from the Greeks to see him (12:27,28, p.73) and finally at the last supper (13:21, p.88). Although I think the Evangelist was aware of the Gethsemane experience, and assumed that his readers would know of it, he puts Jesus's conflict into a specific time sequence, to make his own complex insights clear; he both shows Jesus as fully human, yet also as the perfected channel of God's spirit of love. He is now making the point that, as Jesus went through conflict and agony to come to peace, so will his friends. In fact it will be easier for them to follow him because he has gone before them. He has taken the pioneering course of action, therefore they must trust in God and in him. They will not be let down.

It is possible to translate 'dwelling-places' (14:2) as staging posts or roadside "inns" on the spiritual journey. We may visualise the after-life either as a static place of 'being', embodied in the picture of a large mansion with many rooms for all sorts of people, or as a spiritual journey of numerous stages. I personally prefer the latter image. But whatever the picture, I am certain of one thing and that is the reality of life after death. For me death is only a definite stage in our spiritual journey and Eternity is here and now. Eternal life is above all else a quality of life lived in the realm of the spirit. Of course, Jesus has already qualified what he may mean about his 'Father's house' in his conversation with the Samaritan woman (4:21). Because God is spirit, 'house' in terms of a place of worship has no meaning other than as an inner reality. Our relationship with the divine is a matter of spirit and truth.

In 13:3, Jesus gives the absolute promise of his personal return to his friends. I believe this refers to his resurrection, which the author of the gospel undoubtedly experienced. In this last discourse, Jesus promises at least five times (14:3,18,28; 16:16,22) that he will return to his disciples. While his words may refer to the resurrection experiences, they speak more importantly of the abiding reality of the indwelling Christ, his actual presence within them. I do not believe they have anything to do with an apocalyptic Second Coming, falsely anticipated by so many down the centuries.

The imagery of journeying, of coming and going, departing and returning, is in fact, a typical characteristic of the Evangelist's style, but he tells us that Thomas and probably the others as well, did not understand Jesus' metaphors. The gospel has given the reader a rather clear picture of

Thomas in the episode (11:16) when he thought Jesus was in danger, and the portrait is made even sharper in the resurrection stories (20:24ff; 21:2). He is listed in the synoptic tradition as amongst Jesus' twelve disciples (Mark 3:18). Here (14:4) he says bluntly that the disciples to not know where Jesus is going so how can they know the way? Jesus replies by affirming that he himself is the way, the truth and the life and further that he alone is the way to the Father. This is an absolute and exclusive claim. The only sense in which I can find this exclusive statement acceptable is to refer back to Jesus' own witness to God. He is the way to God because he has revealed that God is Love. He is also the life because he has stripped away the false selves which delude us all and therefore is at one with the vital energy which is the source of the universe. For further discussion see chapter 5 (p.126).

I do not believe that we have yet learnt the nature of true love, either for our neighbour or for ourselves. But the first love, says Jesus, must be for God. I see love as the only motivation that is really effective. I can glimpse a little of the true nature of Love from the way that Jesus treated Judas and was prepared to suffer the personal consequences of leaving Judas free to make his own choice. The divine Love not only lets us learn from our mistakes, from the consequences of our action, despite the cost, but identifies with us in the process. Thus we have a chance to learn, grow and develop if we wish.

The conversation now takes a different slant (14:7). In response to Jesus' statement that he is the true vehicle for knowledge of the Father, Philip, another forthright disciple, whom we have come to know slightly (1:43ff; 6:5ff; 12:21ff) asks for an outstanding theophany or reflection of God which will leave no room at all for doubt. But that is not the way of Love. All true love needs a willing response. Jesus is perhaps sad that his friends have made so little spiritual progress. Have they not understood that he has himself become a channel for the divine love within? Again the Evangelist places special emphasis on the word "in". Jesus is in the Father and the Father is in him and the proof of this 'indwelling' is manifest in Jesus' own words and deeds. Again Jesus disclaims any personal authority, he is simply the vehicle through which the Father has made his will known (14:10).

Human history shows how many false prophets and messiahs have claimed that their message is inspired by God alone. The acid test of a person's sincerity is always the quality of their own life, not necessarily their words. Jesus warns his disciples in the Synoptics about bogus leaders (Matthew 7:15-20, Luke 6:45) and in the Fourth Gospel Jesus contrasts the thief and the good shepherd (10:10). Again it is the quality of love that matters. As Jesus is later to clarify (15:13), when love is the motivation a person is willing even to sacrifice her/himself.

Verse 12 contains the astonishing promise that his disciples and friends will be able to do as he has done if they have faith in him. They will accomplish even more because he is returning to the source of power itself. When he will no longer be limited by human circumstances, there will be no limit to what he may do through us. Through faith, humanity can be awakened to its spiritual destiny. To 'pray in his name' means in accordance with his own revelation of God. Faith is defined in the Epistle to the Hebrews as that which 'gives substance to our hopes' and 'convinces us of realities we do not see'. Faith must come first, to be followed later by confirmation. When Lear demanded proof of his three daughters' love for him he was sadly misguided; the one who loved him most could not produce the kind of evidence that he looked for. Only later was the truth revealed.

The Old Testament bears witness that humanity cannot endure to see or face the divine reality. Moses was quite exceptional because he had conversations with the Lord in the Tent of Meeting (Exodus 33:11) but even his request to see the Lord's glory was refused because he would not survive the encounter (Exodus 33:20). Faith must be based on the truth of our own experience, not on illusion or ignorance. Jesus asked his friends to have faith in him and in the truth about God that he was demonstrating through his life, because they had been with him during the last few years and knew him. Faith of this kind meant holding steadfast to what was known and experienced.

The promise given by Jesus (14:14) that he will grant whatever is asked in his name, is hard to come to terms with. So often our explicit prayers for our loved ones are not answered. A child praying that her mother may not die or parents praying that their child may get better from a terrible disease - these prayers are often unrequited. We pray for the alleviation of suffering because we cannot bear it and it is even worse when suffering continues. However our vision is very limited. We seek above all else to escape from suffering and death and yet these are fundamental realities in human existence. We need a change of perspective. We must simply do what we can do in faith, even if our action seems totally ineffective. Sometimes we have to leave the outcome to others. As Paul says, we now have a clouded vision, but one day we shall see clearly (1 Corinthians 13:11). If we walk the way of love with Jesus, we shall try to exemplify compassion and truth in our lives. Jesus could only act in love and through love so if we ask in Love's name and for Love's sake then the power and the energy of Love is ours.

b) THE SPIRIT OF TRUTH, 14:15-26

In Johannine writings, Jesus is reported as linking love with obedience (14:21,23f; 15:10,14; 1 John 5:3). His own life exemplifies this. He is utterly obedient to what he conceives to be the Father's will for him even if he may not be aware at the time of its full significance. This link is perhaps harder for us than for previous generations who set such store on obedience in religious communities and church government. But Jesus' commandment was to love and to explore inner knowledge in the hope of learning more about the reality of love. It is therefore obedience to the dictates of Love itself.

He promises his disciples that the Spirit of truth will be with them for ever, in contrast to the temporality of human life. Translations variously describe this Spirit in terms of 'Advocate' (REB and New English Bible), 'Counsellor' (Revised Standard Version) or 'Comforter' in the Authorised Version. Although the translation of the Greek word by 'advocate' is technically correct, it smacks too much of a law court for me so I prefer the word 'counsellor' or 'comforter'. However, the phrase the 'Spirit of Truth' has further significance. Does it equate truth with knowledge? Some people may pursue truth/knowledge without any allegiance to Jesus the Christ. Are there different kinds of truth according to the discipline in which a person is presently engaged, such as artistic or scientific truth or at least truth of the scientific process? These are all difficult questions. I believe there is one truth, which is to be found in the divine, but there are many manifestations of this truth and we all see things from a different perspective according to where we are on our spiritual journey. Having the Spirit of Truth within leads to all-important self-revelation and divine revelation. Unless we understand our motives we shall not progress very far in the spiritual life. For me the Spirit of Truth stands for something more than a personal interpretation of truth because it seeks to apprehend objective reality.

John is very clear that the unawakened portion of humanity, 'the world', cannot know the indwelling spirit. I would put it another way. Although we are all equally loved by God, we are not equal in our spiritual development. We are at different stages of our journey. For me, the moment of self-awakening is to realise that God is Love. This moves the indwelling of God into acute realisation or consciousness, whereas before it may have been unconscious. Where there is not Love or an awakening to the reality and purpose of Love, then there is not a proper consciousness of God's indwelling reality.

The relationship between Jesus and the Spirit is difficult to understand. After New Testament times the two realities seem to be treated as interchangeable but this is because Christian orthodoxy established Jesus' divinity which is something I cannot accept. Jesus, for me, was human, mortal, circumscribed by time; he was born and he died. The Spirit is within, is of God, is therefore timeless and cannot die. Jesus talks of this Spirit as illuminating his teaching (14:26). Some people think of the Spirit as Jesus' alter ego, but the Spirit has been present in all human history before and after the time of Jesus and in other faiths or none. The reality of the resurrection experience and later the indwelling presence of the risen Christ made those first disciples of Jesus believe that his spirit had been pre-existent with God since before the dawn of time (cf. Prologue, p.157). I accept that here is a great mystery. For me, Jesus became the Christ through his utter fidelity to God. His indwelling presence is a reality. Paul calls him the second Adam. He is therefore the prototype of what we may become.

Jesus again promises to return. Although the 'world' will see him no longer because of his physical death, his disciples will see him. He will return to them. He will go through the experience of death and emerge on the other side. And because he lives, they will live also. In John's gospel, it is Jesus the Christ who gives eternal life, the reward of faith in Christ. I am convinced this doctrine oversimplifies matters. Humanity has passed through many stages and all the great faiths, not just Christianity, teach the reality of an after life. It is the quality of life now which is all-important. Perhaps the Fourth Gospel is saying that if you enter into relationship with the divine Love as manifest through Jesus, you will begin to live in and experience eternity here and now.

The other Judas (Luke 6:16; the son of James) is concerned about a private revelation to them alone and not to the world (15:22) but Jesus explains that it depends on receptiveness. Those who love him and have accepted the truth of his message will be open to receive him and the Father. There can be no compulsion in Love's dealings with us, otherwise we will not change. In order to grow, we must acknowledge our need to start the spiritual quest and welcome the challenges it brings.

c)   THE GIFT OF PEACE, 14:27-31

Jesus' parting gift to his disciples is the same inner peace which he has found through fidelity to Love. The Fourth Gospel records that the resurrected Jesus actually imparts this gift of peace and the Holy Spirit when he meets his disciples on Easter night, (20:21,22). Jesus' gift of peace has nothing to do with avoiding pain and suffering. It is an inner quality which enables us not to be spiritually destroyed by them; even though pain and suffering will change us, will cause us to die and be reborn into something new. Jesus' peace can be a permanent possession but it has to be continually striven for and then received again and again if we are obedient to the call of Love.

Jesus reverts to the theme of his departure and return to his friends. His disciples should rejoice at his going away to the Father who is greater than himself. He is expounding these things now so that when events actually happen their faith will endure. That their faith was confirmed by subsequent events is the witness of the gospel writers. We have discussed earlier the universal law that through death comes life. The relationship between Jesus and his disciples will become an inner reality - an indwelling. This is perhaps another form of the promise of eternal life for all who learn to love.

Jesus then speaks of the approach of the 'Prince of this world' by which he means the evil which will seem to overcome him through his arrest, trial and death. As befitted a man of his culture, he regularly personified evil and the Synoptics report him talking of Satan (or the devil) and his kingdom (Mark 3:23ff, Luke 4:1-13; Luke 10:18). Evil is only apparently triumphant, for Jesus says that Satan has no power over him; having emptied himself of greed, ambition, hatred, anger, the desire for personal revenge, and the false selves which haunt us, he has become I AM. Events prove this to be true. Jesus' terrible suffering in body and mind does not weaken his resolve or his commitment. He remains steadfast.

The final words in chapter 14, bidding them all to get up and go outside, have led many scholars to suppose that the further discourse in chapters 15, 16 and 17, must have taken place on the walk to the Garden of Gethsemane. The translator Moffat's drastic solution was to insert chapters 15 and 16 before 14:13a! Certainly it does appear as some modern scholars believe, that chapter 16 is virtually the same discourse as we have studied already but in a slightly different form.

3.   John 15

a).   JESUS AS THE VINE, 15:1-10

The image of the vine holds an important place in Hebrew religious thought. The prophet Jeremiah (2:21) likens Israel to a 'choice red vine of pure strain' which has now become an 'wild vine' because of the people's apostasy, while Isaiah (5:1-7) gives us a vivid picture of an unfruitful Israel. God had planted Judah and lavished care upon the nation but when he looked for justice and righteousness there, he found only bloodshed and cries of distress. Isaiah's passage is a prophetic cry of judgement upon a nation unfaithful to its destiny. The writer of a Psalm (80:8-16) from the Babylonian exile, when both the southern and the northern kingdoms had been devastated by conquest, prays that God will restore and tend the vine of Israel (as happened, under the leadership of Nehemiah and Ezekiel). In the Synoptics, Jesus himself uses the vineyard image. The parable of the wicked tenants illustrates the corruption of the religious leadership and their failure to care for God's people (Mark 12:1-12). This particular condemnation with its implicit threat to their status, roused the temple authorities to such fury that they tried unsuccessfully to arrest Jesus (Mark 12:12). The Fourth Gospel takes the symbol of the vine a step further. What was once an image of the whole nation, Jesus now claims as his own in the seventh I AM statement. He is the fulfilment of Israel's purpose (Exodus 19:6) and the true servant of the Lord in his vicarious suffering (Isaiah 53), but he is more than that. He is the source of energy, the lifeblood of the new Israel. The new community he is founding is different, however, from the old Israel with its limitations of race, nation and culture. Although Jesus has his roots in Jewish tradition and history, hence his use of specific imagery, his message is universal. He calls those who follow him to be 'the light of the world' (Matthew 5:14). (For further discussion see the I AM statements. p.118).

The theme of this whole passage is summed up by the word 'dwell' (REB, New English Bible) 'abide' (Revised Standard Version) which occurs at least eight times. The presence of the indwelling Christ was a reality to the writer of the gospel and for him, all power and energy came from this realisation. Jesus repeats the tremendous promise that all requests will be fulfilled (15:7) but the condition of this fulfilment is clear: it depends upon consciousness of the indwelling Christ and his words. That is to say, fulfilment follows when all petitions accord with Christ's teaching, his character and his purpose, which is to reveal that the divine is love. The disciple is bidden to dwell in Jesus' love as he himself dwells in the Father's love.

b)   Loyalty to Jesus means attaining heavenly joy, 15:11-17

Companionship with Jesus brings joy as well as peace (14:27). This cannot mean a superficial experience but one that reflects the state of the soul regardless of external circumstances. We know that Jesus went through great conflict and anguish not only in the Garden of Gethsemane, but before and during his ministry (Luke 4:1-13). Other great ones who have achieved a mystical union with the divine, confirm the joy and peace this brings. If, as ancient mythical wisdom teaches, humanity is made in the image of God (Genesis 1:27), to be united with the source of being must bring peace and joy.

Jesus commands his friends to love each other as he has loved them, adding that the greatest love is shown by willingness to give one's own life for a friend. I see this as John's version of Jesus' saying (Mark 8:34f) that anyone wanting to be his disciple must 'deny himself and take up his cross'. The desire to save one's own life, by implication at the cost of others, would be abortive whereas those willing to die for Jesus would find true fulfilment (ie. life). The Fourth Evangelist makes a more positive affirmation. Jesus' own death was both terrible reality and symbolism. In the new Israel, love must overflow, both in terms of self-knowledge (ie. love of one's self) and in love of one's neighbour; as the parable of the Good Samaritan illustrates, this means anyone we meet who is in direct need.

Jesus' statement that his disciples are his friends (15:14), if they are faithful to his teaching, can be read as conditional friendship, a peer group offering companionship if its members conform. But this reading, I believe, is to misunderstand John's Jesus. He is offering a friendship based on the premise that a disciple knows what she/he is undertaking. The offer of friendship as opposed to the role of servant is important because it highlights the change in the relationship which the growth of love can bring. It is the contrast between these states which John is highlighting rather than any offer of conditional friendship. Jesus has shared with his friends what he has understood of the Father's nature and wishes, but they have to be willing to respond to the overtures of love. In the parable of the Prodigal Son it is the younger son's desire to return to the Father that is the turning point of the story. The Father had never ceased to love his sons and in the end the call of this love overcame the reluctance of the younger son, if not the pride of the elder one.

The phrase 'You did not choose me. I chose you'. (15:16) may strike a very discordant note with us; it smacks of a harsh exclusiveness which has at one time or another featured in both Catholic and Protestant churches. It brings us up against unanswerable dilemmas. How do we resolve the terrible problem of innocent suffering? Why is wealth distributed so unevenly? Does not this kind of statement breed a racial and/or religious superiority that is obnoxious to the concept of God as Love? There is no answer to this kind of question other than as a challenge to change what we can while we can. Perhaps our ability to choose depends on our response to life as we meet it; we may have no choice about the circumstances of our birth and our genetic heredity, but within these limitations we can still choose either to make the most of what life offers or to reject our opportunities. We can accept that some are more greatly gifted and well endowed than others, recognising that much more is expected from them (cf. the parable of the Talents, Matthew 25:14-30; Luke 19:12-27). Faced with the unanswerable, we may recall the prayer of St. Francis asking that we may be able to change what we can, to accept what we cannot change and to have the wisdom to know the difference.

The notion of 'election' by Jesus is something I find very unpalatable but at least we can bear in mind that the purpose of this 'choosing' is for service (cf 1 Corinthians 15:58). To 'bear fruit' means to become the vehicles of light, love and truth and to fulfil our human potential as did Jesus. In biblical, terms this is the challenge of becoming truly daughters and sons of God, even as Jesus was truly the Son of God.

c)   THE HATRED OF THE WORLD, 15:18-27

These are difficult verses because we do not necessarily share the New Testament view of the 'world', i.e of agnostic or atheistic human society. I would transpose these ideas into today's context by saying that the greed, avarice, complete selfishness and exploitation that we find in our particular culture leads to a society that organises itself on a different value basis from that of justice, peace, compassion and the integrity of all creation. It is true that 'the world loves its own' in the sense that those who fight for these latter values run into vested interests and even persecution because they threaten to disturb the established order which gives wealth to the few at the expense of the many.

Jesus then reiterates the truth that his coming has highlighted sin (15:22). In Luke's gospel the old priest Simeon prophesies that Jesus' mission is not simply for the Jews, saying that the hearts (i.e. the motivation) of many will be revealed by whether they accept or reject him (2:34,35). We may define sin as that which separates us from the source of our being, since in the Old Testament sin meant breaking God's law and in the New Testament Jesus summarises the whole law in terms of love (Mark 12:29-31). Jesus in his revelation that Ultimate Reality is Love/Compassion, has deepened the choice. To accept or reject Jesus' truth as opposed to Jesus himself is to accept or reject the source of all true life, by whatever name it is known. Paul was to teach that the law's purpose was to act as a tutor to humanity until they came of age through faith in Christ (Galatians 3:24). It is through Jesus the Christ that true adulthood and liberation is possible (8:32).

It seems rather harsh of Jesus to comment on 'their' law when he is himself a Jew (15: 25 cf. Psalm 69:4) but we can take this remark in two ways. Either the gospel writer has separated the Master from his background, because Jesus himself has founded a new Israel whose one fundamental law is based on Love, or (as we shall see in chapter 16) at the time of writing the Johannine community is suffering under severe Jewish persecution and therefore feels distinctly separate. From the Evangelist's point of view, the Jewish authorities should have recognised who Jesus was. Failure to do so meant failure to understand God.

Jesus further appeals to the Spirit of Truth (15:26,27) who will come from God and who will validate Jesus, as will the witness of his disciples (cf. Acts 1:22f, 5:32).

4. John 16

a) JUDGEMENT BY THE SPIRIT, 16:1-15

The significance of these verses is their immediate relevance for the author and his original readers as they encounter hostile reactions from the 'world'. Jesus assures his disciples that his death will not leave them desolate and leaderless against intense persecution, especially from the synagogue authorities. They will receive the indwelling Counsellor/Advocate, but only when Jesus has returned to the Father. The Counsellor will assuage their grief and will assess the world. According to John this threefold task of showing where wrong, right and judgement lie (vs.8) is part of the illumination which the Spirit of Truth will bring (15:13) as a continuing work down the ages (15:13,14). Jesus talks confidently about evil being exposed for what it is and thus being condemned. It is true that in so far as Christians have been faithful to the message and teaching of Jesus, they have brought enlightenment to humanity. Great spiritual leaders too numerous to list have often been dissidents against orthodoxy and have enlarged our vision and enriched our lives.

We know the Spirit was present before Jesus arrived in history but humanity's capacity for understanding spiritual truth has always been dependent on and limited by recurring revelations of the divine nature. I believe humanity has not yet worked out the significance of Jesus and his knowledge of God. Of course Jesus' life was incomplete because he was simply a mortal man living at a particular time in a specific culture. There is a whole range of human experience - including that of being a woman - which of necessity lies outside his comprehension. I do not share the view of some Quakers that we are living in a post-Christian age. Rather I am dedicated to trying to understand Jesus' revelation in terms applicable to our own time. For me, the principle of what he taught is as relevant now as then, so I can believe that what the Spirit reveals comes intrinsically from Jesus the Christ (15:15) although its application may be totally different from what John would have thought two thousand years ago.

We have noted previously the Evangelist's horror that his own people reject Jesus instead of being the first to acclaim him. The early Christian community may encounter hostility but their joy, peace and knowledge of the indwelling Christ has enabled them to surmount persecution. It is highly likely that Jesus would warn his followers of persecution to come and it is interesting that either Jesus or the Evangelist has the wisdom to recognise that some religious persecutors genuinely believe they are doing what is right; so indeed did Paul before he experienced the risen Jesus (Acts 26:9). Yet if we really absorb Jesus' message, persecution of another must be totally abhorrent. An arrogant and fundamentalist approach is contrary to the essence of Jesus which recognises people are at different stages of their spiritual journey. If Love is to flourish it always needs some mutuality however unequal the relationship may be in terms of giving. God/Love asks for a willing response from humanity so that we may grow to maturity, which is why the use of force (or persecution) to impose a certain course of action is completely alien to the way of Jesus/Love. Even prayer, when used in a manipulative way, can be mistaken. We cannot pray that God will change minds but only that others will be illumined by the Spirit of truth and love.

(Glory, as noted before at 13:31f, I have interpreted as showing the glory of, or showing the true nature of the divine, in the sense of meriting praise and honour.)

b) JESUS' FINAL WORDS TO HIS DISCIPLES, 16:16-33

Some of those present are puzzled by Jesus' continuing references to his leaving them, going to his Father and then returning. They discuss his twice reiterated phrase 'a little while' amongst themselves. Knowing their worry and puzzlement, Jesus explains more clearly that they will experience deep sorrow at his departure (through his arrest and crucifixion) while his opponents will rejoice at having settled for ever this troublesome fellow. However, the transformation in their feelings will be as great as the contrast between a mother's labour pains and her joy at the birth of her child (cf. Isaiah 66:7-9,14 which refers to the coming of the Messianic community). 'A little while' refers to the time between that Thursday night and resurrection Sunday; the transforming joy is amply illustrated in the story of Mary Magdalene (20:18) and the other disciples.

Jesus again promises (15:16) that what they ask the Father in his name, will be granted them (15:23,24). This is reminiscent of the Synoptic advice (Matthew 7:7; Luke 11:9) to ask, seek and knock, because the response will always come. The synoptic version is clearer because it refers more specifically to the kingdom of God. The qualifying phrase is, of course, 'in my name' (14:13f; 15:16). Fullness of joy is once more seen as the result of their relationship with him and the Father.

The Evangelist now claims that at last Jesus resorts to plain speech instead of images (16:25), saying that he will soon be able to talk directly to them about the Father. Presumably the writer means that after the resurrection his disciples will be able to ask the Father direct, without intermediary, because communion between them and the Father will be established. The Father loves them because they love him and believe that he has come from God. Jesus now states explicitly that (16:28) he has come from the Father into the world and is about to leave the world and return to the Father. Now convinced that he knows everything, the disciples respond with added faith; further questions are unnecessary because they think they are sure that he is from God (16:30).

However, events prove otherwise. Jesus knows that they will all forsake him at the crucial test but he will not be alone because he is certain that the Father is with him. He has told them all of this only so that they will eventually find peace. Their future 'in the world' is uncertain for they will meet enmity but they must have courage, for the last word is his. He has overcome the world (16:33).

Despite my respect for the reality of the writer's experience, I have reservations about these last passages. I am not convinced that Jesus actually spoke in this way at his last meal with his friends. The imagery is characteristic of John's way of presenting Jesus' teaching. All the great I AM statements for example relate to the nature of Jesus' revelation of the divine within. Whereas in the Synoptics, by contrast, we get a picture of Jesus' enigmatic sayings and paradoxical style, in this gospel it is the Spirit of Truth who is reputed to clarify issues for the disciples (16:13). Even in this passage Jesus is still not speaking as plainly as he is made out to do, for his arrest, death and their desertion of him have yet to be lived out.

I do not believe that Jesus limited God's love for the disciples by qualifying it according to the love and faith they have for him (16:27). In the parable of the Labourers in the Vineyard (Matthew 20:1-16) Jesus makes it abundantly clear that God's love for us is not nicely portioned out according to merit or what we think we merit. The Father's love is universal because it is Love itself.

As we shall see (p.138), John claims that Jesus did not feel deserted by God on the Cross but was in complete control from beginning to end while the Synoptics report his cry of desolation (Mark 15:34); even if he is quoting the opening Psalm 22, which ends on a note of triumph, this moment of anguish speaks of Jesus' real humanity. That he went through utter desolation and emerged into final renewal of confidence in God is the more convincing and heartening for us all.

It is clear from the Synoptic record that Jesus did predict not only Simon Peter's betrayal but that the others would also run away. Jesus knew them well enough to realise that their expectations of the Messiah did not compare with his own. They would be so heartbroken, so convinced that things had gone terribly wrong, that there would seem nothing left for them to do but flee for their own safety. John actually hints at the Synoptic record by using the word 'scattered' from Zechariah (13:7, cf. Mark 14:27). To be fair to the Fourth Gospel's presentation, the writer has utter confidence that Jesus the Christ has overcome the powers of evil and opened up for humanity a new relationship with God.

I believe that Jesus did personally overcome the evil within himself, which the gospel personifies as an actual evil being, Satan. Although I do recognise evil as a spiritual force, I think it is too easy an option to blame all evil onto a personified being rather than acknowledging the ambiguity within the human personality. Jesus overcame in himself the desire to retaliate. He kept faith with what he believed God was asking him to do. He was empowered to do so by his own relationship with the divine.

As for overcoming the world, Paul also talks in Colossians (2:15) about cosmic powers and authorities which Jesus has made captive. I see such language as the cosmology of the first century Jew. We are not bound to share such a view. Today we are aware of the terror and majesty of the universe, in which our particular sun is a mere speck of light amidst millions of other stars. This change of outlook is something we have to acknowledge and come to terms with. In what sense has Jesus 'conquered' the world (16:33)? Did he actually make this claim, or was it the Evangelist's assessment of him? In any case I see the meaning of these words as expressing Jesus' own personal victory over inner evil; this is what makes him a pacemaker for us. Further, his power and energy can be translated into our own if we have the courage to claim them through the indwelling Spirit.

5. Jesus' prayer, 17:1-26

Only twice before in this gospel is Jesus recorded as praying. The purpose of his prayer at the Raising of Lazarus (11:41-42) is to give God the glory for the miracle which is about to take place; he next prays when deeply troubled in spirit at the end of his public ministry (12:27-28). On this latter occasion he repeats the first line of the Garden of Gethsemane prayer (Mark 14:34) but instead of pleading to be saved from the Cross, he ends 'Father, glorify thy name', an idea not dissimilar from the Synoptic record that Jesus accepted his Father's will for him (Mark 14:35).

The reader may ask two questions. Did Jesus actually offer this prayer at this time? If not, was it composed by the Evangelist or some later editor? Those who accept that Jesus did speak these words point out that it fits with his foresight that his friends will desert him but that the Father will be with him. In fact the theme of the first eight verses is the relationship of complete union between Father and Son. Some commentators call it 'The High Priestly prayer', others simply 'the priestly prayer', as it is certainly concerned with intercession.

Personally I believe that this prayer is the author's reflection on the purpose of Jesus, his relationship with the Father and with his disciples and also their relationship with each other and with the Father through him. It deals with both present and future discipleship. From what we know of the literary conventions of the period, it could be an acceptable literary device for the author to compose not only the prayer but also part of the discourses, especially the last one which we have been considering in this chapter.

It has also been suggested (cf. John Marsh, Pelican Commentary) that this prayer incorporates some of the themes of the Lord's Prayer (Matthew 6:9-13) which Jesus gave his disciples as an example of how to pray. In many ways John 17 does seem to be a meditation on Matthew 6:9-13. For example the term which Jesus uses for God 'Father' (in Aramaic 'Abba') occurs six times (17:1, 5, 11, 21, 24, 25); the 'hallowing' of God's name in the sense of making God's name known and the power of that name occurs four times (17:6, 11, 12, 26). The phrase in Matthew concerning the coming of the kingdom and the fulfilment of God's will on earth, which I interpret as the reign of God/Love in people's hearts, minds and life, could be seen perhaps in Johannine terms as 'glorifying the son' with all that that implies (cf. 7:39). It occurs four times (17:1, 5, 11, 23). Daily bread in Matthew's gospel means meeting our daily needs on every level of existence, including the need to forgive others and be forgiven; this could be seen in John's gospel as Jesus himself being the bread of eternal life (6:35 and 17:2). The idea explicit in the Lord's prayer, that life itself tests us if we are willing to experience it to the full, yet we remain held secure by the very power of God/Love itself (Matthew 6:13), is implicit in various ways in this prayer too (17:12, 15).

I have been impressed by the Fourth Gospel's capacity to illuminate the Synoptics especially on the matter of the Last Supper, but I find the wording of this prayer particularly difficult in many places, whereas I find the Lord's Prayer inspired both in its depth and comprehensiveness. Its brevity and clarity convince me that it must have originated from Jesus himself.

We know from the Synoptics that Jesus was a man of prayer. Mark tells us that at the start of his ministry, Jesus got up early to have time alone to pray (Mark 1:35-39). The strange story of the Transfiguration (Mark 9:2-13) describes Jesus' face illumined by the power of his prayer (Mark 9:2-13). He told his disciples that they had not prayed enough when they failed to heal the epileptic boy (Mark 9:14-29). Mark further gives us three poetic and provocative sayings on prayer (11:22-25), saying that its effectiveness depends upon our ability to forgive. He also includes, of course, the unforgettable prayers of Jesus in Gethsemane.

Matthew, in the Sermon on the Mount, has a specific passage on the heart of Jesus' teaching about prayer (6:1-18). Prayer is private interior conversation with God. It is not a repetitive series of petitions but the expression of a genuine relationship. Jesus is reported as giving the disciples a pattern of prayer (Matthew 6:9-15) as a means by which they could become more aware. Prayer for Jesus is an attitude of mind, a way of looking at life. He also talks about corporate prayer which can be doubly effective (Matthew 18:20) if its spirit is such that it makes his presence a real possibility.

Luke's gospel lays particular stress on both the need and the power of prayer. He tells us of at least three occasions when Jesus prayed (5:16; 6:12; 9:18) besides giving us three parables about prayer: the Importunate Friend (11:5-13) contains the lesson that we must trust God for all our needs; the Importunate Widow (18:1-8), that we must never give up; the Pharisee and the Publican (18:9-14), speaks of the effectiveness of prayer being dependent on self-knowledge and admission of our needs.

In Exodus and Numbers, Moses is recorded as praying a great deal to God especially to avert the Lord's anger upon his sinful people. He is even represented as being able to make God change his mind (Exodus 32:11-14) for the sake of his (God's) reputation. Such changeability cannot truly be one of God's characteristics! What this story must therefore mean is that as Moses prayed, he began to glimpse something more of the nature of the being who had called him and so his own thought developed. Jesus' emphasis on prayer being intimate interior conversation (Matthew 6:6) brings out the same point. Through such dialogue we learn more about ourselves and our own motivation and therefore more about Love itself.

Both in the Jewish tradition of Jesus' day and in Christian orthodoxy, the priestly intercessory role is emphasised as the priest prays aloud, interceding on behalf of his congregation. As Quakers we stress the priestly role of all believers, even if members of the Society may have very varied, somewhat confused and hesitant ideas about the interpretation of this part of our vocation. In the past Quakers prayed aloud a great deal in their Meeting for Worship. Now they do not. We need to ask ourselves in what sense if at all, has spoken ministry superseded prayer and in what sense is the worshipful silence a corporate expression of unspoken prayer?

We will now look at the main points in this chapter regarding it in the nature of a conclusion to the Last Discourse.

a)   THE SON'S RELATIONSHIP WITH THE FATHER, 17:1-8

The Evangelist states clearly his belief that Jesus as Son of God is sovereign over all humanity and as such brings eternal life to those 'men' to whom he has been given. (Note: no mention of women here although they have been singularly important in the gospel itself.) Eternal life is defined as a knowledge of God through the revelation which has come through Jesus. It therefore consists of acknowledging the Sonship of Jesus himself. Jesus has glorified God on earth through completing the task he has been given to do. He asks now to receive again the glory that he had with the Father before the world began.

b)   PRAYER FOR THE DISCIPLES, 17:9-19

This section is quite exclusive. Jesus is not attempting to pray for the world but for the chosen few who belong not only to the Son but to the Father also; through them Jesus' glory will shine. He is concerned for them now that he will no longer be with them and prays that their sense of union with each other may reflect the unity he has with the Father. While on earth he can protect his friends by the power of God's name and thus keep them all safe, bar the one who was destined to be lost. He speaks these words now that he is still with them so that they may experience his joy. He knows that they are 'strangers' to the world even as he is and are hated because of this, but he does not ask for them to be taken out of the world, since they have work to do there; he simply asks that they should be protected from 'the evil one'. They are to be consecrated, i.e 'set apart' or equipped for service, by the truth. As Jesus himself has been sent into the world by God, so now he also sends forth his disciples. As he now consecrates himself by the truth, so they also are consecrated (cf. 'I am the truth', 14:6).

c)   PRAYER FOR UNITY OF ALL WHO BELIEVE, 17:20-26:

The Evangelist looks into the future and indeed to all those in his own community, who believe in Jesus Christ though they have not necessarily known Jesus of Nazareth. He attributes to Jesus a prayer for unity for all those who will come to believe in him. The emphasis is again on the unity between Father and Son and that through the unity of those who believe in him, the world will realise not only that Jesus is from God but that the Father loves his disciples as he has loved the Son. The indwelling of Son/Father/Spirit of truth is the key to the fellowship of love which must abound in all who follow Jesus.

d)   DIFFICULTIES

I am not convinced that Jesus was concerned with his own glory in the accepted sense of the word, but I do appreciate that to the struggling, persecuted, small Christian communities, this was a matter of supreme importance. They accepted Jesus not only as their Lord and Master, Messiah or Christ, but as a bringer of eternal life, the saviour sent by God to his struggling people. They came to worship the Christ and certainly experienced the indwelling of his presence amongst them. He was the source both of their joy and also their power. The resurrection experience which came to Jesus' immediate friends (both men and women) convinced them (according to early preaching) that Jesus had returned to God and was 'seated at God's right hand'. The glorification of Jesus was therefore essential to their faith.

The second difficulty is the whole concept of the chosen few. That the select happened to be exclusively male is an irritation that perhaps I can excuse as a cultural limitation! I know that the degree of choice open to human beings is a question for debate but given that Love is the Creator of the whole situation, the very nature of Love as I understand it demands a willing response. We must therefore be able to choose to respond.

Jesus, for me, is realised human potential. He is quite unique and special and his power to awaken the human spirit is not diminished by two thousand years of human error. By contrast, the theory of the select few being God's chosen instruments can be very damaging to humanity as a whole. The Old Testament is clear that God's choice of Israel to be his special people called them to a vocation of service. They were an instrument through which the divine could work out 'salvation' for the whole human race. This is also the message of Jesus. He was a shining vehicle for God's spirit, as others both before and after him have been to a greater or lesser degree.

The exclusive claims of Christianity have not served the purposes of Love. They need to be the examined in the light of the knowledge we now have of other great faiths and of Love itself working in the human spirit. The emphasis should always be on Love manifested in a myriad ways and the unity which humanity can achieve with the source of its being.

The third problem is the designation of Judas Iscariot as 'lost', or 'wasted' to fulfil the scriptures (17:12). I do not believe that Jesus looked at Judas in this way. He took a risk with him, as God takes a risk with all of us as a species! With some the risk pays off, but with others it does not. The sufferers are those who fail, but God, being Love, suffers with them. We know how we too can suffer when we love someone who deliberately self-destructs. Yet if we can fail and acknowledge our failure, we grow in self-knowledge and can accept grace upon grace.

It is ironic that the writer should consider unity amongst believers to be a major reason for the world believing in the significance of Jesus. Christian unity has never been achieved, not even in New Testament times. However true it is that disunity spreads disbelief, unity cannot be enforced and the various attempts to impose it have led to major disaster for the Christian cause. Unity can only come through change, tolerance and love, when we learn to accept the integrity of each individual's spiritual search.

I am challenged by the chapter's emphasis on joy and by the view that in some circumstances we should be able to see death as the fulfilment of a person's life, not its negation. According to John, Jesus faced death with calmness, complete control and a sense of triumph. The Synoptics do not entirely agree but they do witness that he achieved this serenity in the end. Chapter 17 is portrayed as Jesus' own interior conversation with the Father. Perhaps it is based on some prayer of Jesus during these last hours together.

CHAPTER FIVE – THE SEVEN "I AM" STATEMENTS

	Chapter	Page
The Bread of Life	6:35-40	111
Discussion on the significance of this statement for later Christians		114
Comment	6:59-71	117
2. The Light of the World	8:12-20	118
Comment		119
3. The Door	10:9,10	120
Comment	10:1-18	121
4. The Good Shepherd,	10:11-16	122
5. The Resurrection and the Life	11:25	124
6. The Way, the Truth and the Life	14:6	125
7. The Vine	15:1-10	126

CHAPTER 5:

The Seven "I AM" Statements

This chapter recapitulates the text so far through comment on these seven majestic statements which have all appeared in John chapters 6-15. For orthodox Christians they speak of the divine Christ in all his power as the name for God in the Old Testament is 'I AM'. I have separated them out because I believe they speak to us not only about the uniqueness of Jesus but also in certain cases, they speak about human potential, when the seed of God within is allowed to develop and grow.

1.   "*I am the bread of life*: he who comes to me shall not hunger, and he who believes in me shall never thirst" (6:35).

Background: The scene has been set by the fourth sign, feeding the multitude in the wilderness and the controversy which awaits Jesus at Capernaum (6:1-34, see p.32). The crowd, many of whom have been fed by Jesus, now want a further sign from him that he is the Messiah. In 6:35 the conversation suddenly takes on a different tone, almost as if the Evangelist is writing for a wider audience. Jesus states categorically that he himself is the bread of life. The person who comes to him and believes in him (for in John the words 'coming' and 'believing' stand for discipleship) will not hunger or thirst again (cf. words to the Samaritan woman, 4:14). As the essential part of a human being is spirit, the real food is spiritual sustenance.

This is the first of the great 'I AM' statements in John's gospel. Did the historic Jesus really talk in these terms? He does not appear to have done so in the Synoptics. We can only speculate but, whether we are dealing with Jesus' own words or John's mature reflection on the significance of his Lord and Master, our job is to attempt an interpretation of meaning.

When Moses is called by God and told of his extraordinary and unenviable commission (Exodus 3:1 - 4:17), he raises various objectons. These can be summarised as 'Who am I?' and 'Who are YOU?' or at least 'What is your name?' which for the ancients had the same significance. The answers God gives are simply that Moses is 'I will be with you' and the name of the divine being who has called him, is 'I am that I am' or 'I cause to be what I cause to be', or 'I will be what I will be'. The name of God is thus explained in terms of the Hebrew verb 'to be'. For the Israelite, however, the name for God was too sacred to be uttered, so in the text the title 'Lord' was substituted for the divine name.

If, therefore, Jesus did express himself as John represents, his use of I AM was bound to cause great offence; to say 'I AM' in a definitive way would appear to be arrogant and blasphemous. But just as Moses' authority and power came from the fact that he was to be truly 'God with him', the same applies to Jesus. He repeatedly says that by himself he is nothing, being only there to do the Father's will. This is the very opposite of Isaiah (47:8-10) where 'I am, and there is none other' represents Babylon, whose fate is destruction. The unpleasant death suffered by King Herod Agrippa in Acts (12:21-23) is ascribed to his blasphemous acceptance of divine honours from the people of Tyre and Sidon. In the ancient literature of all great religions it is recognised that the sin of hubris or pride brings nemesis or disaster.

But John saw Jesus as emptied of self - in Jungian terms, the ego or the many false selves which present themselves in the personality. Only so could he be filled with the Eternal Spirit of Love. He was completely centred in God and from that source and no other, could he say 'I AM'. The gospel's claim that he and the Father are one is another way of expressing this truth. Jesus wishes his disciples to enter into the same kind of union with him (17:20-23).

All the hard and paradoxical sayings in Mark's gospel (8:34-37) about renouncing self and being prepared to 'take up a cross' to follow Jesus point in the same direction. These are sayings about wanting to save one's life and therefore losing it; of losing one's life for Jesus' sake and thereby saving it; of the futility of gaining the whole world at the cost of losing one's self (life). The individual who constantly grabs at what brings immediate selfish satisfaction regardless of others' welfare, in the end becomes diminished as a person. For we receive by giving and we find ourselves by losing ourselves in some loving relationship or creative commitment. Jesus was most truly a whole and perfected human being because he was able to overcome the egocentric and ignoble promptings of his lesser self. This is the way of completion for humanity even though it is a hard and seemingly almost impossible path.

For John, faith in Jesus the Christ is the total fulfilment of the life of the Spirit, but the Galileans, despite their experience of the sign in the wilderness do not believe (vs.36). Their motives are so mixed that they cloud recognition of the divine indwelling Spirit within Jesus.

The problem of unbelief concerns the Evangelist greatly. It is a mystery which he cannot resolve. For him the only thing to do is to trust in the divine will. He presents belief or unbelief as being under God's control even though each person is given their own choice in the matter. Those who do believe, do so because the Father has touched, taught or called them - it is difficult to find adequate words for this 'selection' by God. Jesus will cherish all who are so 'given' to him and will bring them to eternal life. The words 'the last day' (6:39) probably refer to the final consummation - the end of all things. They recur in 6:54.

I find the hint of predetermination offensive but I believe that behind the words we can discover the truth of how things are in human experience; faith is not something which can be determined by a person's will. Much depends on temperament, background and education in its widest sense. Each individual has to work with integrity to understand and find their own level of being and then to be prepared to grow and change accordingly. If there is judgement, it must be an assessment of this effort of self-knowledge and growth, starting from where a person is.

For me the Evangelist is mistaken in his exclusive claim about Jesus, but again, if we look at a deeper level I believe we can arrive at another profound truth. Jesus declares (6:38) that he has come from God solely to do God's will and that God is Love. As we can see that Jesus is filled with the Eternal Spirit of love, therefore the route to our spiritual source is via the paths of love which Jesus personified, but, of course, not literally through his name alone. For example the Sufis, the mystical sect of Islam, recognise a universal law, which our spiritual nature calls Love, but for them the way to eternal life lies through Islam, not Christianity. The person, message and significance of Jesus is for the whole world but it is his inner and spiritual reality which is important, however variously this may be interpreted.

What the bread of life costs the giver, is explored in 6:41-58.. A critic of this gospel might be excused for pointing out how repetitive are John's various statements, but on each occasion he adds something new to the argument. Contemporary readers (or hearers) familiar with the way Hebrew poetry used the rhythm of parallel statements rather than rhyming sounds, would readily accept the recapitulation of significant points, appreciating the further elucidation of meaning by additional phrases.

The change of tone mentioned above, is underlined by the fact that the Galilean crowd now becomes 'the Jews' (6:41); by their disbelief they have become the opposition. Knowing his human origins, they object strongly to Jesus' claim that he has come from God. He is Jesus, the son of Joseph; they know both his father and his mother. Jesus stops the argument because he sees it will lead nowhere. He quotes the vision of the prophets (Isaiah 54:13, Jeremiah 31:34) that the time will come when God will teach everyone himself. Even now those who already listen to the Father and are receptive to the Spirit's promptings in their hearts, will recognise that he has come from the Father and will believe.

By contrast to the manna given to the Israelites long ago, the bread now offered contains the seeds of eternal life. Jesus goes on to say that this bread is his own flesh, his self offering for the life of the world, even if it means his death. Not surprisingly, his audience react very negatively. Far from helping them at all, he reiterates the image even more strongly; the Son of Man's flesh and blood must be eaten and drunk for eternal life. His words about blood would be highly objectionable to a Jewish audience, only allowed to eat animal flesh from which the blood had been drained. As blood contained the life principle, it belonged to God and was untouchable (Genesis 9:4). In sacrificial language however the phrase 'flesh and blood' was understood to mean a giving and a taking of life. Jesus' listeners, therefore, could interpret his words as referring to his own self-offering, especially as he concludes with the phrase that those who eat and drink in this sense will dwell in him. As he lives in the Father who sent him, so whosoever eats him will live for ever because of him.

The significance of this statement for later Christians

These precise words of Jesus, as presented by John, caused great problems at the time and indeed have continued to do so down the centuries. One of the most bitter controversies in Christendom has centred on how far and in what way the believer could spiritually eat Jesus' flesh and blood. On the one hand the doctrine of transubstantiation was formulated as early as the ninth century. This held that by a miracle, the bread and wine of the Eucharist celebration, became the actual body and blood of Christ. The doctrine received final official sanction in the thirteenth century and remains part of Roman Catholic teaching. On the other hand, this idea has been denounced by other scholars from its inception and later by many others including Wycliffe and Luther and is not accepted by the Protestant wing of the Christian church.

There are two questions to consider here. Why did John not include the Synoptic tradition of Jesus' words at the Last Supper about the bread and the wine being his body and blood? What is the spiritual significance of this particular symbolic language?

There can be little doubt that at the Last Supper Jesus knew that his arrest and death were imminent. Having accepted that death was the inevitable outcome of the course of action he felt impelled to pursue, he spoke of his voluntary self-offering in terms of the Jewish sacrificial system. We have general evidence not only from Mark (14:22-25), Luke (22:15-20) and Matthew (26:26-29), but also from Paul (1 Corinthians 11:23-25) that this is so, even if there are verbal variations.

We have seen that John omits much which is found in the Synoptic record and have assumed in this book that he does so knowing that his readers are familiar with the oral if not the written Synoptic tradition. He considers strict chronology secondary to his main concern i.e. the theological meaning of events in Jesus' life.

Furthermore John treats the Feeding of the Five Thousand as a sign, in the same category as the Water into Wine at Cana. Although he does show Jesus' compassion for the hungry crowd, he deliberately sets the feeding in the context of subsequent discourses. Its meaning is spiritual; it shows Jesus as giver of life to the world and therefore personally distributing the bread and fish, leaving the disciples to collect the leftovers so that nothing is wasted. As Peter later declares, Jesus speaks the words of eternal life (6:68). Belief in him will give this quality of life to every human being who seeks it.

As discussed before (p.34), we can rationally interpret the Feeding in Mark's gospel, arguing that Jesus' teaching and the disciples' example encouraged the crowd to share what they had with each other and consequently all had enough. John teaches a different lesson. If humanity would absorb the spirit of Jesus' teaching about the significance of each individual and would draw energy from the deep springs of eternal love within, human beings would reorganise available resources and there would be no desperate hunger, poverty and deprivation in the world.

In the Genesis parable of creation, men and women are made in the image of God, (1:26) but the biblical record then shows how disobedience to the will of God distorts this original likeness with its inherent spiritual potentiality. I interpret the Fourth Evangelist's vision to mean that if the seed of God, the Spirit within each person, is given the chance to develop and grow through assimilating Jesus the Christ, a spiritually mature and developed humanity will emerge. This vision is shared by other New Testament writers (cf. Ephesians 4:13).

The Jewish Passover festival probably originated as thanksgiving for newborn lambs. Ancient people believed that firstborn of humans, animals and crops belonged to God (Exodus 13:1,2) so in Jesus' day the firstborn male child was customarily offered to God and then bought back ('redeemed') by a substitute offering in his place (cf Luke 2:22-24). Since the Passover festival coincided with the miraculous escape from Egypt, (according to Exodus) the festival was also celebrated as a commemoration of that supreme deliverance from bondage. Later on it became obligatory to sacrifice the paschal lambs in the Temple in Jerusalem on the 14th Nisan. The meal was eaten on the following night.

Although John notes that (6:4) it was Passover time, in no way does his language suggest the blessing and distribution of the bread is a ritual foretaste of the Eucharist. Nor is the lamb mentioned in any of the gospels, even though Jesus is traditionally thought of as "the Lamb of God", John Baptist's title for him (1:29). However, the concept of a God of love demanding a sacrificial victim is quite abhorrent to me. Deliverance from bondage surely signifies freeing our inner disposition. In any case it appears that John's Last Supper was not a Passover meal but antedated it by twenty-four hours. The Evangelist is making a different point (cf. ch. 13, p.84) and his omission of Jesus' words may mean that he wishes to emphasise the more universal and less sacramental meaning of Jesus' self-offering and death.

There is a further point to consider. The writer of the First Letter of John, (in all probability the Evangelist himself) deals with the serious heresy which has arisen in his community ie. the belief that Jesus the Christ only seemed to be human (ie. the docetic Christ). John vehemently affirms the absolute humanity of Jesus (1 John 1:1) on the grounds that he personally saw, heard and touched him. In John ch.6, when Jesus identifies the bread with his flesh, he emphasises his humanity. In ancient times, worshippers sometimes sought to assimilate the power of the gods or the totem animal by eating and drinking the flesh and blood of the sacrifice. The Israelites themselves had several rituals associated with peace offerings, penitential offerings and so on, in which various parts of the animal were eaten by offerer, priest and, as a burnt offering, by the divinity. However, in the Last Supper Jesus asked his friends to be bonded with him in his service to others and symbolised his self-giving by the actual bread and wine. This is the precise point which John makes in his account of the last meal they had together.

Having miraculously supplied bread and fish to the Galilean crowd in the wilderness, what Jesus offered them was something quite other than physical nourishment. It was a deeply spiritual concept dependent on their assessment of the person of Jesus himself. Given that the Evangelist was an eyewitness to the Jesus event and a beloved disciple, the reality of this offer was not in doubt. He had surely experienced both the risen Jesus and, through many years, the indwelling spirit of Christ. For a short time he had encountered the human Jesus and had been one of his closest friends. Now he had come to understand that the actual physical presence of his master had somehow been translated into the ever living Christ of faith.

As the above discussion illustrates, I believe John's version of these words helps to put the Christian rite of the Mass, the Eucharist or Holy Communion into a quite different setting, one which is certainly compatible with Quaker beliefs. I am reminded of the fourth beatitude (Matthew 6:6) when Jesus talks about hungering and thirsting for right to prevail. His imagery implies that the passion for justice and harmony, whether social, political or spiritual, is as fundamental to the human spirit as food and drink is to the body. I personally see the essential Jesus as the spiritual bread of life for the believer, although I recognise that many other people would not agree. Wherever we find the nourishment of the Spirit of love, we need to acknowledge our spiritual hunger and thirst. If we also can become a means by which the Spirit of God/Love manifests itself, we too can nourish and support others.

Comment on 6:59-71.

John tells us all this happened in the synagogue at Capernaum. Probably Jesus taught there over a number of days and John strung several discourses together (cf. the Sermon on the Mount). It is not only the Galilean crowd who reject Jesus' words about his body and blood, but also many of his disciples. Jesus is aware of their shocked reaction but instead of helping them, he talks of the Son of Man ascending, presumably to the Father from whom he has come.

It is Luke (Acts 1:9-11) who records that Jesus' actual departure into the heavens ended the resurrection appearances, an event later named the ascension and celebrated as such in the Christian calendar. Today we do not believe God dwells in any special place, but for the disciples it was necessary to know definitely that the resurrected Jesus would no longer be present. They were now to experience the indwelling Christ and the Spirit, so we can say that the Ascension establishes a clear break with what had gone before, even if we cannot identify with the imagery used in Acts.

On the other hand Jesus may have used the word 'ascending' in John's gospel simply to mean going up to Jerusalem; the same Greek verb applies, in which case he was referring to his death. John talks in 7:39 about believers receiving the gift of the Spirit after Jesus' glorification. As is so often the case in his gospel, the meaning is ambivalent, but as the Ascension experience was given only to Jesus' intimate friends, we may assume John was again contemplating evidence of the mystery of unbelief. Marvels do not convince nor are they ever intended to do so. Jesus is suspicious of those who follow him merely because they are impressed by what he can do. They are like the seed in shallow ground (Mark 4:5,16); scorched by the hot sun, it perishes after its first growth, having no depth of root. The parable of the sower may well have been in the Evangelist's mind because, although he does not refer directly to it, he now makes its meaning explicit. Jesus' spoken words are both spirit and life. They contain the truth about God and humanity. The fact that some initial followers fall away can only mean that faith itself is a gift from God. In Mark's gospel (9:24), the father of the epileptic boy glimpsed the truth of this when he cried out to Jesus, 'I believe; help my unbelief!'

Jesus is obviously saddened although not surprised by the desertion of some disciples. When he asks the twelve (mentioned only here and in 20:24) 'Do you also want to leave?' Peter answers for all of them. They are committed to Jesus because they recognise him as 'God's Holy One' and know his words have eternal life-giving power. In Mark (8:29) Peter confesses that Jesus is the Messiah and later he is harshly rebuked by Jesus ('Out of my sight, Satan!' 8:33) for his misunderstanding of the nature of Jesus' messiahship. In John's gospel it is Judas Iscariot who is called 'a devil' (6:71) because, despite his calling by Jesus, he will betray his master.

2. *"I am the light of the world* he who follows me will not walk in darkness, but will have the light of life". (8:12).

Background: This second I AM saying comes in the midst of controversy (see p.62) and marks the second stage in the great debate when Jesus is attending the Feast of Tabernacles in Jerusalem. The questions at issue centre on Jesus' origin and nature, his relation to the Father, and the judgement which is falling on his opponents, the Jews.

The location for the whole discourse was important to the Evangelist. One of the striking symbols in the festival was the lighting of the four brilliant candelabra in the Court of Women, near the Treasury, to remind worshippers of the Pillar of Fire in the wilderness wanderings (Exodus 13:21).

Light is an important biblical symbol in both Old and New Testament. Its power is dominant in the Priestly creation hymn (Genesis 1: 3,15,17). The psalmist in Psalm 27 declares that if the Lord is light and salvation (27:1), there is nothing to fear and later (43:3) implores the Lord to send out his light and truth to be his guide. As God called Israel to be a light to all the nations, (Isaiah 49) it became a Messianic title. Certainly the old priest Simeon identifies Jesus with 'the light' which will bring revelation to the Gentiles and glory to God's people, Israel (Luke 2:32, cf. Isaiah 49:6).

There are several references to light in the Synoptics (cf Mark 4:21,22; Luke 11:33-36) including the image (used in John too) that a man who walks in darkness is without guidance. Hence healing the blind symbolises healing of inner person (cf. the fifth sign, p.36). Of paramount significance for us is the fact that Jesus calls his own disciples "the light of the world" (Matthew 5:14-16) urging them to shine before all humanity so that God may be glorified. The writer to the Ephesians tells his readers: "now you are light in the world; walk as children of light" (RSV, 5:8) and the First Letter of John states categorically that God is Light (1:5).

Comment on text 8:12-20

When Jesus says he is the light of the world, the Pharisees react with hostile incredulity. They again accuse him of invalidating his claim by being his own witness. Deuteronomy 17:6 and Numbers 35:50 ruled that the evidence of at least two or even three witnesses was required to condemn a man to death (see discussion on p.56). Jesus replies that even though he is his own witness, the Father who sent him is his witness too. He knows where he has come from and where he is going. He accuses them of judging by superficial and wrong standards. He does not claim to judge anyone himself but judgement is happening all the time through him because of the One who has sent him. When the Pharisees ask where his father is, Jesus retorts that to know him is to know the Father also. They are ignorant of both. The Synoptics clearly show that the Kingdom of God is an inner spiritual state, not an outward one at all (Luke 17:21), therefore knowledge of God is inward knowledge. His questioners are unaware of their lack of true being and their need for inner transformation. In spite of the bitterness of this controversy, Jesus was not arrested at this time.

In what sense can we accept Jesus as the light of the world? I believe that through Jesus has come great illumination and power. He constantly emphasises the need to understand the inner motivation which drives us. He always appeals to the Inner Authority, to the God within as well as without. He trusts the testimony of spiritual sensitivity not the judgement of outward appearances and criticises the Pharisees for judging by externals. Jesus has no intention to judge but to save (3:16-21). Those who reject the Light come under judgement by that act, not by Jesus' decision.

George Fox writes in his journal; 'Christ, who has enlightened me, gave me His light to believe in,' also stating that Christ has enlightened everyone so that those who believe in him may become 'children of light'. Fox felt his mission was to turn people to the Inward Light. In one of his epistles (1652) he ascribes to the Light the ability to see sin and evil inwardly and credits to it the 'humbleness of mind' which creates the capacity to learn from Christ's teaching. Another letter says that to walk in the Light, to love Christ, brings unity with each other. 'Children of Light' was one name given to those first followers of George Fox. It is the theme of John's gospel that a person who comes to believe in Jesus the Christ, walks in the light and becomes a child of God.

I do identify the Inner Light as another name for the Spirit of God within, which, for me, can mean the indwelling Christ. As discussed elsewhere, I know that the Spirit of God is boundless, regardless of race, religion or tradition, but for me as an individual, Jesus the man so identified himself with the spirit within that he became a totally transparent vehicle of the Light which is God. I also believe that to be children of the light is our human destiny. In Jesus' own words, we are called also to be the light of the world, even as he was.

3. '*I am the door*; anyone who comes into the fold through me will be safe. He will go in and out and find pasture. A thief comes only to steal and kill and destroy; I have come that they may have life, and may have it in all its fullness.'(10:9,10)

Background: Following the healing of the man born blind, John 10 deals with the whole question of leadership and contains the third and fourth 'I AM' statements: Jesus is the door of the sheepfold and also the Good Shepherd. His whole purpose and aim is life-giving and enhancing for all humanity, for his followers come from 'other folds'. His ministry is not simply for his own people, the Jews: he has universal significance.

Jesus first tells a parable which is probably based on a passage in Ezekiel. This charismatic prophet came from a priestly family and was deported to Babylon c.BC 597. Active for about twenty years, he saw the Exile as the direct result of sin but his vision of a restored people of God illuminated his utterances. In Chapter 34 he described the people as helpless, a scattered and suffering flock, thanks to their shepherd's corruption. He foretold that God himself would instal a true shepherd of the house of David as the valid leader of his people.

The ambience of Jesus' story is culturally unfamiliar to us but not to his original hearers or to early readers of the gospel. The sheep of several flocks would be kept together in a fold overnight for safety probably in the enclosed courtyard of a house. The only legitimate entrance door would be opened by an independent doorkeeper who would know the rightful shepherds of the various flocks. Any nefarious person would have to climb over the wall or enter indirectly. In a culture where sheep are the major source of wealth and where adequate pasturage has to be constantly sought, the shepherd has to be with his sheep all the time and directly lead them. He thus establishes a personal relationship with his animals which is all-important. He knows the animals of the flock by name. They are familiar with him and prepared to follow where he leads. A stranger, whose voice and person are unknown, would frighten them into running away. John says that the parable (or 'figure') was simply not understood by the Pharisees.

Comment on 10:1-18:

After speaking generally, Jesus states first, that he is the door of the sheepfold (vs,7,9), then that he is the good shepherd (10:11,14). The solemn intensity of his whole thought is indicated by the twice repeated 'In very truth, I tell you' (10:1 and 7).

The image of a door is timeless. An Eastern shepherd would experience this quite literally by lying down across the opening of the fold to keep the sheep within and a ravening beast without. He would need to be courageous and faithful when danger threatened, putting the safety of the flock before his own, and when the night was over, he would have to take the sheep to fresh pasturage.

Then Jesus draws a contrast between the thief and himself: the former has only his own interest to serve, so he steals, kills and destroys. Examples of the destruction caused by selfish behaviour and corrupt leadership abound in the world about us. Always it is the innocent who suffer and are exploited, from the child killed by an incompetent driver in a stolen car to the thousands of prisoners of conscience throughout the world. By contrast, Jesus says that he comes to bring abundant life to all; he means this in the here and now, as well as in any future existence. The door to the inner life must be recognised and opened: only so can the outer life be enriched and fulfilled. If we are unaware of our spiritual resources we only half exist. The rhythm of 'coming home' and 'going out again' needs to be a constant spiritual as well as a physical element of the truly balanced life.

For John, Jesus is the meeting point for heavenly and earthly, the divine and the human. This is made clear by Jesus' conversation with Nathanael (1:51) when Jesus referred to the descent and ascent of angels on the Son of Man (cf Genesis 28:10-22, see comment p.14) but this meeting place is also located within each one of us. The biblical vision is that human beings are made in the image of God; in other words, there is that in us which can respond or withhold our response to the divine initiative. As Moses was truly You are 'God with you' so Jesus was 'I am the one whom the Father has sent' or 'the one whom Love has sent'. Jesus expresses the relationship between Love and the lover. And Jesus makes clear later in the gospel that this is our destiny and fulfilment also.

The picture of a door remains relevant in the contemporary world for we open the door to reach the relative safety of our homes and open it again when we pass to the outside world. Unless we are totally incapacitated we have to go out for the necessities of life, for work and pleasure. The two faces of the door represent also the inner life and the outer, that which is within ourselves and that which is without in our daily contacts with other people. As Quakers we speak of the Inner Light, that of God within, which can sustain our spirits. The reality of the spiritual experience within illuminates all that we do without. We may resist the exclusiveness of the claim that Jesus is the door but if we take the claim to mean his way of totally loving compassion and truth, the exclusiveness vanishes.

Thinking of the door in these terms, we can see how we also may become the way in which the Spirit of Love and Truth can be manifested in the world. If we have the self-knowledge to be true vehicles of the Spirit we too may become the door. Seeking the divine, creative way will demand searching self-analysis and honesty. To follow the analogy further, we open the door to "thieves and robbers who approach by another way" when we entertain mixed motives for taking responsibility and leadership, when we desire to be always in the right, when we love power for its own sake, when we suffer from self-satisfaction and unreality.

The promise of the door is that once we enter the fold we shall be safe (10:9). This refers to the inner calm and tranquillity which we experience at the still centre of our being. We need to return to that point even in the midst of anxiety, fear, danger and terror. Those who have encountered people of violence and survived, have told of the power of prayer and the sense of being upheld which steadied them and which, in some mysterious way, affected the situation. The absence of fear and aggression is a powerful antidote to violence.

4. "*I am the good shepherd.* The good shepherd lays down his life for his sheep" (10:11).

"*I am the good shepherd*; I know my own and my own know me, as the Father knows me and I know the Father, and I lay down my life for the sheep. And I have other sheep that are not of this fold; I must bring them also, and they will heed my voice" (10:14-16).

Background: Good Shepherd was a title which could be used in Jesus' day of gods, kings, great men and morally upright leaders of every description; 'good' is perhaps understood in the Platonic sense as representing all that is beautiful, just, true and balanced. Myths speak of the divine ruler who dies for the sake of his people - hence the dying, rising saviour god exemplified in the cycle of nature.

In Second Isaiah the faithful servant of the Lord was prepared to give his life for the many. It is clear from the Synoptics that Jesus identified strongly with these servant songs (cf. Mark 10:45) and saw his mission in terms of the Servant of the Lord.

Comment on text, 10:11-16

Jesus, in familiar terms, contrasts the good shepherd as true leader with the hireling. The former is prepared to give his life for his sheep, the latter runs away at the suggestion of danger. (For further discussion of the controversy this arouses, see p.67).

The fourth 'I AM' saying has two implications. The relationship between Jesus and his disciples, is likened to that between Jesus and the Father. It is a reciprocal relationship based on enduring knowledge and love of each other. This is in sharp contrast to the false shepherd who does not know his sheep at all and who cares nothing for them. Of vital significance is Jesus' categorical statement about having other sheep who do not belong to this fold (10:16), but who nevertheless know his voice and must be given his care. John sees Jesus as the Saviour of the whole world, contrasting the inclusiveness of his mission with the exclusive claims of Judaism. It is tragic that the Christian church itself became wrongly exclusive and imperialist in outreach for so much of its history. The key to this impressive statement by Jesus about his 'other sheep' is that they recognise him and respond to what he stands for. As he makes clear in the Lucan parable of the Great Feast (14:15-24), those who are excluded are not left out by the host but remain outside by their own choice. Their self-selection or rejection is apparently a matter of their inner perspective.

Of course many walk the way of compassion and truth without acknowledging any adherence to Jesus. They have responded to the inner light and to the teachings of other great religious leaders and faiths. Between all people truly guided by the Spirit of compassion and truth, there exists a unity which is world saving.

Do we want to be compared with sheep? On the surface it perhaps seems offensive to some as the aim of the spiritual life is to make us truly adult. On the other hand we are a very vulnerable species; humanity on the whole does seem gullible, impressionable, easily led and capable of disaster unless there is a selfless and wise guide. When humanity achieves full maturity, perhaps the sheep metaphor will become obsolete.

I do believe that those who are truly spiritually awakened of whatever race, gender or religion are called to give moral and spiritual leadership in the world. This leadership is a matter of the individual's quality of life not their office, although the two can be combined.

5.   *"I am the resurrection and the life*; he who believes in me, though he die yet shall he live, and whoever lives and believes in me shall never die" (11:25).

Background: The fifth I AM saying is set in the midst of the Lazarus story (cf. p.39). Arriving at Bethany, Jesus discovers that Lazarus has been dead four days. When he tells Martha that her brother will rise again, she replies that she believes this will happen at the final judgement.

Jesus' statement about himself goes far beyond the Pharisaic beliefs, which Martha has expressed. We know from Mark (12:18-27) and Luke's parable (16:19-31) that Jesus himself believed strongly in life after death. In the Marcan account, Jesus is asked a ridiculous question by the Sadducees, who believed a man only lived on in the blood of his descendants. Jesus makes two clear points in return. First, he shows that the Sadducees are ignorant both of the Scriptures and the power of God. Second, he is certain that the conditions of life after death are very different from this one. The physical body is translated into a spiritual body, presumably like that of the angels!

The whole theme of the Fourth Gospel is that belief in Jesus as the Christ will bring the disciple eternal life. Whether or not the actual historical Jesus spoke the resurrection words to Martha it is impossible to assess. Presumably, too, the Evangelist has personally experienced the life-giving power which this brings. He has knowledge of the indwelling Christ.

By his supreme self-offering and his witness to the truth of ultimate reality, Jesus has become the dynamo for resurrection and new, awakened life. What we are now and can hope to become in this mortal existence, will fit us for life beyond death.

The paradoxical statement about dying and living reminds me of the Marcan account of Jesus' six sayings after Peter's confession of faith (8:34-38) which have been discussed before. The theme is loss and gain. It contains a fundamental truth about human experience. Physical death is not the end, but, says Jesus, we can destroy our true selves, our own personal integrity, by the pursuit of false goals and temporary gain.

We cannot say that we are the resurrection and the life but we can say 'I am reborn to a new life through Jesus or the indwelling Christ/Spirit'.

(For further discussion, see the Sixth sign, p.40).

6. *"I am the way, and the truth, and the life*; no one comes to the Father, but by me" (14:6)

Background: The Sixth saying comes in the middle of Jesus' last discourse with his disciples (see p.94). The exclusiveness makes it one of the most difficult and controversial of all the sayings. It has surely been partly responsible for the Christian church's claim to the monopoly of truth and has even been an excuse for persecution of other faiths. Even if it does sum up all that the Evangelist believed about Jesus the Christ, we do not have to accept it as right for us today.

I am not convinced that the historic Jesus ever made such a claim for himself. Its historical authenticity is all the more questionable because this gospel repeatedly represents Jesus as saying that he is only the instrument through whom the Father speaks (14:10, cf. 7:10; 28; 8:29; 43; 54). Admittedly in this intimate final time with his disciples, he does say he is in the Father and the Father is in him (14:11), thus indicating that he speaks with the Father's voice.

The only way in which I can begin to come to terms with this sixth I AM saying is by a radical change of emphasis. In my belief, Jesus is the way to God only in the sense that he has revealed the truth that God is Love. Nevertheless I recognise that other faiths have emphasised the importance of love too.

I can envisage him as the life because he has stripped away all the false selves which make the human personality so complex and he is at one with the vital energy, the source of the universe. If absolute reality is Love, then the only way to that reality of the spirit is the way of love, which Jesus personifies. However, in so far as all the great religious leaders and faiths also teach this, they too are the way, the truth and the life. And when the

Christian church has betrayed essential reality by seeking worldly power, then it is Christian structures and not other faiths, which have become part of the opposition.

It is tempting to paraphrase the saying more acceptably as "I am the true and living way", but to do so would still not mitigate the exclusiveness of the next claim. 'No one comes to the Father but by me' is generally applied solely to the historic Jesus and the Christian church which grew out of his community of disciples, yet his way of love is universal in application and can be practised by any non-Christian, as Gandhi demonstrated.

Jesus has claimed on a previous occasion (8:32, p.63), that his disciples will be liberated by knowing the truth. He has also said, in the intimacy of the last meal together, that they will receive the Spirit of truth after his death (14:17, 15:26; 16:13), when the Spirit will on its own authority guide each of them into truth (cf. p.95).

'Life' in the Fourth gospel means the deep, inner, enriched life of the spirit. We can grow into it and can experience its eternal quality.

7. "*I am the vine, you are the branches*. He who abides in me and I in him, he it is that bears much fruit." (15:5)

Background: Scholars disagree about when this part of the last discourse actually takes takes place (see p.00). William Temple argues that Jesus and his friends are on their way through the Temple Court to the Garden of Gethsemane. He visualises Jesus stopping by Herod's temple and pointing to the decoration of the great golden vine which trailed over the holy of holies, its huge clusters of grapes symbolising the life of Israel entwined about the Sanctuary of God. Thus in claiming to be the vine, Jesus claims Messiahship.

My own view is that the conversation presented by John on this last night together must have happened within the Upper Room. Nevertheless they would all know this decoration on the Temple Porch and the Old Testament image of Israel as a vine which God brought out of Egypt and planted in Palestine. In such soil the vine should have brought forth good fruit but it did not. Isaiah 5:1-7 gives a picture of careful viniculture in a harsh landscape and the bitter disappointment when the vine reverted to its wild state. Prophetic warnings down the centuries record the infidelity of God's people, John Baptist being the last in the line of great prophets who called his people to repent before the coming Day of Judgement.

Jesus' disciples would be very familiar with the life-cycle of the vine and more immediately aware than we are of the significance of this symbolism. When Jesus rescued the marriage feast at Cana by turning water into wine, the Evangelist called this the first (and principal?) sign and claimed that through it Jesus manifested his glory and his disciples believed in him. Here, the Evangelist states clearly that Jesus is the vine, the source of the wine for the Messianic celebration. Although Jesus' disciples thought of themselves as the new Israel or people of God (Mark 10:37), Matthew 19:28, Luke 22:30), Jesus does not say "we are the vine". Instead he uses about himself an image formerly applied to the nation. For the Evangelist, therefore, Jesus alone embodies the true Israel and is founding a new world order, a new and living community.

Perhaps the key to this passage lies in the world "dwell" or "abide". Jesus Christ is the whole vine, not just the stem. The disciples as branches are part of him. His energy, spirit, and vital force pulse through them. Their bonding with him gives them the power to be creative or 'fruitful'. The love which is the heart of the relationship between Father and Son, is also the essence of relationship between Jesus and his friends/disciples. Their relationship is reciprocal and they are mutually dependent. Paul uses a similar image when he talks about the wholeness of the body in 1 Corinthians (12:12-31) and Romans 12.

For me, John has illuminated Mark 14:24,25, in which Jesus describes the shared wine cup as symbolising his blood of the new covenant poured out for many. In reading Mark's account, it is clear that blood is mentioned because for the Jew, blood is quite literally sacred to God as containing the life force of a person or animal. Jesus uses the word 'blood' to symbolise his total self-offering in order to establish a new understanding between humanity and its Creator. Although deeply shocked, his friends would know that the wine represented his complete self-giving.

By focussing on the incident where Jesus washes his disciples' feet (see p.81) and using the powerful image of the vine to illustrate his interconnectedness with those who acknowledge his way of love, the Fourth Evangelist has spiritualised the concept of bread and wine. He has gone back to the root, which is a matter of internal and abiding relationship. Jesus' saying that he is the bread of life occurs after the Feeding of the Five Thousand, in the very controversial setting of the Capernaum synagogue (see p.34). So in no way does John represent these words (spoken at the Last Supper in the Synoptics) as a rite or sacrament. In giving us 'I am the bread of life' (6:35) and 'I am the Vine and you are the branches' (15:5) the Evangelist has concentrated on the image of a relationship.

We need to consider the context of this last I AM statement as 15:1-10 are difficult. The picture of God the gardener busily pruning, cutting away dead branches and burning them, vividly portrays how things are in the reality of life as we know it. It may not appear to be a picture of love, with its unending desire to rescue, renew and restore, but it actually describes the facts. It is like Jesus' cryptic remark (Mark 4:25) that if you don't use, you lose. Life does 'prune' us; we cannot avoid the experience of suffering, grieving, failing, becoming despondent and afraid. But if we are willing, we can learn through all these experiences and grow in the life of the spirit. God draws us by love. On the other hand we can refuse to grow and we can remain barren. To bear fruit, for me, is to become what we have the potential of being. We need to discover in our roots, our spirituality, our essence. From that base, we can accomplish many things.

We must also query the exclusiveness of 'apart from me you can do nothing' and ask about those who do not acknowledge Jesus, who find they have no place in Christianity or who belong to another great faith. I believe there is a great inclusive network of the Spirit of love and truth, even though for me it is personified by Jesus. I may and do identify Jesus as the Vine, but I can well appreciate that others do not and I find it a great sadness when the name of Jesus the Christ is made the cause for bitter feuds, wars and oppression. One of the joys of a Quaker Meeting for Worship is the diversity of beliefs held by the many who attend. Yet in the silence, we can find the Inner Light, a common source which is beyond words. For many as for George Fox, it is the Light of Christ Jesus, but others today would be unwilling to define it in words. Yet the Vine of the Spirit of Truth and Love is a constant reality.

What name we attach to the living Spirit of love and truth which is active throughout the world, is not necessarily significant; its activity and its interconnectedness are all-important. We often underestimate its power because we hear so much of its opposite but community life is only possible because ordinary people everywhere love and cherish others. Jesus makes the tremendous claim: "ask whatever you want and you shall have it", but there is a crucial condition attached. We need to 'dwell' in him first. Verses 9 and 10 tell us that 'dwelling' means a quality of Love like that between Jesus and God, whom he called Father. He was utterly obedient to the commands of Love as he understood them. Despite all setbacks, it is Love which has the power, the creativity and the energy because it is the very source of the universe.

CHAPTER SIX – THE SEVENTH SIGN

	Chapter	Page
1. The arrest, trial and death of Jesus,	18,19	131
a. The Arrest,	18:1-11	132
b. A preliminary trial before Annas, and Peter's denials,	18:12-27	132
c. Trial before Pilate,	18:28 - 19:16	134
d. The Crucifixion,	19:17-30	138
Discussion points		139
e. The Burial,	19:38-42	142
f. Summary		142
2. The Resurrection,	20,21	143
a. The Empty Tomb,	20:1-9	144
b. Mary Magdalene's Encounter with the Risen Jesus,	20:10-1	146
c. The Evening of the First Day,	20:19-23	148
d. The Appearance to Thomas,	20:24-29	151
e. Conclusion,	20:30,31	152
f. Chapter 21		153

CHAPTER 6:

The Seventh Sign, John 18, 19, 20, 21

1.   The arrest, trial and death of Jesus

John's account of these last days is, as we have come to expect, quite different from that of the Synoptics. He portrays Jesus not as victim but being in complete control. This being John's mature consideration, years after the events, I have to start by accepting that this is how it appeared to him; then I need to get what I can out of such a presentation. Clearly John believes that the crucifixion brought the old world order to an end and created a new one. The last discourse (see p.90) has told us the nature of the new order with its new commandment of love for one for another, based on Jesus' love for his disciples. His followers will be able to do greater work than he has achieved because he is returning to the Father. They will also be enlightened by the gift of the Spirit of truth. Through his witness, humanity can find a new relationship with God, fulfilling the prophecy of Jeremiah (31:31-34) that the law of Love can be written on people's hearts. Jesus has warned his followers of persecution but assured them that the consciousness of his indwelling presence will enable them to endure it. The unity between Father/Son/Spirit is the model for the unity between Jesus and his disciples.

What is not discussed, of course, is the world community whose existence is outside the necessarily narrow vision of the Evangelist. New Testament writers considered the 'world' needed rescue from the powers of darkness, therefore (John 3:16) the sign of God's love for the world is to give his son for its redemption (see p.16). They believed the new order was confined to those who followed the way of Jesus until his Second Coming and the end of the age. Our twentieth century perspective is very different; we are rightly aware of 'our global village' and our planet earth. Nevertheless, I believe that humanity needs the essence of Jesus' power and spirit to survive successfully.

a) JESUS' ARREST, JOHN 18:1-11

It is helpful to compare this passage with that found in Mark (14:43-53). The striking thing about John's account is that Jesus takes the initiative throughout. Crossing the Kedron valley, he goes to the garden (of Gethsemane), a familiar meeting place for his followers, known to Judas. There Jesus advances to meet Judas' company of Roman soldiers and police and initiates the arrangement that only he will be taken while his disciples go free. John alone hints at the power of Jesus' presence as he declares' I am he', even perhaps 'I am'. The awe produced by this announcement momentarily halts his arrest.

John does not mention the Judas kiss as a means of identification for it is superfluous to his account. Indeed Judas plays a very subordinate role in the whole affair. John's account (by implication that of an eye-witness) names Simon Peter as the one who draws his sword to lunge at the High Priest's servant, cutting off his ear and he alone names the servant as Malchus. We read in Luke of the disciples having two swords between them (22:18) and that Jesus immediately heals the injured man (22:51).

Perhaps a fragment of Jesus' agonised prayer (Mark 14:32-42) is reflected here in Jesus' words that he must drink the cup his Father has given him (18:11). He knows, even if his disciples have not yet realised it, that suffering (symbolised by 'the cup', cf Mark 10:38; 14:36) is the inevitable consequence of Love and is voluntarily accepted for the sake of Love. It is not, however, the end of the matter. Jesus believes his own death will lead to a new relationship between humanity and God, just as we know through experience that the death of the false self leads to rebirth. Jesus has already said that his return to the Father (14:28) is a matter for joy and is to the disciples' advantage (16:7-13). Therefore the image of the cup also carries overtones of blessing and joy, as in Psalm 23, where the writer's journey through a valley of deepest darkness leads to assurance of the goodness and unfailing love of the Lord.

b) A PRELIMINARY TRIAL BEFORE ANNAS: PETER'S DENIAL, 18:12-27

Let us look first at the Synoptic record. Mark (14:53-72) recounts a Jewish and a Roman trial. Overnight Jesus is accused before the High Priest and the Sanhedrin of blasphemy, but as the Council can only meet constitutionally during the hours of daylight, they meet again at dawn (Mark 15:1) to legalise their decision. Peter, waiting for news in the courtyard below, has denied his master three times before the cock crows for a second time, as Jesus had prophesied. At the second trial before Pilate (15:2-15), the charge is altered to sedition or treason, since Pilate would not have been interested in blasphemy. Pilate gives the crowd a choice between Jesus and Barabbas. Barabbas is released and Jesus is delivered up for crucifixion.

Matthew adds to this an account of Judas' suicide (27:3-10) and the dreams of Pilate's wife. Her warning that her husband should have nothing to do with Jesus leads to Pilate's public hand-washing and his declaration of innocence regarding Jesus' death. The people accept responsibility for Jesus' execution (27:19-25).

Luke (23:1-5; 15-25) combines the two Council meetings into one, held legally in the morning. He places Peter's denial of Jesus before the trial and records the soldiers indulging in brutal mockery. The Jewish authorities list three specific charges against Jesus in the trial before Pilate: perverting the nation, inciting people to withhold tribute to Caesar and claiming he is Christ, a King. Luke who has previously indicated that he had private information about Herod's court (Luke 8:1-3), also includes the story that Pilate sent Jesus to see Herod before his final condemnation (Luke 23:6-12).

John recounts that Jesus is first taken to Annas, the father-in-law of Caiaphas (cf. 11:51), whom he entitles High Priest, presumably because Annas had held that office from AD6 to AD15 before being deposed by Valerius Gratus, Pilate's predecessor. Perhaps he was still regarded as High Priest in certain quarters, for Luke talks (3:2) of the High Priesthood of Annas and Caiaphas (cf. also Acts 4:6 where the two are again bracketed together with others of the high priestly family). Annas' judgement was clearly still important although Caiaphas had been appointed High Priest by Valerius Gratus in AD18 and remained in office until AD36. John reminds his readers that it was Caiaphas who told the Sanhedrin it was expedient that one man should die for the sake of the nation as a whole (18:14).

I find John's use of details an impressive indication that he is following his own independent oral tradition. He further mentions that the unnamed disciple had connections with the High Priest and was therefore not only able to gain access to the courtyard but could gain admission for Peter. Assuming that the unnamed disciple can be identified with both the beloved disciple (13:23,24, 19:26, and 21:7, 20) and the one who claims to be an eye-witness to events (cf. 1:14, 19:35, 21:24), we have some pointers to the Fourth Gospel's source.

If Peter had attacked a servant of the High Priest, it must have taken some courage even to follow, let alone enter the courtyard, where he could easily have been recognised and arrested. Apparently the maid who opened the gate and was with those standing round the fire quite casually assumed that he was another disciple of Jesus, as was the unnamed man he accompanied. At this point it need not have been very difficult for Peter to admit his discipleship yet he denied it twice, so that when he was actually asked by a relation of the wounded Malchus whether he had not been with Jesus at the arrest, he inevitably denied it a third time. Perhaps the Evangelist intends his readers to note the difference between Jesus' "I am (he)" (18: 5) and Peter's "I am not" (18:25). It certainly highlights the sharp difference between Jesus' fully integrated human personality and Peter, who does not as yet know himself but is capable, through the impact of love, of great change, for it is to Peter that the risen Jesus later entrusts the care of his followers (21:17).

Meanwhile, Annas has been questioning Jesus about his teaching. When Jesus replies that he has always taught in the synagogue (cf. 6:59) or Temple (2:13ff; 7:14, 28; 10:22f) and has nothing to hide, so why not question his hearers? He is struck on the face by a Jewish official who obviously thinks he is being insolent to Annas. Jesus again stands up for himself; if he is guilty of an offence, then this should be clearly stated in evidence, and, if not, why has he been struck? He will not be intimidated by violence. Annas, failing to find any incriminating evidence, sends him bound to Caiaphas. We hear nothing of Caiaphas' interrogation, simply that he passed Jesus on to Pilate but it is worth recalling that the Sanhedrin had already condemned Jesus to death in his absence (11:47-50, p.69).

c) THE TRIAL BEFORE PILATE, 18:28- 19:16

This is an impressive and dramatic scene. Much has been made by commentators of Pilate's alternating movements between the interior of the Governor's headquarters, (possibly the fortress Antonia, or the old palace of Herod), where he addresses Jesus and the exterior where he talks to the Jewish leadership who will not enter the praetorium for fear of defilement at Passover time.

Passover is due to start around six pm at sunset. It is now very early on the Friday morning. The Jews make it clear that Jesus' offence deserves the death sentence and that they have brought him to the governor because Roman law gives them no power to execute. Pilate then questions Jesus about being king of the Jews. In the discussion which follows Jesus simply asserts that his kingship is not of the worldly variety. In fact, the whole question of kingship had always been a deeply controversial issue in Israel; its institution was opposed by Samuel, the last judge over all Israel (1 Samuel 7:2-8:22; 10:17-24; 12:1-25). Strictly speaking, Israel was a theocracy with God as king. It is very likely that Jesus would never have used the word king because of its wrong associations.

To clarify these matters for Pilate, Jesus says that if he were the kind of aspiring leader that Pilate would recognise as kingly, his followers would be fighting for him now. He describes his mission as declaring the truth, but makes no attempt to elucidate this for Pilate. The reader however knows that Jesus has described himself as the truth (14:6) and has promised his disciples the advent of the indwelling Spirit of Truth (14:15-26, see p.95). From our vantage point we can see that his life and teaching do reveal the truth about God and the Creator's relationship with humanity. Jesus' personal example makes him the great liberator, freeing people from the vicious circle of retaliation and revenge.

Lacking this background, Pilate responds by asking for a definition of truth, but he does not wait for an answer. Instead he goes to tell the Jewish leadership he finds no guilt in Jesus. As a compromise he recalls that at Passover time, the governor may release a prisoner - presumably a goodwill gesture to a conquered people, although there is little extra-biblical evidence to support this statement (cf. Mark 15:6). He therefore gives the Jews a choice between Jesus and Barabbas, whom John describes as a bandit. At the time Jesus' own supporters are unaware of anything amiss, so they have not rallied in support. The crowd, presumably packed with ill-wishers, shout for Barabbas to be released.

Mark calls Barabbas a rebel leader in a recent uprising and suggests that the crowd outside the governor's headquarters has been influenced by the chief priests (15:7-11) and makes it clear that this was all part of the Sanhedrin's plan to have Jesus done away with as quietly and quickly as possible. That Jesus had a strong following is evident from his rapturous reception at the triumphal entry and the people's reactions to his teaching in the temple precincts. This obvious popularity may have alarmed the authorities just as much as his teaching, as John indicates. Although the Fourth Gospel differs from the Synoptics in many interesting details, the essentials are the same. John was either following his own oral source, or using his skill as a dramatist and theologian to draw out his own significant points. I believe the evidence for an oral source is strong.

Before passing sentence Pilate hands Jesus over for flogging (John 19:1-2), an unusual and possibly irregular occurrence. On the other hand the Romans did use torture to extract confessions from non-Roman citizens or slaves. Sometimes also a man who had been sentenced was flogged in order to weaken him before crucifixion. What Pilate hoped to gain from this flogging is not clear. He must have known that the Jewish authorities would not be moved by pity, having expressly said they wanted Jesus executed. If the Johannine account is correct (as opposed to Mark who says Jesus was flogged after sentence), it raises some interesting speculation about Pilate's mixed motives. We know from extra-biblical sources that the Jews considered Pilate to be 'merciless, inflexible and obstinate' and that he was recalled to Rome in AD36. Perhaps, motivated by weakness or by unconscious envy of his inner spiritual power, Pilate hoped to break Jesus' calm resolve and make him admit to something which would render judgement easier.

The themes of power, powerlessness and vulnerability are some of the most interesting sub-topics of this gospel. Jesus is depicted as exercising great power in turning water into wine, multiplying bread and fish, healing the incurably sick and raising the dead. I personally value these incidents for their spiritual symbolism rather than their apparent magical quality. I believe Jesus had great power over people but that he used his power selflessly to awaken the seed of God within. He has indicated to Pilate that his realm is a matter of inward reality not the external trappings of power which Pilate represented. At this moment Jesus is physically powerless, a prisoner with his hands bound behind his back, accused of a capital offence by his own people before a pagan official. As such, he exemplifies the vulnerability of a love that is willing to sacrifice itself for the sake of others. He epitomises both the voluntary vulnerability of Love itself and the very real inner power of the spirit.

Human beings have assumed that their hierarchical structures derive from God. They are obsessive about power, hence they project on to God the qualities of omniscience and omnipotence, then reject a God who apparently does not live up to his reputation. The lesson of Jesus is that we need to grow up into a more adult concept of the Spirit of truth and love. The real power base is something other than we had supposed. Thus John presents Jesus as very much in control even while he is superficially impotent; even when he is physically beaten and finally crucified, he is not intimidated but chooses his own path.

John follows Luke in suggesting that Pilate tried three times to release Jesus because he was not convinced of his guilt. After flogging, the soldiers crown Jesus with thorns and deck him in purple to mock his royalty. Pilate then shows him to the Jews, reiterating that he can find no case against him. Jesus must have been looking quite terrible, battered, bruised and bleeding. "Behold the man," says Pilate. Jesus' identification with suffering humanity is never more apparent.

The real reason for Jewish hostility to Jesus now comes to the surface. He has infringed their law by claiming to be Son of God. Such blasphemy is punishable by death (Leviticus 24:16), therefore they demand that he be executed by the governor, since they cannot do it themselves. Their accusation of blasphemy is unfounded. In all the great confrontations with the Jewish authorities recorded in this gospel, Jesus has said repeatedly that his authority comes from God (see p.60). To equate oneself with God is spirit-destroying arrogance, a sin of which Herod Agrippa I was guilty (Acts 12:22,23). Jesus, in fact, was a true vehicle for the glory of the divine and as such was Son of God.

Mark reports that Jesus admitted to the Sanhedrin that he was the Christ, the Son of the Blessed (Mark 14:62) while Matthew adds that the high priest put Jesus under solemn oath before asking him the vital question (Matthew 26:63). In both gospels, Jesus quite deliberately calls himself the Son of Man using a quotation from Daniel (7:13) and further declaring with words taken from Psalm 110:1 that God will vindicate him.

To return to the Fourth Gospel, the pagan Pilate is alarmed at talk of a god's son and asks Jesus "Where have you come from?" (cf the theme of the bitter controversy at the Feast of Tabernacles 7:28, 4lf; 8:14. see p.61). When Jesus does not reply, Pilate sharply reminds him that he, Pilate, has the power of life and death over him. Despite the agony and exhaustion of his flogging, Jesus finds the strength to clarify the nature of Pilate's authority. It is merely derivative (as a Jew, Jesus would consider all temporal power as derivative for the whole world belonged to God). He goes on to add that Pilate is less blameworthy than the one who had delivered Jesus to him, presumably meaning that Caiaphas, as Jewish High Priest ought to have recognised Jesus' origins. If Caiaphas had not been so hidebound by tradition and interested in maintaining the priestly hierarchy and power, he would have discerned the movement of the Spirit of God within Jesus. By handing Jesus over to the Roman governor instead, the Jewish authorities had betrayed their nation's religious heritage, a fact John makes clear in 19:15.

Jesus' mission was to establish within himself and then others a different power base or authority, that of the indwelling Spirit of truth and love. The imposed authority of law might be necessary in 'childhood' or when the seed of God was not awakened, but it did not enable humanity to mature and thus to become sons and daughters of the divine. Pilate has merely the limited power to enforce the death sentence, whereas Jesus' inner power of compassion could bring liberation and eternal life.

Having tried a third time to procure Jesus' release by declaring him innocent of a capital offence, Pilate buckles under the threat that he is no friend of Caesar's if he frees someone who has claimed to be a king. He agrees to judge Jesus, doubtless worried lest an adverse report reach the Emperor Tiberius if he does not now take action. John gives precise details about the judgement seat and the time, saying it was about noon on Friday when

Pilate delivered judgement. Mark states (15:25) that Jesus was crucified about the third hour (i.e. 6 am). We have to accept ancient discrepancies about time-keeping. Determined to have the last word, Pilate asks the Jews 'Shall I crucify your king?' Perhaps he intends the irony of evoking the response which he gets: "We have no king but Ceasar"; in their determination to reject Jesus, the Jewish leadership deny their historic birthright. For John, Paul and other early Christians this means that the community created by Jesus is the true inheritor of Israel's past.

d) THE CRUCIFIXION, 19:17-30

It is probably useful to compare Mark's account (15:16-41) with that given by John. One of John's most notable omissions is the detail that Simon of Cyrene was commandeered to carry Jesus' cross, after he had collapsed under its weight. It is very likely that Jesus would set out bearing his own cross-bar to the place of execution (named The Place of the Skull: Hebrew, Golgotha; Latin, Calvaria) but later be unfit to carry it. Simon of Cyrene, in North Africa, may have been visiting Jerusalem for the Passover. The fact that Mark is able to name his two sons suggests both that Simon later became a follower of Jesus and that his two sons were well known in the Christian community in Rome. That John should omit this incident is in keeping with his presentation of Jesus as being completely in control, even though physical weakness is one thing and spiritual vigour another.

Perhaps John's most striking omission is Jesus' cry of desolation from the cross, also missing from Luke's account. Jesus quotes (Mark 15:34, cf. Matthew 27:46) the opening line of Psalm 22. Although this psalm expresses the deepest grief and wretchedness, the psalmist wins through to faith in the Lord's abiding providence and ends with the affirmation "The Lord has acted". This was truly Jesus' conviction. Unlike the psalmist, he knew that he had to pass through death, but he did believe that he would be vindicated by the Father. John's faith is based on the experience of the indwelling presence of Jesus the Christ. Perhaps this is why he omits Jesus' cry. However he is conscious of Psalm 22's relevance to the crucifixion; commenting (19:24) that the soldiers dicing for Jesus' seamless garment was a fulfilment of scripture, he actually quotes Psalm 22:18. There was probably a quaternion of soldiers under each of the three crosses. A condemned man's clothes were the soldiers' perquisites and a seamless robe would be worth keeping intact.

John does not specify the crime of the two men crucified with Jesus but most likely they were accomplices of Barabbas. He also omits the offer of drugged wine, the mockery of the passers by (cv. Mark 15:22-32), Luke's account of Jesus' forgiveness of the soldiers in the very act of crucifying him (Luke 23:34) and his conversation with one of the criminals (Luke 23:39-43).

John's additions to the synoptic record are as fascinating as his omissions. It was Roman practice to nail a notice of criminal record to the cross. John gives greater detail about the wording (19:20,21) "Jesus of Nazareth, King of the Jews", and Pilate's obstinate refusal to alter it to 'he claimed to be King of the Jews' at the request of the Jewish high priests. The fact that the inscription was in Hebrew, Latin and Greek may have been Hellenistic custom, but for the Evangelist it demonstrates the universal nature of Jesus' ministry.

John's list of the women at the cross is interesting. Mark has named three (15:40) out of a group of women from Galilee watching from a distance - Mary Magdalene, Mary Mother of James (the younger) and Joseph, and Salome. Matthew records that the mother of Zebedee's sons was also present (27:56). If we suppose that the Fourth Evangelist is mentioning four women - Jesus' mother, (who is unnamed, cf. 2:4), his mother's sister (also unnamed), Mary wife of Clopas and Mary Magdalene, it is reasonable to suppose that mother Mary's sister was called Salome and that she was also the mother of Zebedee's sons, in which case John was Jesus' cousin. To read into 19:25 that there were only three women present is to assume that the sisters had the same name Mary, which would be unusual and confusing.

John's additions include Jesus' entrusting his mother to the care of the beloved disciple and mention of his parched throat and plea for the drink which enabled him to raise his voice at the end in great cry of triumph - 'it is finished' or 'it is accomplished'. His tortured position, stretched out to the physical limit, would mean that when he bent his head he could no longer breathe so his last moment was to some extent a voluntary action and it could be said that Jesus relinquishes his spirit into the Father's care.

Traditionally these Johannine additions are considered to arise from the fact that the beloved disciple was John the Apostle, the eyewitness on whose testimony the gospel was written (see 19:35 where the writer claims to be present at the horrifying event). I personally tend to give credence to this ancient evidence, but whether or not it is so does not nullify the psychological and spiritual message the Evangelist is conveying.

Three points for discussion

i) How best can we deal with grief? I am reminded of two women who both lost sons in tragic circumstances. The first one made a shrine of her son's room and belongings, keeping them as exact as she could. The second opened her house to all her son's friends and gave herself to a cause which benefited young people, thus gaining many adopted sons and daughters. Of course there can be no replacement of a dearly loved person. Each is unique and special and their dying means that those who love them experience a kind of death too. Afterwards the relationship has to be internalised, which means letting go of outward forms and accepting spiritual reality. Jesus' mother had had to let her son go his own way. The Marriage at Cana story indicates (see p.27), that she had learnt to trust him completely even though she must have been aware of the possible consequences of his teaching. His closest friend too had to let Jesus go his own way and trust him profoundly. He did not try and interfere to prevent Judas' betrayal, as Peter surely would have done. These two people who loved him so dearly, were given to each other by Jesus in his dying moments, so that their love for him could grow and enrich their own lives, which is what Love is all about.

Mark's gospel (3:31-35) indicates that Jesus' family in general did not really understand either his ministry or his teaching. John bears this out by reporting a conversation showing that Jesus' brothers (7:1-9) frankly did not believe in him. Although we know on the evidence of Paul and Acts that his brothers did believe later, it is interesting to note that Jesus commends his mother to his dearest friend (and, probably, cousin) in accordance with his teaching that his true family are not necessarily blood relations but those with whom he has an affinity of spirit and commitment.

ii) Although the Fourth Evangelist interprets Jesus' actions as fulfilment of scripture, it is hard to conceive that Jesus in extremis would have the energy to think of anything at this moment, other than his physical need. The writer/witness to these events probably recalled Psalm 69:21 much later. Jesus' thirst was temporarily quenched with some sour wine. How this was conveyed to Jesus' lips is immaterial This moisture enabled Jesus to summon the strength to give the cry 'It is accomplished.' His work was done. He had completed the task set by the Father. Probably his enemies also thought that the matter was now over and done with. Having disposed of this trouble-maker they could rest secure in their orthodoxy.

iii) John then adds a further significant detail, unrecorded elsewhere. According to his chronology Jesus was crucified on the eve of the Passover, which that year fell on the Sabbath and therefore began at 6 pm on Friday. The Synoptists strongly indicate a Passover setting for the Last Supper held on Thursday evening, but there would be many problems in accepting that Jesus was crucified on Passover day. Instead it could be argued that what Jesus and his friends celebrated was a Chaburah meal - a meal of fellowship.

Many scholars would agree that John's chronology is right. He reports that the Jewish authorities were anxious to hasten death because of the religious importance of the forthcoming day, being both the Sabbath and the Passover. They therefore ask for the men's legs to be broken, thus increasing the difficulty in breathing. They want the bodies taken down and disposed of before the Sabbath, according to Jewish law (Deuteronomy 21:22f). However, when the soldiers come to Jesus they find him already dead and do not break his legs. In order to make sure of death, one soldier stabs Jesus' side with a lance; water and blood pour out. For the Evangelist this event is so significant that he verifies it with the stamp of eye-witness testimony and further underlines its importance by claiming it is fulfilment of scripture (19:37 refers to Psalm 34:20 and the second quotation could be from Zechariah 12:10).The modern mind is not impressed by the idea of scripture being fulfilled when it seems that clearly the event has sent people in search of an appropriate text to be tagged on to the action.

There are two other points which we need to discuss. First, the Evangelist is probably testifying to Jesus' humanity by making it absolutely certain that he was dead. We know from the First Letter of John that this needed saying because the author was faced with gnostic heresy about the docetic Christ. This stated that an emanation from the divine descended upon the man Jesus at his baptism and left him at the crucifixion, because the Christ spirit could not suffer or die. John gives personal witness that this interpretation of Jesus' death is wrong.

Second, the 'water and blood' theme has run through the gospel from Marriage at Cana story, to the Woman at the Well, and the Feeding of the Five Thousand. Jesus claims that his body and blood are spiritual food; in some way, the Evangelist sees the flow of water and blood as symbolic of the total self-offering of Jesus, which was to bring the gift of eternal life to those who believed in him. Orthodox Christians see the flow as symbolising the sacraments of baptism and the Eucharist and they place the same interpretation on 1 John's words (5:8), that to the testimony of the Spirit must be added the testimony of water and blood.

Water and blood could stand for both Jesus' baptism and his death. Strangely John's gospel does not record Jesus' baptism by John Baptist, although it is implied (cf. 1:32). Mark implies that when Jesus was baptised, the vision of the dove descending and God's voice in blessing and confirmation, came to him alone (1:9-11). However the symbolism may be interpreted, I see the lance-thrust as confirmation that Jesus, the completely human man, dies a human death on the cross. I have no difficulty in accepting that the Evangelist believed that Jesus' self-offering completed his ministry and life, enabled humanity to enter a new relationship with the divine and with sources of eternal life but, as a Quaker, I prefer to identify the symbols with an inner meaning rather than with an outward rite.

e)   THE BURIAL, 19:38-42

We know from the Synoptic gospels (Mark 15:42-47, Matthew 27:57-61, Luke 23;50-56) about the courage of Joseph of Arimathea, the Jewish aristocrat who went to ask Pilate's permission to bury Jesus' body. According to Luke, he was a man of character and integrity who had dissociated himself from the Sanhedrin's decision to do away with Jesus. Matthew and John claim that he was a disciple of Jesus but, John adds, 'in secrecy, for fear of the Jews'. John also mentions the presence of the Pharisee Nicodemus (cf 3:1-15; 7:50), who is now brave enough to accompany Joseph of Arimathea and who brings a large amount of myrrh and aloes to embalm and perfume the body. (This contradicts the Mark/Luke account that the women brought and prepared species to embalm the body.)

The Fourth Evangelist is at pains to point out that Jesus was buried according to Jewish custom, perhaps in order to explain the arrangement of the empty grave clothes which are discovered on the First Day by the disciples (20:5-7).

The two men place Jesus' body in a new tomb in the garden near the crucifixion spot. Matthew adds that Joseph uses his own rock-hewn tomb for the purpose and Mark (Matthew also) describes how he rolls a stone against the opening to make it secure. In Matthew we read that Pilate gave the Jewish authorities permission to place a guard at the tomb for fear of the disciples' stealing the body, but John does not record this.

f)   TO SUM UP THIS SECTION SO FAR:

Had Jesus wished to be a national liberator, he could have rallied considerable popular support, although others such as the Sadducees, would have been less enthusiastic because they held power by Roman patronage. Jesus must have presented an incongruous figure to Pilate and yet he had such impressive strength and courage that Pilate wanted to set him free. Jesus' authority was from God alone, from the Spirit of truth and love within, so he could not - and would not - fight with physical weapons to establish his inner realm. It was, nevertheless, a reality. Here is the sharp contrast between external control by force and armed might and the control of the heart, mind and will by Love and Truth. In a profound way the Fourth Gospel illuminates the Marcan account of Jesus' messiahship. Jesus did not claim 'kingship' or messiahship without defining what that meant. His purpose was to bear witness to the truth which would liberate humanity from its false images of power and glory. Jesus found mastery over himself. He could have achieved mastery over others but his purpose was not to dominate or possess. He wanted to awaken the spiritual potential within, so that people would grow in love and truth and so find their true selves. Political power is a necessary element in human society, but it is not what Jesus was seeking.

2. The Resurrection, John 20 and 21

We have already discussed the cosmic law that through death comes life and have seen how the ministry of Jesus embodies this in precise human terms. Now we find the fulfilment of this law displayed on a profound spiritual plane. Jesus' death was final in a worldly sense. It removed him from the historical scene as death removes us all but that was not the end of the matter. The resurrection appearances were an essential experience to those first friends of Jesus as they made the transition from contact with their human master to consciousness that his indwelling presence was a lasting reality. The theme of resurrection has been universal since the dawn of time when human beings first buried their dead with certain rituals. We find it in the cycle of natural events and in the myths of a dying and rising fertility god or goddess. But so far as I know from my study of other faiths the particular form of Jesus' resurrection was unique. No wonder he was later deified and translated by Christian orthodoxy into God the Son. Nevertheless I believe this redefinition of Jesus robs humanity of its dignity and its potential. What he was and is, including his testimony to life after death, is open to all of us if we follow his way.

It is impossible to know from this distance in time what actually happened at the resurrection, but I believe there was a truth in the resurrection experience sufficient to change completely the lives of those who had loved the mortal man. I also know through faith that when those whom we love die, we can internalise our relationship with them so that they live within also. I am convinced too that we shall meet again in the hereafter and continue to grow in love.

We have seen how the six previous great signs provoked different reactions from different people and were never absolutely convincing in their own right. Some believed and some disbelieved, depending on their sight or insight. To see the inward meaning of the outer happening, we must first have faith that there is an inner significance to be searched for. This is equally true of the seventh and greatest sign. The risen Jesus only appeared to those who loved him. According to Paul, whose letters are the earliest written record of the resurrection experience (cf. 1 Corinthians 15:3-8), the risen Jesus appeared to Peter and then to the Twelve, then to five hundred 'brothers', most of whom were still alive when Paul wrote his letter, then to Jesus' brother James, then to all the apostles and finally to Paul himself. According to Matthew's gospel (28:16,17), the eleven disciples went to the Galilean mountain where they had been told to meet Jesus. There some greeted him by kneeling before him, but others were dubious. So even at the heart of the gospel story some doubt is expressed about the precise nature of the event. The Fourth Gospel itself deals with Thomas' doubt as we shall see later.

Possibly the Galilee event (28:16,17) was not confined to the eleven but included the five hundred 'brothers' mentioned by Paul. The mountain setting for the final meeting and the instruction to baptise in the name of the Father, Son and Holy Spirit, fits Matthew's presentation of Jesus as greater than Moses the law-giver. The baptismal instruction reflects the thinking of the later Christian community to which Matthew belonged, rather than Jesus' own commission.

a)   THE EMPTY TOMB, 20:1-9

All four gospels record this central fact and Mark's gospel actually ends with it. (It is generally agreed that Mark 16:8b-20 was added at a later date, since the two oldest Greek manuscripts omit these final verses, their style is quite unlike the rest of the gospel and their contents summarise material drawn from the other three gospels.)

I think it worth recounting the Synoptic story in detail to highlight John's handling of the same event. The Synoptics tell us how the faithful women visited the tomb very early in the morning. They all specifically mention Mary Magdalene. In Mark and Luke they go to anoint Jesus' body. Mark recounts the presence of a young man dressed in white, within the tomb, who tells the women the miraculous story of the risen Jesus. The women are bidden to tell the disciples and Peter that Jesus will meet them in Galilee as he has promised, but the women run away too terrified to say anything to anyone. Luke records that two men in dazzling garments appear to the women in the tomb and ask them why they are seeking the living in a tomb, reminding them that Jesus himself had prophesied he would rise again on the third day. Filled with joy, the women tell this to the disciples, but are not believed.

In Matthew the women go to see the tomb and are subsequently terrified by a great earthquake, which Matthew attributes to the descent of an angel of the Lord. The angel has rolled away the stone before the tomb and is sitting on it. He tells them Jesus has risen, shows them the empty tomb and informs them that Jesus is gone to Galilee where he will meet them all. As the women run off to tell the disciples they encounter the risen Jesus on the way and worship him. Jesus tells them not to be afraid but to tell his friends to go to Galilee where they will see him. The interesting discrepancies in these accounts do not nullify the main fact: the women were the first to visit the tomb, sometime between 3 am and 6 am and they found the great stone blocking the tomb entrance had been rolled away. The tomb itself was empty.

John mentions only Mary Magdalene, but she would not have gone to the tomb alone. On finding the tomb empty she runs to the house; presumably the beloved disciple and Mary the mother of Jesus would be staying there as well as Peter. Her cry of anguish suggests that, going with the other women, she has seen that the tomb is empty and suspects the body has been stolen. At her news, the two men run to the tomb, the younger arriving first. He looks in but does not step inside until Simon Peter arrives, whereupon they both enter. When the unnamed disciple sees the position of the graveclothes, he believes. But he says nothing to Peter; presumably what he believes is that his master has risen and therefore is the Christ. We are not told what Peter thinks. Then the two men return to the house.

By attaching great significance to the position of the empty, undisturbed grave clothes, John concentrates on the essential contrasting fact between the resurrection of Jesus and the resuscitation of Lazarus (cf. p.46). Lazarus needed help to free him from his wrappings, but the risen Jesus has simply transcended them and left them flat yet in position. If the tomb had been rifled and the body stolen, the graveclothes would have been taken as well, or at least left in disorder. No one actually saw Jesus rise from the dead. They simply encountered the risen Jesus and this brought utter conviction. Scriptural endorsement came later. The Fourth Gospel leads us to believe that this convincement was based on eyewitness memory of the events. I find the incidents so vividly arresting as to be true.

Throughout the gospel and at four particular points, the Evangelist has been preparing his reader for the tremendous fact of the resurrection. In the first place, he tells us that it was on the third day that the marriage at Cana took place, when Jesus turned the water into wine (see p.27). Secondly, when the Pharisees challenge him about the cleansing of the Temple (2:19-22), Jesus says the sign of his authority will be to raise 'the temple' in three days time. His disciples came later to understand that by 'temple' he was referring to his own body which would be raised from the dead by God. Thirdly, Jesus tells Nicodemus (3:14) that the Son of Man will be lifted up in order to give eternal life to those who believe in him. The Greek word lift up can mean either physical raising as on the cross, or exaltation in the sense of enhancing one's moral or spiritual stature. Through the resurrection, Jesus was exalted. Fourthly, when Jesus returned to Bethany the third day after receiving news of Lazarus' mortal illness, he called himself the resurrection and the life and raised Lazarus from the dead. In all these incidents we are dealing with symbols that speak of the spiritual reality that through death comes life. At the death of someone whom we love, we can be conscious that the veil between this life and the next is very thin and can be aware of the lasting worth of the loved one. In Jesus' case the experience was qualitatively different. Through his ministry and death he showed his friends a new approach to life, a new way of living. By his resurrection he also was able to energise them into action.

b)   MARY MAGDALENE'S ENCOUNTER WITH THE RISEN JESUS, 20:11-18

This scene is moving in its simplicity yet profound in its implications. It is to a woman that the risen Jesus first appears. We know nothing from this gospel of the Magdalene's history, nor is it material. As Jesus' disciple, she is utterly faithful and courageous. She was previously mentioned as being with the other women at the cross (19:25). What more we know about her from the Synoptic Gospels only adds to the richness of the story.

Although Mary is inconsolable in her grief, she is able to 'see' two angelic beings sitting where the body of Jesus had lain, one at the head and the other at the feet. When they ask why she is weeping, her reply shows her total concern to find the body of Jesus. Without waiting for any comment from them she turns to see standing outside the tomb a figure, which she presumes to be the gardener. Perhaps the early morning mist obscured her vision, or she was blinded by weeping so much, but she does not instantly recognise either Jesus or his voice when he first speaks. We may suppose that Jesus' body had undergone some transformation or translation into a different sphere of being, as it was not apparently subject to normal laws. Mary's loving heart responds immediately when Jesus says her name. With unbounded joy she calls him 'Rabboni', an Aramaic term which the Evangelist translates as 'Teacher', but it is a stronger word than Rabbi, and may be taken to mean 'my Lord'.

Jesus tells Mary not to cling on to him for he has not yet 'ascended' to the Father. Perhaps he is not yet established in his new being. People who claim to have psychic gifts say they can see quite clearly people who have died but they do not touch them as their forms must be insubstantial to appear and disappear at will. However, the risen Jesus can later invite Thomas to touch him and can cook breakfast by the lakeside for his friends (ch. 21). Jesus, however, bids Mary go back to his 'brothers' (the first time Jesus has used this term of his disciples, implying a change of status) and to tell them he is about to ascend to his and their Father and God. Mary joyfully obeys. Her words 'I have seen the Lord' surely imply both physical sight and inner understanding.

Luke's Gospel also records a resurrection episode where Jesus is at first unrecognised. The two disciples walking to Emmaus know him only when he breaks the bread with them (Luke 24:13-35). Luke also describes his appearance to his disciples in Jerusalem (24:36-49) and his taking them out to Bethany where, after blessing them, he leaves them (24:50-53). Acts (1:1-11) places the ascension of Jesus forty days after the resurrection and describes it in spatial terms (although the best manuscripts omit that Jesus was carried up into heaven). However, Luke is simply stating that after a time, the physical presence of Jesus left his disciples permanently. From now on they are aware of his spiritual presence in their midst and the gift of the Holy Spirit (Acts 2:1-4) occurs ten days later when they are together in the Upper Room.

John describes these events very differently. He concentrates the resurrection, the ascension and the gift of the Spirit into a single day - the first day of the week - although he is clear that the Spirit is not given until Jesus has been glorified (7:39; 16:7). It is futile to try and harmonise these variations and at a deep level, the discrepancies are not important. For me, they only add veracity to the story. The gospels all state the main facts that the tomb was empty and there were unusual appearances of 'men' or 'angels' at the site. Matthew, Luke and John all state that the risen Jesus was seen by those who loved him, that he empowered them to continue his work and that they received or became aware of the gift of the Spirit. They somehow identified this Spirit with their consciousness of the indwelling Christ Jesus, even though they also felt it as a separate experience.

As we no longer think of God in spatial terms, we find Jesus' ascension difficult, but for New Testament minds the sky/heaven was the dwelling place of a God who was and is an outer reality. The Old Testament makes clear that God was distinct from and other than his creation (Genesis 1). In this he was unlike the divinities worshipped in the natural world, although he was also seen to be active in the forces of nature. As we have discussed, the Greek word 'ascent' has a dual meaning, so Jesus' ascent to the Father really means his glorification. Peter indeed proclaims in his apostolic preaching that Jesus, having been raised by God is now sitting at his right hand in the place of supreme honour (Acts 2:33). This is proved by the power of the Spirit which his disciples are experiencing and which now is available to those who believe in Jesus as Lord and Messiah. We are not comfortable with this language but alternatives are not easy to find.

John seems to be saying that by returning to the Father from whom he once came, Jesus is empowered to give the spirit to his disciples (20:23). Therefore, however much Luke and John may disagree about the timing of events, for both of them there are two elements in the resurrection experience. Initially his friends knew that their master had somehow gone through a terrible death and had been translated into a different kind of being; later they received an inner power or energy, which they identified as the Spirit of truth and love which enabled them to proclaim Jesus' radical and innovative message that humanity must find a new relationship with its Creator, the source of its being. Because those first disciples were Jews, they then searched the Jewish scriptures to find prophetic statements which would identify Jesus as the promised Messiah and they expressed their beliefs about him in terms appropriate to their cultural and religious inheritance - hence the emphasis in Jesus' words to Mary, 'I am ascending to my Father and your Father, to my God and your God'.

We see in the gospels and Paul's letters how this witness to Jesus was built up; these records indeed are themselves 'proofs' of the reality of the resurrection experience to the disciples. Despite gross misunderstanding through the centuries, the essence of John's message still has power to enable humanity to find its true destiny and to create a better world.

In the final discourse (ch. 13-16, see p.81), Jesus has promised his disciples that he will return, not leaving them desolate (14:18,28); that they will actually 'see' him and grief will turn into joy (16:16-22); that he is going to the Father (14:12); that they will receive the gift of the Spirit (14:26, 15:26; 16:7) and peace (14:27, 16: 33), and that they will be able to do what he has done (14:12). The encounter with Mary fulfils some of these promises. Her grief is turned to joy. The relationship is now not an external one but an inner reality, therefore she must not cling to him. She has no doubt at all that she has actually seen Jesus and as the first bearer of the good news, she is truly an apostle.

c) THE EVENING OF THE FIRST DAY, 20:19-23

The disciples are together behind locked doors for fear of Jewish reprisals. Fear that they will be accused of stealing Jesus' body and guilt at deserting their master probably make them doubly afraid. They are unchanged as yet. Quietly the risen Jesus comes to them. Perhaps the energy levels of his resurrected body are quite different from solid matter for he is able to pass through doors. He gives them the conventional greeting of 'Shalom' - peace be with you - but it is his actual presence which has the power to impart peace. He has come back to them as he promised (14:18) and he shows them his wounds. It may be that they needed this sign of identification, but in my view the wounds of Jesus are symbolic of his humanity. William Blake says human beings are made for joy and woe. We need to recognise the fact that we experience both deprivation and fulfilment, dark patches of depression and glorious illumination. Jesus' message has been that through following the way of love which can lead to death, comes also life. The reality of Jesus' presence on this occasion cannot be doubted. According to Paul, one of the first Christian prayers was "Marana tha", which means "Come, Lord!" (cf 1 Corinthians 16:22). The experience of millions down the ages is that the Spirit does come.

Jesus commissions his disciples to be his messengers in the world as he himself was sent by the Father (cf. 17:18). He has already said that he has given them everything he himself received from the Father (15:15). He now breathes into them the Spirit, thus energising them for their task. The parallel between wind/breath and Spirit/rebirth occurs in his conversation with Nicodemus (3:8, see p.13). Paul also compares God giving Adam the breath of life (Genesis 2:7) and Jesus giving the Spirit. He describes Jesus as the last Adam, who has become a life-giving spirit (1 Corinthians 15:45).

The Synoptics agree that Jesus charges them to proclaim the gospel (Mark 16:15); they are to preach to all nations repentance and the forgiveness of sins in his name (Luke 24:47,48: Acts 1:8); they are to make disciples of all nations and baptise in the name of Father, Son and Holy Spirit (Matthew 28:19). According to John however, Jesus instructs his disciples to withhold as well as to forgive.

This is a difficult statement for us to stomach. The power to forgive or withhold forgiveness by virtue of priestly office could be open to misuse. The only place in the Fourth Gospel where Jesus refers to 'a guilt remaining' is in conversation with a group of Pharisees after healing the blind man (see p.39). On this occasion, it is clear that Jesus is referring to lack of self-knowledge, the spiritual blindness which prevents a person from recognising their need for change and forgiveness. This is totally different from giving his friends (how many were in the room? Did they include the faithful women? I hope so!) the authority to grant or withhold forgiveness. Orthodox Christians made absolution from sin a necessary precondition of eternal life; it could be a fearful thing to die 'unshriven'.

Perhaps we can look at this statement another way. Each of us can forgive or withhold forgiveness from those who wrong or injure us. The power to love, forgive and to be compassionate is ours alone. Of course if we withhold forgiveness we diminish ourselves as well as the other. As a Quaker, I believe in the priesthood of all believers and there is a sense in which we all fulfil our priestly function by mutual forgiveness. If Jesus' words are taken personally, they can make sense. Love offers forgiveness, but it requires response from the individual to be truly effective. We have to be aware of our need before it can be met. We can forgive those who harm or injure us even if they do not ask or want our forgiveness. To do so liberates us from the burning desire to retaliate and to take revenge. Our liberation frees us from bitterness whatever the response of the other. It is not a sign of weakness but of change and growth. In the same way, if we seek forgiveness we are liberated from guilt, for Love itself forgives whether the injured person does so or not. Love does not ask us to judge but shows us our task in the ministry of reconciliation.

Forgiveness is the keynote of all Jesus' teaching. He lived it out by forgiving the soldiers as they nailed him to the cross (Luke 23:24). Forgiveness requires us to let go of bitterness, the right to be outraged, hurt pride, anger or hatred. It is not only central to Jesus' ministry but is also a fact of life learnt by countless noble men and women. Held hostage for several years, Terry Waite found that he and other hostages had to go beyond anger to survival. He had to learn to look upon the enemy as a fellow human being. Laurens van de Post discovered in a Japanese P.O.W. camp during the Second Wold War that "forgiveness was as fundamental a law of the human spirit as the law of gravity... If one broke this law of forgiveness one inflicted a mortal wound on one's spirit and became again a member of the chain-gang of mere cause and effect..." (*The Night of the New Moon*, Hogarth Press, 1970, p.157). To learn this truth can be a long hard process if we have been deeply wronged. Sadly it is to our own profound detriment if we do not manage it.

It is a major Fourth Gospel theme that we need to let go the false self so as to find God within and become, like Jesus, a channel of the divine light. The motivation for this effort is Love and with love comes truth. The gift of the Spirit of Truth (16:13) brings much needed discernment (14:28; 16:7) for self-knowledge leads to a more compassionate understanding of others. If we can see ourselves as we truly are and learn to accept ourselves and others with this new perspective, we shall be able to forgive both ourselves and others.

John squeezes not only the resurrection, ascension and gift of the Spirit into the same day, but also Jesus' great commissioning of the disciples, here presented as the beginning of a new age and creation. The new order's hallmark is the presence of the indwelling Christ. Perhaps he felt all these things were so inexpressibly bound up with each other that the only way to express their unity was to incorporate them all in the same day.

d)   THE APPEARANCE TO THOMAS, 20:24-29

We know nothing of Thomas apart from the Fourth Gospel's account. Evidently he was an utterly loyal disciple, prepared to die for his master (11:16); he was also rather literal minded and blunt, as shown when he told Jesus the last time they were together, that they did not know where Jesus was going so how could they know the way?

Thomas was not present on the first day when the risen Jesus came to his disciples, so he has not yet received the empowerment and illumination of the Spirit. He resolutely resists what the others tell him of their experience. His devotion is not in doubt but perhaps his longing for verification is so great that he can only trust the evidence of his own senses. He speaks for many of us who by temperament are logical and clear-headed, not easily swayed by others. Jesus meets his need. A week later, they are again together in the same locked room (evidently the yeast of the Spirit has not yet liberated them from fear) when Jesus comes as before and gives the greeting of peace. Then he turns to Thomas and invites him to touch the wounds in his hands and side. Thomas does not need to touch Jesus; his response is an immediate declaration of faith. His words, "My Lord and my God!" are the only place in the New Testament, apart from the Prologue (1:1) where Jesus is actually equated with God. As I believe that Jesus was truly a human being, I would interpret this by saying that through the transparent and glorified Jesus, Thomas sees the Father. To a greater or lesser degree, we can all reflect the divine within as we grow in love.

Jesus' last words on this occasion reflect the reality of Christian experience. Only the privileged few could know Jesus as an historical person but millions have known his presence in their hearts, lives and worship. The First Letter of Peter also speaks movingly of the faith of those who love Jesus the Christ, and find great joy in their faith although they have never seen him (1:8).

All the gospels record some scepticism about the resurrection (Mark 16:13, Matthew 28:17, Luke 24:22ff, 38,41) but given Thomas' genuine love for Jesus we cannot equate his doubts with those of the Pharisees who demanded a sign from him (Mark 8:11,12) out of their dislike and suspicion. Jesus only appeared to those who loved him because Love refuses to compel. It gives freely and waits for a genuine response. If Jesus had forced acknowledgement by appearing to Caiaphas and/or Pontius Pilate, his profound revelation about the nature of ultimate reality would be null and void. In his earliest recorded mental conflict, Jesus faced and overcame the temptation to win adherents by the false methods of satisfying people's physical needs, employing force, persuasion, propaganda or brain-washing techniques. Despite his great personal charisma and influence, he relied only on reflecting the glory of God within and consequently gave humanity a new concept of the divine as Love.

John deals with doubt and scepticism in his own terms. He shows people's very mixed response to Jesus' signs, and reports that Jesus himself did not greatly value faith which came as a result of a sign (2:23,24; 4:48). Jesus' early conversation with Nathanael (1:50,51) is interesting in this respect. Unlike faith based on miracles, faith which comes by experience leads to illumination; it opens a new dimension, the interaction between heaven and earth, spirit and body.

Whenever John relates miraculous happenings he is asking us to look beyond the sign to the intrinsic meaning behind it, hence his emphasis on insight rather than physical sight. This means that I can accept the symbolic meaning of the incident he records, even if I doubt Jesus' ability (or intent) to override the laws of nature.

e)   CONCLUSION, 20:30,31

Many scholars believe that the Evangelist meant to end his gospel here, where John explicitly states his purpose in selecting material and writing the gospel: he wishes his readers to find what he has found, faith in Jesus as the Christ, the Son of God and hopes that through this faith they will possess eternal life here and now. According to Jewish thought, a person's name signified character, persona, the sum total of what that person was, hence the significance of 'by his name'. We are reminded of the great I AM statements in the gospel and the Exodus statement that the sacred name of God is 'I AM that I am' (3:14, cf. p.112).

I note that the Evangelist does not here endorse Thomas' declaration that Jesus is God, but rather encourages his readers to have faith in Jesus as the Messiah and God's son. This is in full accordance with the Synoptic tradition as well as Acts. Peter proclaimed at Caesarea Philippi that Jesus was the Messiah (Mark 8:29) and before Lazarus was raised (11:27), Martha expressed the belief that Jesus was the Messiah, the Son of God. Paul also subscribed to the Synoptic tradition (2 Corinthians 4:5,6). Jesus himself said that the Spirit's function is to illuminate, to show us right and wrong and to give us a true scale of values (16:8ff). In this sense we experience the ongoing understanding and insight which Jesus foretold.

f) CHAPTER 21

We must first ask whether this is an appendix/epilogue to the gospel or whether it is by another hand. Some scholars say categorically that it was written by a disciple of the beloved disciple after his death; others regard it as an essential part of the gospel.

Those who regard it as an appendix, point to the fact that the Evangelist seems to have rounded off and completed the gospel in chapter 20:31. However, he could have had second thoughts and felt them important enough to add later, a technique used in Paul's letters and in the First Letter to John (5:13).

Those supporting the theory that it is an essential part of the gospel point out that it appears in one of the oldest manuscripts. If it was added, therefore, it was added very early. While some scholars say the content and style of writing is different from chapters 1-20, others see no significant change at all. The situation cannot be compared with that of Mark's gospel, where the ending is quite clearly by another hand.

For me the crux of the matter is theological. What do we believe about the actual resurrection? If one regards the resurrected body as intangible and insubstantial, the last chapter is extremely challenging, since Jesus appears to make a charcoal fire and cook fish on it for his friends. Of course, in Luke too (24:41ff) the resurrected Jesus actually eats with his disciples.

The second question we have to ask is what this chapter adds to the gospel. I can list five points.

i) This chapter re-establishes Peter as shepherd of the newly formed fellowship, a role we find him fulfilling in the early part of Acts. There are good reasons why James, the brother of Jesus, later seems to take over the leadership of the Jerusalem community and is in charge at the Council of Jerusalem. We realise that Peter leaves the scene because his life is in danger following his arrest and escape (Acts 12:1-17). Presumably he goes away on missionary work for he returns temporarily to be present at the Council and makes an important speech (Acts 15:6-11). He was well known abroad for he is mentioned, under the name of Cephas, in Paul's Letter to the Galatians and in the Corinthian correspondence.

ii) It clears up a mistaken belief that the beloved disciple would not die until Jesus had come again. Mark reports Jesus' words (9:1) that some of those present would not die until they had seen 'the Kingdom of God come with power'. Some disciples had misinterpreted this to mean Jesus' Second Coming with glory at the end of the world. Paul's correspondence with the Thessalonians (1 Thess, 5:1-11) shows that the early Christian community did mistakenly think Jesus would return in glory soon. Some commentators on this chapter speculate that the beloved disciple, the last of the Twelve left alive, had now died, and this had caused anxiety and dismay among the faithful because the Second Coming has not taken place.

Jesus' words about the coming of the Kingdom with power could of course be interpreted to mean that his way of love was vindicated by his death, resurrection and the gift of the Holy Spirit, all of which empowered his disciples to work for the coming of the Kingdom.

iii) The chapter also clears up any misunderstanding which may have arisen about the roles of the John and Peter. Peter is the Rock, the Head Shepherd of the community. The beloved disciple is John, who saw and believed and whose gospel testifies to his own witness and perception of Jesus.

iv) It would appear that Peter and six others had gone home to Galilee and that Peter, uncertain of his future role, especially after his failure in time of crisis, resumes his everyday routine. He decides to go fishing and the others opt to go with him. Apparently none of them had grasped their new vocation. The six consist of Zebedee's sons (their first mention in the Fourth gospel), Thomas, Nathanael and two unnamed men, one of whom presumably would be Andrew, Peter's brother. It has been suggested that this chapter is actually the lost ending to Mark's gospel: it would fit in with the fact that in Mark, Jesus promised to meet them in Galilee (14:28; 16:7). Perhaps the Fourth Evangelist wanted to let his readers know that such a meeting did take place.

The episode is sometimes compared with the strange story of a miraculous draught of fish (Luke 5:1-11) in which Peter declares he is not fit for Jesus' company, a remark more appropriate after his denial of Jesus than before. But Luke's main point is that Jesus commissions Peter to become a fisher of men and that Peter and Andrew, with their partners, James and John, all decide to leave everything and follow Jesus.

The miraculous draught of fish is not the main point of John's story either, despite the unbroken net, but he does attach significance to the number and kind of fish caught (21:11). Fishermen would naturally ply their trade at night but as usual the Evangelist uses facts symbolically. He has made constant use of the symbolism of night (3:2, 9:4; 11:10; 13:30) to stand for the darkness of the soul lacking Jesus' presence in contrast to the daylight when he is there. It is the beloved disciple who recognises the man on the beach as Jesus and Peter who impulsively jumps into the water when he hears who it is.

After the meal Jesus asks Peter three times if he loves him. John uses two Greek words for love: agape on the first and second occasion, phileo, which stands for 'friend', on the third. One supposes that Peter is asked three times because he is reported as having denied his master three times. He needs healing from the denial and it has to take place at a deep level. Peter can now be sure that Jesus knows him through and through, yet still wants him as leader for he is bidden on each occasion to feed Jesus' lambs. Jesus' apparent prophecy of Peter's death by crucifixion (21:18) could only have been written after the event was already known to the gospel readers (21:19).

When he is finally bidden to follow Jesus, Peter sees the beloved disciple also following and asks what will happen to him, only to be rebuffed with the astringent comment that it is no concern of his. This seemingly harsh treatment may be explained by reflection on the contrasting behaviour of the two men. The beloved disciple had been completely faithful. He had stood by the cross and comforted Jesus' mother. On seeing the grave clothes he had believed that his master had risen. Peter had to learn to be faithful to his own task, which was simply to follow his master and become the shepherd of his flock.

It is fair to deduce from verse 23 that the beloved disciple had died by the time this was written and that the writer is deliberately clarifying the point that Jesus had never said he would not die but simply that his future was not Peter's concern.

The authorship of the gospel, or the inspiration behind it, is firmly attributed to the beloved disciple. Then follows confirmation that "we" know his testimony is true. Tantalisingly the gospel simply does not say who "we" are but presumably they are the Elders of the Ephesian community amongst whom the beloved disciple lived and died.

The final verse emphasises the selective character of any gospel; much more could have been included but material was chosen for a definite purpose, as has been made clear (20:31).

CHAPTER SEVEN – THE PROLOGUE, JOHN 1:1-18

		Page
a	Origins	157
b.	Background: Jewish, Greek and the Synoptic Gospels	158
c.	Summary of the text	162
d.	Problems	164
e.	Concluding Summary	166

CHAPTER 7:

The Prologue, John 1:1-18

I have left the Prologue to the last because I believe that it was a later addition to the gospel and that other readers may find, as I, that one can more appreciate this poetic and difficult passage having studied the gospel first. I give below a few comments on the debate about authorship and the cultural background to the Prologue itself.

a)   Origins

As usual there is a controversy amongst scholars! Some say that it was originally a Christian hymn to which the Evangelist made some prose additions, i.e. the verses which mention John Baptist. In support of this view, it has been pointed out that the Prologue is different in style and vocabulary from the remainder of the gospel: eg. 'Word' as a title of Jesus the Christ, is only used in Chapter 1:1 and 14 and 'Grace' is only used in Chapter 1:14 and 16f. The origins of the hymn are not known but as the Prologue contains a well developed Christology, it would certainly have to be late in the first century AD. It could have originated in the Christian community at Ephesus which had gathered round the immensely prestigious figure of the Apostle John, or the unnamed beloved disciple, either of whom may have been the inspiration behind the gospel, even if not its actual author.

Other scholars would ask: 'Is it an addition to the original gospel, but by the same author'? They would suggest that it may have been written as a preface to the second edition and therefore contains a summing up of the main themes of the gospel.

Lastly there are those who regard the Prologue as an integral part of the gospel in which the author announces in advance his themes of Light and Life.

As it now stands, the purpose of the Prologue is to introduce the reader to Jesus as the Word, who existed with God before the creation of the world, who was the agent of God in creation and who is the Life of everything and the Light of humanity. It is one of the best known passages in the new Testament, frequently read aloud as part of Christmas celebrations and it forms the basis of one of the most popular carols, 'O come all ye faithful'. Its sheer beauty and majesty strike a chord of response which is beyond the rational.

b)   Background

Whatever the Prologue's origins, some minimal understanding of both Jewish and Greek thought helps to put it into its cultural background. There are three strands of Jewish thought of which we must be aware.

i) In the twentieth century when we are inundated with words visible both in print and on screen, it is easy to forget the power of the spoken word in ancient traditions. The Old Testament begins with the Priestly creation hymn in which God speaks and creation immediately results. Subsequently, in the Patriarchal stories, it is clear that words spoken in God's name and on God's authority are thought to have power to bring events to pass. This is particularly true of blessings and curses. For example, when his death approaches, the aged Isaac (Genesis 27), tells Esau, who is his elder and favourite son, to make him a savoury dish so that he may have the strength to give him his due blessing. What is then said cannot be unsaid, even though Jacob tricks his father and brother, thanks to Isaac's poor eyesight. Later, Jacob in his turn (Genesis 49) utters deathbed oracles concerning his twelve sons. Although modern scholars may show that these oracles were written at a later date and therefore reflect contemporary tribal confederacy, they were regarded for centuries as prophetic and self-fulfilling.

It was the 'word of the Lord' which came upon the prophets - including John Baptist in the New Testament period - so that they not only received knowledge of God's will but also declared his divine purpose to the people in God's name.

ii) The rabbis regarded the Torah, the sacred Law contained in the first five books of the Old Testament, as God's word. They taught that through the Torah, both light and life can come to humanity. By contrast, Jesus summarised the whole law in terms of Love, and Paul argued in his Letter to the Galatians, that the Torah did not bring life and light because it was restrictive and arbitrary. He likened its role to that of a tutor necessary to humanity's childhood phase. It was only in Jesus the Christ, himself the Son of God, that humanity could grow to maturity and have fulness of life.

Christian literalists have always regarded the whole bible as the word of God. However New Testament writers (particularly Paul and John) affirm that it is only Jesus the Christ who is the word, not any written text. I personally regard any religious text, however sacred, as either an interpretation of an experience of the divine or an intuitive understanding of truth expressed in images and poetry. In either case, it will be clothed in terms that are appropriate to a particular culture.

iii) The third strand, Jewish Wisdom literature, is found in the biblical books of Proverbs, Ecclesiastes, Job and probably some Psalms, and in the extra-canonical books, Ecclesiasticus and the Wisdom of Solomon. Although the above-mentioned books are post-exilic in date, the genre is very ancient indeed and its writers would undoubtedly have been influenced by the cultures of Babylon, Egypt and Greece.

In some of these writings, we find the Wisdom of God personified, as feminine in gender; she is presented as being with God from the beginning (Proverbs 8:22,23), even before time (Ecclesiasticus 24:9). In the same chapter of Proverbs (8:30,31) she is called God's darling and delight while in the Wisdom of Solomon (7:26), she is described in terms which I would use for Jesus: 'the radiance that streams from everlasting light, the flawless mirror of the active power of God, and the image of his goodness'.

The aim of later Jewish Wisdom literature was to inspire the individual to lead an honest, good and upright life, caring for poor and dependent relatives and refusing to exploit others for personal gain. Jesus in Luke and Matthew's gospels shows his knowledge of this literary/religious tradition (cf. Luke 7:35; 11:31; 11:49) and even makes the same kind of appeal in his preaching. It is worth the reader comparing Ecclesiasticus 51:23-26 with Matthew 11:28-30, though the latter quotation shows the degree to which Jesus' insight transforms what is said.

Paul specifically identifies Jesus with 'the power of God and the wisdom of God' (1 Corinthians 1:24), but the author of the Prologue, although obviously influenced by various strands in Jewish thought, does not choose to think of Jesus in terms of wisdom, nor does he use the word 'Sophia' -probably because it is feminine in gender, nor does he use 'gnosis' for knowledge, which had many connotations with Greek mystery cults and gnosticism. He prefers 'Logos' which stands for word/reason/intelligence/thought.

So far as **Greek thought** is concerned, the most influential philosophical and ethical movement in the New Testament period, and for several centuries later was Stoicism, founded by Zeno (c.336-263 BC). Stoics maintained that Rational Principle, or Right Reason permeated all reality and was the same as Zeus (God), the Supreme Head of the universe. In effect, although acknowledging the existence of other deities, the only God they worshipped was the divine Logos. Later Stoics believed a spark of this divine Logos, Reason, was found in the best and wisest of people, even if not in all humanity. Epictetus (a lame slave, later emancipated, active as a philosopher in AD.89), wrote in Discourses II, viii.6 'You are a principal work, a fragment of God himself, you have in yourself a part of him'.

In Plato's *Apology of Socrates*, Socrates himself says he must obey God rather than humans; by 'God' he probably means either the Delphic oracle or that divine spark within.

Philo of Alexandria (c. 20BC - AD45), a very influential Hellenistic Jew who studied Plato and other Greek philosophers, attempted a synthesis of Hebrew Law and the world of Greek ethical philosophy. He believed that God's thought was the means by which creation took place.

Thus we can see that both Jewish and Greek thinkers struggled to articulate the mystery of creation and life, and that for both Jewish and Greek readers of John's gospel, the term Logos could mean the self-expression of God.

If we assume that the Synoptic gospels preceded John, we must also look at the way in which they introduce the advent of Jesus. Mark begins his gospel with a declaration of faith - Jesus is the 'Son of God' By referring to the mission of John Baptist and to two Old Testament oracles, from Malachi and Isaiah, he then places his gospel beginnings in the prophetic period. Matthew uses Mark, but prefaces John Baptist's mission with Jesus' genealogy, and then with birth narratives exclusive to him. His genealogy traces Jesus back to Abraham, making Jesus the son of Abraham and of David, therefore heir to the promise of Genesis 12:3. He is the Messiah.

Luke addresses his preface to Theophilus, then gives events leading up to John Baptist's conception and birth, exclusive birth narratives from his own source, including the family's visit to the Temple where the infant Jesus is met by Simeon and Anna. It is not until Chapter three that he attempts to place John Baptist's mission within contemporary history and gives us his own version of Jesus' genealogy going right back to Adam.

For Luke, therefore, Jesus is the Saviour of all humanity. Jesus is thus implicit in both the creation of Adam and the call of Abraham.

It seems that John's purpose throughout is not only to deepen the Synoptic concept of Jesus but also highlight specific truths about him. In the Prologue, the same process takes place. Using Hebrew and Greek thought, the author goes further than Luke, taking us back beyond time. He identifies Jesus with the Word who was the agent of creation, the source of Light and Life and who was manifest in the man, Jesus of Nazareth.

Those first century men and women who regarded Jesus as their Lord and Master were utterly changed by the resurrection experience and their awareness of the indwelling presence of the Risen Christ. They also believed in the Spirit of God, which had been present and active throughout Jewish history. Some of them, at least, came to the conclusion that Jesus' own spirit must have been pre-existent with God. To avoid any duality of deity, which was completely alien to their culture, they followed Jesus' own teaching about the Fatherhood of God and went on to see him as uniquely the Son.

The gospels do express the special relationship between Jesus and God in terms of 'sonship', as Jesus himself does at his baptismal experience. For him and for his disciples this Father/Son image was a natural cultural expression. In thinking about it today, those of us who are female have to divorce the image from overtones of exclusiveness, male dominance and hierarchy, in order to look at the reality of relationship which it is expressing. I believe that while we may reject terminology unsympathetic to us, we must not disregard the fact of the relationship with the Other. When the Genesis hymn declares that human beings were made in the image of God, male and female were created together, it is in fact talking about relationship, the need of one for another, the responsibility of one for another in love. As human beings, we find our happiness and fulfilment in relationship with each other and with the divine.

The Prologue, of course states that Jesus was not only the Son of God but God the Son. In AD 381 Christian theologians met in Constantinople at a conference called by the Emperor Theodosius to combat various 'heresies' which disputed either the complete humanity or divinity of Jesus. They eventually formulated the credal statement, now known as the Nicene Creed, which established the Trinity of Father, Son and Holy Spirit, three persons in one God, as an article of Christian faith. Whilst accepting the reality and mystery of totally inexplicable experience, which originally lay behind the formulation of the doctrine, I reject the doctrine itself.

c)   **Summary of the text**

In beautiful and poetic phrases (1:1-5) the author states his faith in terms echoing the Genesis Priestly hymn of creation. Time has no meaning for the divinity, yet we mortals are bounded by time so inevitably we think in terms of a beginning of creation and of humanity. The Word of God was a reality with God before time began but through him all things (as we understand them) came into existence. And he is the source of all life. The darkness of the original chaos still surrounds and penetrates creation but does not and cannot extinguish the Light of the World, which shines out as a beacon for all humanity.

The first prose section (1:6-8) deals with the advent of John Baptist whose role was of great significance to the early church. From the Synoptic gospels we learn that he preached repentance in view of the Messiah's coming and his imprisonment and death. Luke and Matthew record his doubts about Jesus and Jesus' comments on him (L. 7:18-35; M.11:2-19) We know from Acts (19:1-7) that his disciples continued after his death. The Jewish historian Josephus, refers to John Baptist too, so that he has an assured place in Jewish history regardless of biblical writings.

John's treatment of the Baptist is interesting especially as he draws from his own source. We hear very little about the Baptist's preaching or even his baptising (3:22-30, 4:1). He calls himself 'the best man' to Jesus 'the groom' (3:29). Everything is concentrated on the fact that he was sent by God, like an Old Testament prophet, to proclaim truth. His task is to be the forerunner of the Messiah, testifying to the coming of the Light, who is Jesus (1:6; 1:19, 29, 32). How well he fulfilled his mission is demonstrated by the fact that Jesus' first followers were directed to him by John, (1:35-42) having originally been the Baptist's own disciples. John Baptist is emphatic that he is not the Messiah (1:20 et al).

The New Testament viewed the universe as largely under the power of the evil one, whom Christ had conquered. Mark's gospel reports Jesus stilling the storm (4:35-41) as if he had muzzled a demon of the elemental forces. Illness was often attributed to demon-possession. In Luke's and Matthew's temptation narratives, the devil boasts of having all the kingdoms of the world at his disposal (Luke 4:6; Matthew 4:9). Jesus himself (John 12:31) talks about the prince of this world being driven out. So in the Fourth Gospel (see Introduction) the word 'world' as in 1:9, stands not only for the universe but also for humanity, organised in societies and nations which were largely hostile to God and his purposes. See also 1 John 5:19 which contrasts God's family with those others who are under Satan's powers.

The irony of the situation for Jesus as the Word, is expressed in poignant terms (1:10-14). Although the world was created by him, it did not recognise his arrival. Even his own people, whose prophets had prepared them to acknowledge God as their King and to look for the coming of His kingdom, did not see in Jesus, the Son of God. The Jewish rejection of Jesus as Messiah is amply demonstrated in the gospel (7:40-44; 8: 12-14, 37-43, 58-59; 10:19-21; 11:46) and causes Jesus and his disciples great pain and persecution.

However, those who do believe receive the gift of a new creation. The Prologue is emphatic that being a child of God has nothing to do with race or human parentage. As the story of Nicodemus illustrates (3:9,10) the essential element is spiritual rebirth. I would interpret this as a voluntary response within the individual, a personal act of will, therefore, which awakens the seed of God.

The author uses strong negatives to contrast human conception with spiritual birth leading some commentators to interpret 1:13 as the gospel's sole reference to the virgin birth. However I would conclude that the theory of virgin birth is irrelevant to this gospel (nor is it mentioned in Mark); it is perfectly clear from the gospel, particularly in the story of Nicodemus, that John means to emphasise Jesus' concern and mission is to reclaim that of God within individuals and start them again on their spiritual journey. It is common among New Testament writers, particularly Paul in Romans 8, to think of this self-reorientation in terms of a new spiritual creation.

The crowning statement of the Prologue comes in 1:14. The Word became flesh, which means fully human. For many, Greek and Jew alike, the concept of the divine Logos, or Wisdom, or First Principle becoming flesh would be horrifying. But the Prologue states categorically that the Word became a tangible, historical person, who 'made his dwelling' with 'us', i.e. the writer and his contemporaries. The apostolic witness is confirmed again by the phrase 'we have seen his glory.' For the Jew the glory of God was manifested in the history of Israel, particularly the escape from bondage. In Old Testament thought, God's glory was veiled at the present time, but would be revealed later in the latter days (Haggai 2:9). For the Christian, the latter days were here. The brightness of the Light seen in the Shekinah and the Law was now superseded by the glory found in the Incarnate Son.

The glory of the unique son is described in terms of 'grace and truth' (REB). While grace is a very important Pauline word (Romans 5:15, 1 Corinthians 1:4; 3:10; 15:10) and stands for the ultimate compassion of

God in rescuing humanity, in this gospel it only ever appears in 1:14 and in v.16. However, truth is the key word in the gospel. Jesus says he is the truth (14:6), that knowing the truth is liberation (8:32) and that through him, who is the truth, comes real freedom (8:33). And in his conversation with the Samaritan woman he says that God is spirit and his worshippers must worship him in spirit and truth (4:23,24).

1:15 returns (in prose) to John Baptist. By 'crying aloud' or proclaiming, he is fulfilling his prophetic function of declaring the pre-eminence and pre-existence of Jesus the Christ. 1:16-18 speak of 'grace upon grace', a phrase which stands for me as the basis of renewal which is possible through personal relationships: There follows a sharp contrast between Moses, through whom came the Law, and Jesus the Christ, through whom comes grace and truth. This is similar to the Pauline argument found in Galatians and endorses the experience of those who encounter Love.

The God of the Old Testament is invisible but manifests himself in the Patriarchal stories via anthropomorphic (Genesis 18:1-2 to Abraham) or angelic forms (Genesis 32:30 to Jacob). Moses begs to see God, but because God knows he could not humanly survive the encounter with his glory, God hides him in a cleft of the rock, where he is able to see the glory of God when it has passed by (Exodus 33:20-23). However, God does talk to Moses in the tent of meeting face to face (Exodus 33:11) and not in riddles (Numbers 12:8), an experience which means Moses was quite exceptional. Moses is in fact the greatest man in the Old Testament and one of the humblest. Nevertheless for the author of the Prologue, Jesus, the unique Son of God reveals the truth about the Father to humanity.

d)   Problems

1. The Prologue is difficult. I can accept that Jesus is the Son of God, which indeed is the theme of the gospel, but not that he is God the Son, any more than I can say of myself that I am God the daughter or God the child. Nor can I say God the Creation or God the stone, flower or mountain although I believe that creation took place through divine will. For me God is the Other although I believe both in God's transcendence and immanence. There is that of God in human beings, the seed of God, as George Fox would put it, which is their spirit. In all living creatures both in the animal kingdom and in the realm of nature, rivers, trees and vegetation, there is life and power - the blessings of God. The elements of earth, fire, water and air are life-giving. I wish to identify with these and perhaps I can say - with Matthew Fox - 'Earth I am, Fire I am; Air, Water and Spirit I am' to express the spiritual and natural energy within us.

Also I know that the Spirit of God has life-giving power, has been active since the dawn of time. History is full of examples of extraordinary people who have helped humanity forward along its spiritual path. We find in all the great faiths acute awareness of the spiritual life: in some Buddhist thinking the dharma (the Law) is all-important, but for others the Dao (the way) has ultimate significance and for Zen Buddhists life is all about the search for the Isness of all things, whether human, rock, plant or any aspect of the natural world. So I cannot accept the exclusive claim of orthodox Christianity, although I can understand how first century people, unaware of the great civilisations which existed beyond the Middle East, thought of their cultures as central.

2. There is a great cosmological gulf between us and people living two thousand years ago. We need to ask whether this is of significance to faith. Some people reject the biblical witness because of our totally different awareness of the universe. I believe we must face the fact of this gulf, feeling free to disagree with the biblical record where it is plainly outdated but also seeking to find the common basis of experiential truth. I cannot believe the New Testament view that the cosmos is under the power of evil whom Christ has conquered, although I do believe that Jesus, the innovator, has shown us the way out of the terrible cycle of retaliation and revenge which has bedevilled humanity. I see the universe as having its own immutable laws which we are in the process of discovering. In our century we have made the grave error of assuming only physical laws exist, but there are moral and spiritual laws as well. They are not necessarily different from each other, but may be different in application. One of these laws, that through death comes life, is exemplified in the Jesus story. Another is the law of cause and effect which operates both in the physical and moral world despite the fact that Western culture does not always recognise its moral application. Paul expresses this law of cause and effect in Galatians (6:7), 'Everyone reaps what he sows'. In the East it can be seen in the theory of reincarnation which is held throughout the Hindu and Buddhist world.

3. I cannot believe that humanity is under a curse. This is not to underestimate the power and the spread of evil or the recognition that it is a negative spiritual force. But for me the most important fact about human beings is our ability to adapt, which is why we have survived as a species so far. Our strength lies in our plasticity, yet it is also our weakness; we are easily influenced and we suffer corporately from each other's misguided beliefs and motives. As I see it, humanity is on a voyage of true self-discovery. We have to learn the life of the spirit expressed through the glory of the flesh.

The New Testament's attempt to explain the mystery of the man Jesus may have, in part, prevented us from reaching adulthood. Salvation is not something which is necessarily done for us but something in which we willingly co-operate, otherwise it will not be truly effective. I cannot be healed unless I willingly co-operate. I cannot be taught unless I am eager to learn, nor can I experience new things unless I am open and receptive. It is not all up to God or the devil but to our willingness as a species to grow and learn from past mistakes. I believe we are called to be channels of the Light, of the Spirit of Love, compassion, truth and forgiveness. It is not adult behaviour to swing between abasement and pride and yet that is what is sometimes asked of us in our relationship with God and God the Son i.e. abasement to the divine, pride in our superiority over the unbeliever. If we blame the state of the world on the personification of evil, we can shelve our own responsibilities for the events within it. We are perhaps beginning to glimpse this in the latter half of this century.

4. Believing, as I do, that Jesus' supreme revelation was to disclose that God, Ultimate Reality, is Love, I begin to glimpse the suffering of God when humanity turns away from the course which would bring fulfilment and joy. God is not the arbitrary and omnipotent ruler of the world. Certain laws and creative purposes have been set in motion in order that humanity may evolve into what we potentially can become. There are incalculably many creative options open to us all. It is the hardest thing imaginable to continue loving support to those who deliberately self-destruct, yet this is what Love/God is doing all the time.

e)   **Concluding Summary**

The gospel itself is full of paradox, a feature which seems part of the Evangelist's style. For example, Jesus says on the one hand that he has not come to judge or to accuse, that their accuser is Moses (5:45), whereas God has sent his Son as saviour of the world (3:17). On the other hand in controversy with the Jews, Jesus has much to say about them in judgement (8:26).

The greatest paradox of all is in the Evangelist's picture of Jesus. Many orthodox commentators claim the Evangelist sees Jesus as the Eternal Word. His divinity is declared in the great I AM statements. Yet the gospel also shows Jesus as a true human being whose family and background is known to the crowds and who has a conversation with his brothers (7:3-6). Further, Jesus himself in the gospel continually asserts that he is sent by God, can do nothing by himself (5:19), and speaks on God's authority only (7:16,18; 28,29,39; 8:13) and specifically (8:28). Even after Thomas' declaration to the risen Jesus 'My Lord and my God' (20:28 compared with 20:31), the gospel continually presents Jesus as the Son of God. Of course, in the gospel Jesus does claim on several occasions, that he has come down from heaven not to do his own will but the will of the One who has sent him (6:38). But Jesus is simply saying, in terms according to his culture, that he has come from God. We have to keep in our minds the New Testament cosmological picture which is quite different from our own.

One phrase in Jesus' prayer seems to endorse the claims of the Prologue; it speaks of reinstating Jesus to the glory he had with God at the beginning (see p.161 for comment on this). Even so, it is still the relationship of Father/Son and all that this signifies, which is important in the prayer. This is surely not quite the same thing as the Prologue's assertion that the incarnate Jesus is God the Son. If we have within us the seed of God, which is immortal, we may all be said to be in some sense incarnate.

Jesus, for me, is an historical reality. He is realised human potential, which we can become if we do not destroy ourselves first. He is the supreme innovator. In John's gospel he offers us his friendship. He is our companion along the way and his strength and power are ours if we can open ourselves to the Light. There is so much that is hopeful about the human scene as well as so much that is horrific and terrible. We cannot seek to absorb the sufferings of others, for we do not have the capacity. Only divine Love itself can identify totally with human misery and heartache without being overwhelmed. We can however become vehicles of God's light, as was Jesus.

Bibliography

THE FOURTH GOSPEL, Sir Edwyn Hoskins, edited by Frances Noel Davey, pub. Faber Faber, 1947

THE FOURTH GOSPEL, C.H Dodd, Cambridge University Press, 1953

THE JOHANNINE EPISTLES, C.H. Dodd, The Moffat New Testament Commentary, C.U.Press, 1953

THE PRIORITY OF JOHN, John A.T. Robinson, S.C.M. Press, 1985

REDATING THE NEW TESTAMENT, John A.T. Robinson, S.C.M., 1976.

READINGS IN S. JOHN'S GOSPEL, William Temple, Macmillan, 1939.

BEHIND THE FOURTH GOSPEL, Barnabas Lindars, SSJ, S.P.C.K.1971

THE GOSPEL ACCORDING TO S.JOHN, Alan Richardson, S.C.M.Torch Bible Commentaries,1959

THE GOSPEL ACORDING TO JOHN, A. M. Hunter, The Cambridge Bible Commentaries, 1965

THE GOSPEL ACCORDING TO JOHN, J.C. Fenton in the Revised Standard Version,NewClarendon Bible, Oxford Clarendon press, 1970.

THE GOSPEL OF JOHN AND JUDAISM, C.K Barrett, S.P.C.K, 1975

THE GOSPEL AND EPISTLES OF JOHN, Raymond E. Brown, The Litturgical Press, Minnesota, 1988

THE COMMUNITY OF THE BELOVED DISCIPLE, Raymond E. Brown, Geoffrey Chapman, London, 1979

THE YOGA OF CHRIST IN THE GOSPEL OF JOHN, Ravi Ravindra, Element Books, 1990

PORTRAITS OF JESUS, -JOHN, William Domeris & Richard Wortly ,A conceptual approach to bible study, Collins, 1988

RESCUING THE BIBLE FROM FUNDAMENTALISM. John Shelby Spong. Harper San Francisco, 1991